Jun 21

The New Enlightenment

AND THE FIGHT TO FREE KNOWLEDGE

The New Enlightenment
AND THE FIGHT TO FREE KNOWLEDGE

Peter B. Kaufman

Seven Stories Press
New York • Oakland • London

Library of Congress Cataloging-in-Publication Data

Names: Kaufman, Peter B., 1963- author.
Title: The new enlightenment and the fight to free knowledge / Peter B. Kaufman.
Description: New York : Seven Stories Press, 2021. | Includes
  bibliographical references.
Identifiers: LCCN 2020044684 (print) | LCCN 2020044685 (ebook) | ISBN 9781644210604
(trade paperback) | ISBN 9781644211250 (hardcover) | ISBN 9781644210611 (ebook)
Subjects: LCSH: Knowledge, Sociology of--History. | Freedom of information.
  | Enlightenment--Influence.
Classification: LCC HM651 .K385 2021 (print) | LCC HM651 (ebook) | DDC
  306.4/209--dc23
LC record available at https://lccn.loc.gov/2020044684
LC ebook record available at https://lccn.loc.gov/2020044685

Printed in the USA.

9 8 7 6 5 4 3 2 1

For you, Ellen.

Contents

Preface

This book is one I began more than ten years ago.

It's now one I'm finishing in the middle of a plague.

It began as a vision of our knowledge institutions—our universities, libraries, museums, archives, public broadcasters, and others—recognizing the immense power that they have, especially with the Internet in each of their arsenals.

It began, also, as a call to action for them all to come together and with the power they have—we all have—as publishers to purvey verifiable truths. To have our knowledge institutions put knowledge online. To have us publish facts into a world gone mad.

It's being completed as a health and information pandemic rages around the world. As three hundred thousand newly dead from the pandemic here are buried and cremated.

It's being completed as criminal men try to tighten their grip. As the number of unemployed rises to and passes Depression-era levels. As universities, libraries, museums, archives, and schools worldwide are shuttered and staying closed.

And as fewer and fewer people can even discern truth from fiction anymore.

But this is also a book of hope. How can one possibly write a book of hope now? Jean-Jacques Rousseau, the author of *The Social Contract*, wrote in his memoirs, during the original Enlightenment: "If I want to describe the spring it must be in winter; if I want to describe a fine landscape I must be within doors; and as I have said a hundred times, if ever I were confined in the Bastille, there I would draw the picture of liberty."[1]

The competition for our attention on our screens and our speakers, and the allure of false and malign information, has begun to intensify in ways that were almost unimaginable even a few years ago. The pandemic has provided us with incentives to change the form and frequency of our knowledge conveyance. We are also in a new time, a video age, where the opportunities for free-thinkers can only grow.

How knowledge institutions will handle the challenge of working with video—and with their new responsibility generally—remains to be seen.

Peter B. Kaufman
Lakeville, Connecticut
December 11, 2020

---

1 Jean-Jacques Rousseau, *The Confessions*, trans. J. M. Cohen (London: Penguin Books, 1953), 166–167.

Part I

The Monsterverse

1. *The Monsterverse*

William Tyndale, born in 1494, killed in 1536, believed that the structure of communication during his time was broken and unfair, and with a core, unwavering focus, he sought to make it so that the main body of knowledge in his day could be accessed and then shared again by every man alive. He engaged in an unparalleled act of coding (not for nothing do we speak of computer programming "languages"), working through the Latin, Greek, Hebrew, and Aramaic of the Bible's Old, then New, Testaments to bring all of its good books—from Genesis 1 to Revelation 22—into English for everyday readers. He is reported to have said, in response to a question from a priest who had challenged his work—a priest who read the Bible only in Latin: "I will cause a boy that driveth the plough shall know more of the Scripture than thou dost." And he worked with the distribution technologies of his time—the YouTubes, websites, and Twitters back then—by connecting personally with book designers, paper suppliers, printers, boat captains, and horsemen across sixteenth-century Europe to bring the knowledge and the book that contained it into the hands of the people.[2]

It wasn't easy. In Tyndale's time, popes and kings—Roman pope Clement VII and English king Henry VIII, in partic-

2 John Foxe, *Actes and Monuments of These Latter and Perillous Dayes, Touching Matters of the Church* (more generally known as *Foxe's Book of Martyrs*) (London: John Day, 1563), http://www.ccel.org/f/foxe/martyrs/home.html.

ular—had decreed, out of concern for keeping their power, that the Bible could exist and be read and distributed "only in the assembly of Latin translations" that had been completed by the monk Saint Jerome in approximately 400 CE. The penalties for challenging the law were among the most severe imaginable, for such violations represented a panoply of civil transgressions and an entire complexity of heresies. In taking on the church and the king—in his effort simply and solely to translate and then distribute the Bible in English—Tyndale confronted "the greatest power[s] in the Western world." As he "was translating and printing his New Testament in Worms," his leading biographer reminds us, "a young man in Norwich was burned alive for the crime of owning a piece of paper on which was written the Lord's Prayer in English."[3] Moreover, the text he was translating alone was not the work of one creator. The Bible, as one of its modern translators has said, is "a work assembled by many hands, reflecting several different viewpoints, and representing literary activity that spanned several centuries," and the text assembly involved in its original production "a process akin to collage." "There are other instances of works of art that evolved over the centuries, like the cathedrals of medieval Europe," this modern translator reminds us, but bringing the Bible into English involves "an elaborate process of editing" akin to the work behind "some of the greatest Hollywood films."[4]

---

3 "Christians almost from the beginning knew their book only in translation, and even then, for over half the life of the Faith, had their book taken away from them. . . . It remained inaccessible in Latin for a thousand years, and . . . . [t]o translate it for the people became heresy, punishable by a solitary lingering death as a heretic; or, as had happened to the Cathars in southern France, or the Hussites in Bohemia and Lollards in England, official and bloody attempts to exterminate the species." David Daniell, *The Bible in English: Its History and Influence* (New Haven, CT: Yale University Press, 2003), 11, 136, 157.

4 Robert Alter, *The Hebrew Bible: A Translation with Commentary*, vol. 1, *The Five Books of Moses Torah* (New York: W. W. Norton, 2018), xlix, 9.

Tyndale knew seven languages—Greek, Latin, Hebrew, and Aramaic among them—and with them all he sought to accomplish mainly this one thing: to translate the non-English Bible into English. He was a devout Christian. "Such was the power of his doctrine, and the sincerity of his life," one biographer tells us, "that during the time of his imprisonment"—some twenty months, before he received the capital punishment for his crimes—"he converted, it is said, his [prison] keeper, the keeper's daughter, and others of [the keeper's] household."[5] But hopeful or not, devout or not, Tyndale met his violent end: "executed by strangling," as his Wikipedia biography reads, "and then, burnt at the stake."[6] This was his lot after he was pursued across Europe by a king and church determined for decades to capture and destroy him; after he was caught following an act of gross and itself almost biblical betrayal; and then after close to two years of privation in a cold and wet cell outside of Antwerp, Belgium, where he was held, often in solitary confinement. This poor scholar and polymath to whom, it is now known, we owe as much as we owe William Shakespeare for our language, this lone man sought and slain by church and king and holy Roman emperor—his initial, official strangling did not go well, so that when he was subsequently lit on fire, and the flames first lapped at his feet and up his legs, lashed tight to the stake, he came to, and, while burning alive in front of the crowd of religious leaders and so-called justices (some seventeen trial commissioners) who had so summarily sent Tyndale to his death and gathered to watch it, live, he cried

---

5 Foxe, *Actes and Monuments*; David Daniell, *William Tyndale: A Biography* (New Haven, CT: Yale University Press, 1994).

6 "William Tyndale," Wikimedia Foundation, last modified June 19, 2020, 6:27, https://en.wikipedia.org/wiki/William_Tyndale.

out, less to the crowd, it would seem, than to Another: "Lord! *Lord!* Open the King of England's eyes!"[7]

Grim, the fate of the people who spread knowledge.

This was not an uncommon thing during Henry VIII's time—or Pope Leo X's or Clement VII's time—in and around the 1500s. Tyndale's most rapacious pursuer, Sir Thomas More, himself met a similar end. Henry VIII lost patience with More and initially wished for him to be hanged until he was half-dead, then castrated, then disemboweled and forced to watch his own intestines being burnt in front of him, and *then* (and only then) beheaded and burnt up whole. But, on the advice of counsel, he relented in favor of a much simpler decapitation:

> About Nine [More] was brought out of the Tower; his Beard was long, his face pale and thin, and carrying a Red Cross in his Hand, he often lift up his Eyes to Heaven [. . .]. When he came to the Scaffold, it seemed ready to fall, whereupon he said merrily to the Lieutenant, Pray, Sir, see me safe up; and as to my coming down, let me shift for myself. Being about to speak to the People, he was interrupted by the Sheriff, and thereupon he only desired the People to pray for him, and bear Witness he died in the Faith of the Catholic Church, a faithful Servant both to God and the King.

---

7 Foxe, *Actes and Monuments*, emphasis added. See also Melvyn Bragg, "Melvyn Bragg on William Tyndale," *Daily Telegraph* (London), June 6, 2013, https://www.telegraph.co.uk/culture/tvandradio/10096770/Melvyn-Bragg-on-William-Tyndale-his-genius-matched-that-of-Shakespeare.html. Bragg's BBC film, *The Most Dangerous Man in Tudor England*, directed by Anna Cox, was originally broadcast on BBC Two on June 6, 2013, and can be viewed online, https://vimeo.com/139898687. See also "Jacobus Latomus," Wikimedia Foundation, last modified April 24, 2020, 17:20, https://en.wikipedia.org/wiki/Jacobus_Latomus; and Jacob Latomus, *Confutations Against William Tyndale*, trans. James A. Willis (Leuven, 1542), https://web.archive.org/web/20080517104730/http://www.tyndale.org/Reformation/1/latomus1.html.

Then kneeling, he repeated the Miserere Psalm with much Devotion; and, rising up the Executioner asked him Forgiveness. He kissed him, and said, Pick up thy Spirits, Man, and be not afraid to do thine Office; my Neck is very short, take heed therefore thou strike not awry for having thine Honesty. Laying his Head upon the Block, he bid the Executioner stay till he had put his Beard aside, for that had committed no Treason. Thus he suffered with much Cheerfulness; his Head was taken off at one Blow, and was placed upon London-Bridge [after being boiled—and to a black mass], where, having continued for some Months, and being about to be thrown into the Thames to make room for others, his Daughter Margaret bought it, inclosed it in a Leaden Box, and kept it for a Relique.[8]

Imagine, then, the head of a television news network today— any TV network, really, but take for example Rupert Murdoch, Bill Shine, or Jack Abernethy at Fox News—garroted, disemboweled, drawn and quartered, and auto-da-fé'd in this way. Would *they* manage to endure, as Tyndale did back then? What is (or, when history judges them, was) their personal commitment—above and beyond the here and now—to making the world a better place through the media: through the power, the instruments, the weapons that they wield? Or, let us address even Johannes Gutenberg and the early printers—would they have had themselves strapped to a stake for the sake of knowl-

---

8 Edward Hall, *The Union of the Two Noble and Illustre Famelies of Lancastre and Yorke* (commonly called Hall's *Chronicle*) (London: John Grafton, 1548), vol. 2, S. 2, quoted in Claire Ridgway, "The Execution of Sir Thomas More," *The Anne Boleyn Files* (blog), July 6, 2010, https://www.theanneboleynfiles.com/the-execution-of-sir-thomas-more/.

edge?[9] Guglielmo Marconi and all the radio pioneers? Philo Farnsworth and the other inventors of television? Tim Berners-Lee?

Today there is a new movement—nothing short of it—galvanizing around freeing knowledge. Its success is neither universal nor assured—various countries block its progress, still, wholesale; various forces and personalities seek to stifle and sometimes even to strangle it. But it has billions of catalyzing engines powering it now, and those engines are people, screens, speakers, pages of paper, and all the networks that together comprise the modern Internet. And while there have been purposeful, focused, grandiose efforts before now—around the Bible, in Tyndale's time; around the first encyclopedia of knowledge, during the original Enlightenment; amid the Soviet revolutionary experiment, when there was even a government Commissar of Enlightenment; and at the foundation of public-media experiments much closer to home—to make knowledge grow and take root everywhere, there may be a true chance now to realize the hope that has lain at the heart of these grand visions, and to make all these advances over the centuries somehow more significant and permanent.

This then is a book of hope—and fire. It is set in the modern-day version of Tyndale's Monsterverse. Every age has had its evil—and history shows us that tuning into that evil is central to succeeding in acting against it. Tyndale's Monsterverse had Thomas More. More is best known today for his 1516 work *Utopia* and his flattering portrait as a principled and courageous

---

9 They used to beat each other over the head back then, trying to eliminate partners and competitors throughout the sixteenth century. It was a rough profession; they developed quite a thirst for blood. See "The history of media & social change - Anthony Grafton in INT's ENLIGHTENMENT MINUTES," Intelligent Channel, September 8, 2013, YouTube video, 6:38, https://youtu.be/VosaOdqbVf4.

Catholic in the play and film *A Man for All Seasons*. But More was heinous—a savage—and, as King Henry's chief ideologue, the man who really singularly led the effort to capture Tyndale. He wrote close to a million words—two thousand "heavy pages," as Tyndale's biographer puts it—bubbling with bile and venom, and also fulminating with scat.[10] Typical was More's accusation that Martin Luther—another contemporary heretic, in his view—had claimed the right to "bespatter and besmirch the royal crown with shit."[11] "You kissed the ass of Luther, the shit-devil," More wrote to our man Tyndale on one not atypical occasion. "Look, my fingers are smeared with shit when I try to clean your filthy mouth."[12] Such were the defenders of their own orthodoxy and own worlds in the 1500s (not unlike those you would find today in comments on the Internet).

And Tyndale worked in an environment that spawned other februations, as another scholar has put it, more "penitential public theater": the ceremonial execution of *texts* as well as of the purported heretics and transgressors who wrote or trafficked in the worst of them. Burning books, ripping out their pages (itself a kind of disembowelment), imprisoning them— all that was common in the sixteenth-century Monsterverse. One author of the time was sentenced to have his ears cut off and have his books

> consumed before his eyes in a fire tended by the public executioner. The sentence was carried out . . . with

---

10 And "gallons of ink." Daniell, *William Tyndale*, 275, 375.

11 Constance M. Furey, "Invective and Discernment in Martin Luther, D. Erasmus, and Thomas More," *Harvard Theological Review* 98, no. 4 (October 2005): 486, https://doi.org/10.1017/S0017816005001069.

12 Bragg, *The Most Dangerous Man*, 43:15. More, in his rantings, also called Tyndale "a hellhound in the kennel of the devil" (Daniell, *William Tyndale*, 277).

Prynne in the pillory and his books in flames before him. According to one observer, the smoke from the burning almost suffocated the author, which was hardly surprising since each volume had more than a thousand pages.[13]

Hardly surprising, indeed.

▨ ▨ ▨

With the Aaron Swartzes of the world as suicides, the Julian Assanges pursued into prison, the Edward Snowdens chased into exile, our time in many ways is no different. There will come a moment again soon to consider how to limit all of the damage we are doing to our world through our media and communications policies and norms, and that we are doing—and allowing to be done—to our world by allowing our political leadership such free rein. The damage is altogether too stark and blinding to see at once—like black lightning, if there were such a thing. Today the most powerful offices in the world are once again involved in a relentless effort to crush freedom of thought, independent thinking, expertise—and to stanch progress toward open, civil society. The cabinet of daemons installed in Donald Trump's White House has been extraordinary, in historical perspective, for its share of felons, accused felons, and just general mountebanks nominally in charge of stewarding a sector of society—education, labor, the "interior," health and human services—but each more keen than the next on deregulating and commercializing his fief, all

13 David Cressy, "Book Burning in Tudor and Stuart England," *The Sixteenth Century Journal* 36, no. 2 (Summer 2005): 359–374, https://doi.org/10.2307/20477359.

to keep in lockstep with the moneyed interests that, perhaps more subtly, have been steadily and systematically steering our society toward this point for decades.

⬛ ⬛ ⬛

In 1536, Tyndale had been in his basement cell for 450 days, the first weeks of which "would have been punctuated by long visits from the procurer-general and a notary"—both of whom facilitated the preparation and documentation of the full accusation against him—and the last weeks of which involved an examination-cum-trial replete with apostolic inquisitors and theologians, university rectors and faculty, lawyers and privy councillors: "heresy-hunters," as his biographer calls them. When, at the end, he was condemned, he suffered what they would choreograph as a formal degradation, led in public and in his priestly raiment to a high platform outdoors where oils of anointment were scraped symbolically from his hands, the bread and wine of the Eucharist situated next to him and then just as quickly removed, and then his vestments "ceremonially stripped away," so that he would find himself, and all would see him as, no longer a priest.[14] Death came next. Actually there remains some question whether he shouted out to the king before he was strangled or after (and thus whether the whole botched-strangling account is true or not), but his words—of warning, of prescience, of (what matters here) selflessness—as so recorded were his last.

When we speak of the thirst for access to knowledge, *our* knowledge, we needn't look as far back as William Tyndale for

14 Daniell, *William Tyndale*, 374–384.

an exemplar. We can connect to the life of a real martyr from the modern age, one whose story is tied to almost all of the issues we address in this volume, one who is perhaps the closest modern figure to Tyndale we have, hounded down in our own day just as Tyndale was in his: pursued, captured, arrested, locked in.

Hounded quite literally to death.

Aaron Swartz was a progressive computer programmer, hacker, and activist—an entrepreneur, a genius, a young man of hope—who downloaded scholarly publications illegally. Massachusetts Institute of Technology (MIT) Police arrested Swartz in an MIT closet where he had deployed his laptop and connected it to the MIT system, and in 2013, at twenty-six years old, he took his own life—hanged himself by the neck—during the investigation and prosecution that ensued.[15] His suicide, under pressure from the academy and the government, prompted worldwide examination and reflection. His death and the official government pursuit that led to it contributed, as part of his legacy, to a push by scholars and activists to craft an even more aggressive agenda of publishing reform—a reform, indeed, of the research and action agenda itself, such that MIT's visionary director of libraries, Chris Bourg, could ask of us all, five years later, "How can we create a world where Aaron Swartz's act of disobedience was just . . . research?"[16]

Swartz downloaded copies of academic articles—4 million

15 Harold Abelson, Peter A. Diamond, Andrew Grosso, and Douglas W. Pfeiffer, "Report to the President: MIT and the Prosecution of Aaron Swartz," July 26, 2013 (Cambridge: MIT), http://swartz-report.mit.edu/. It wasn't MIT's finest hour. See also Cory Doctorow, "MIT Blocking Release of Aaron Swartz's Secret Service Files," *Boing Boing*, July 18, 2013, https://boingboing.net/2013/07/18/mit-blocking-release-of-aaron.html; Michael Morisy, "After Pledging 'Spirit of Openness,' MIT Delays Release of Aaron Swartz's Secret Service Files, Pending Review," Boston.com, July 18, 2013, https://www.boston.com/news/innovation/2013/07/18/after-pledging-spirit-of-openness-mit-delays-release-of-aaron-swartzs-secret-service-files-pending-review.

16 Chris Bourg, "Open as in Dangerous," (talk, Creative Commons Global Summit, Toronto, ON, April 14, 2018), https://www.youtube.com/watch?v=6JN3EGpraAY.

or 4.8 million; millions, at any rate—with the objective of publishing them freely online, so that anyone could read them anywhere, at any time. His target and source was JSTOR—a "digital library," as the company describes itself, "for scholars, researchers, and students"—and one that holds, as of this writing, some 12 million digital articles, books, and primary documents across 75 disciplines or fields of study.

The hounding Swartz endured as a result was unbelievable. Some 14,500 pages of the US Secret Service's files on him are available online.[17] The original indictment against him—the charge—featured this language:

> Between September 24, 2010, and January 6, 2011, Swartz contrived to:
> a. break into a computer wiring closet at MIT;
> b. access MIT's network without authorization from a switch within that closet;
> c. connect to JSTOR's archive of digitized journal articles through MIT's computer network;
> d. use this access to download a major portion of JSTOR's archive onto his computers and computer hard drives;
> e. avoid MIT's and JSTOR's efforts to prevent this massive copying, measures which were directed at users generally and at Swartz's illicit conduct specifically; and
> f. elude detection and identification

---

17 These Secret Service documents can be viewed at https://swartzfiles.com/. See also Kevin Poulsen, "First 100 Pages of Aaron Swartz's Secret Service File Released," *Wired*, August 12, 2013, https://www.wired.com/2013/08/swartz-foia-release/.

all with the purpose of distributing a significant proportion of JSTOR's archive through one or more
file-sharing sites.[18]

Among the laws he was charged with breaking were 18 U.S.
Code § 1343 (committing wire fraud); 18 U.S. Code § 1030 (a)
(4), (b) (computer fraud); 18 U.S. Code § 1030 (a)(2), (b), (c)
(2)(B)(iii) (unlawfully obtaining information from a protected
computer); 18 U.S. Code § 1030 (a)(5)(B), (c)(4)(A)(i)(I), (VI)
(recklessly damaging a protected computer); 18 U.S. Code § 2
(aiding and abetting); and 18 U.S. Code § 981(a)(1)(C), 28 18
U.S. Code § 2461 (c), 18 U.S. Code § 982 (a)(2)(B), and 18 U.S.
Code § 1030 (i) (criminal forfeiture).[19]

Swartz believed that knowledge should be set free when
and where it could be—and he so proselytized. "Information
is power," he liked to say. He wrote a tract and treatise—the
'Guerilla Open Access Manifesto'—in July 2008, where he
reminded his readers:

> But like all power, there are those who want to keep
> it for themselves. . . . Those with access to these
> resources—students, librarians, scientists—you have
> been given a privilege. You get to feed at this banquet
> of knowledge while the rest of the world is locked out.

---

18 See *United States v. Swartz*, United States District Court, District of Massachusetts, Criminal No. 11-10260-NMG, Document 2, July 14, 2011, viewable at https://www.wired.com/
images_blogs/threatlevel/2011/07/swartz_indictment.pdf. A second indictment added nine
more felony counts; see *United States v. Swartz*, United States District Court, District of
Massachusetts, Criminal No. 11-10260-NMG, Document 53, September 12, 2012, viewable at
https://www.wired.com/images_blogs/threatlevel/2012/09/swartzsuperseding.pdf.

19 See "18 U.S. Code § 1343. Fraud by wire, radio, or television," Cornell Law School Legal
Information Institute, accessed October 13, 2020, https://www.law.cornell.edu/uscode/
text/18/1343.

But you need not—indeed, morally, you cannot—keep this privilege for yourselves. You have a duty to share it with the world.[20]

In its own review of the matter after Swartz's death, MIT's Review Panel stated that "the Review Panel views the question of what [Swartz] intended to do with the information that he was downloading from JSTOR as remaining open." The Review Panel also stated that "Federal law enforcement apparently took the first sentence [of one paragraph of the 'Guerilla Open Access Manifesto'], 'We need to take information, wherever it is stored, make our copies and share them with the world,' as the motive and purpose behind his extensive downloading—some 4.8 million articles, or 80% of JSTOR's database of journals."[21]

Apparently so.

In many ways William Tyndale and Aaron Swartz were just trying to accelerate events, the realization of eternal truths they knew, but knew in the wrong time.

In many ways they were just trying to accelerate freedoms that will be as obvious to us in the future as the Thirteenth,

---

20 Aaron Swartz, "Guerilla Open Access Manifesto," July 2008, Internet Archive, https://archive.org/stream/GuerillaOpenAccessManifesto/Goamjul. See also *The Internet's Own Boy*, a film of Swartz's life, directed by Brian Knappenberger (Beverly Hills, CA: Participant Media, 2014), described at "*The Internet's Own Boy*," Wikimedia Foundation, last modified May 27, 2020, 11:47, https://en.wikipedia.org/wiki/The_Internet%27s_Own_Boy (how a free version of this film is not available legally is a mind-blower); John Naughton, "Aaron Swartz Stood Up for Freedom and Fairness—and Was Hounded to His Death," *Guardian*, London, February 7, 2015, https://www.theguardian.com/commentisfree/2015/feb/07/aaron-swartz-suicide-internets-own-boy; Larissa MacFarquhar, "Requiem for a Dream," *New Yorker*, March 4, 2013, https://www.newyorker.com/magazine/2013/03/11/requiem-for-a-dream.

21 Abelson, Diamond, Grosso, and Pfeiffer, "Report to the President." See, for contrast, Carl Malamud, "On Crime and Access to Knowledge," Internet Archive, March 30, 2013, https://archive.org/details/org.resource.public.crime/mode/2up (a published version of Malamud's memorial speech for Swartz at the Internet Archive, San Francisco, CA, January 24, 2013).

Fourteenth, and Fifteenth Amendments to our Constitution are today.

But Swartz—the Monsterverse took his life away, too.

Part II

The Republic of Images

2. *The* Encyclopédie

When the ideas that matter most to us—liberals, democrats, progressives, republicans, all in the original sense of the words— were first put forward in society in order to . . . *change* society, they were advanced first and foremost in print. New rules, new definitions, new codicils of human and civil rights that undergird many of the things that we value today, that undergird the rights we know we have—rights, now that we have won them, that in turn protect us in the fight for more—had as their heart text and its delivery mechanism, the printing press, beating in every struggle of the original Enlightenment. The ubiquity of text today—words and writing are everywhere in our everyday lives—has helped to render the magical centrality of printing, of the mechanical duplication of word and image, for the networks of ideas that matter most to us as more of an "unacknowledged revolution" than a violent one: an "elusive transformation."[22]

Some thirty years after Johannes Gutenberg built the first printing workshop in Germany, that country had print shops in only forty towns. By 1500, a thousand printing presses were in operation in Western Europe, and they had produced roughly 8 million books. But by the end of the century, William Tyndale's century, between 150 and 200 million books were circulating.[23]

---

22 Elizabeth L. Eisenstein, *The Printing Press as an Agent of Change: Communications and Cultural Transformations in Early Modern Europe* (Cambridge: Cambridge University Press, 1979), 1, 3–42.

23 Lucien Febvre and Henri-Jean Martin, *The Coming of the Book: The Impact of Printing 1450–1800* (New York: Verso, 1976), https://books.google.com/books?id=9opxcMjv4TUC&printsec=-

The French Revolution—an ultimate moment of the Enlightenment—featured the liberation of the Bastille prison in central Paris, an act whose significance has often been lambasted as overblown because, as one historian encapsulates the matter, that fortress "contained only seven residents: four men accused of forgery, two 'mental cases' and the Marquis de Sade." But the 1789 liberation involved more than people: it involved ideas; it involved ghosts; it involved freeing some texts. "Over eight hundred authors, printers, booksellers, and print dealers had been incarcerated [in the Bastille] between 1600 and 1756," the historians tell us, as well as "thousands of copies of the *Encyclopédie*, the masterpiece of the Enlightenment, between 1770 and 1776."[24] And that *Encyclopédie*, the fetish of this book, was enormous. It comprised 28 folio volumes, 71,818 articles, 2,885 illustration plates, and more than 20 million words—and, of course, beneath its "bulk," as its physical presence has been described (callous!), an "epistemological shift that transformed the topography of everything known to man."[25]

The publishers of the original brochure—or "prospectus," as it was then called—for one of the greatest media enterprises of all

---

frontcover&source=gbs_ViewAPI#v=onepage&q&f=false; Elizabeth L. Eisenstein, *The Printing Revolution in Early Modern Europe* (Cambridge: Cambridge University Press, 1993), online in part at http://assets.cambridge.org/052184/5432/frontmatter/0521845432_frontmatter.htm. See also "Global Spread of the Printing Press," Wikimedia Foundation, last modified June 2, 2020, 03:38, https://en.wikipedia.org/wiki/Global_spread_of_the_printing_press.

24 Eisenstein, *The Printing Press*, 147. See also Ithiel de Sola Pool, *Technologies of Freedom: On Free Speech in an Electronic Age* (Cambridge, MA: Harvard University Press, 1983); Elizabeth L. Eisenstein, "Some Conjectures about the Impact of Printing on Western Society and Thought: A Preliminary Report," *Journal of Modern History* 40, no. 1 (March 1968): 52. The *Encyclopédie*'s original publisher, André Le Breton, did a stint in there, too. See John Lough, *The Encyclopédie* (New York: David McKay Company, 1971), 29.

25 Robert Darnton, *The Business of Enlightenment: A Publishing History of the* Encyclopédie, *1775–1800* (Cambridge, MA: Harvard University Press, 1979), 7. See also John Lough, *The* Encyclopédie *of Diderot and D'Alembert: Selected Articles* (Cambridge: Cambridge University Press, 1954), ix.

time, one of the original truth engines, was built upon a fib, a bit of fraud, even a "whopping lie."[26] Seeking subscribers for the *Encyclopédie* project—a complete catalog of the world's knowledge, as it was defined back in the eighteenth century—the publishers wanted you to shell out 60 French livres, or "pounds" (named for pounds of silver, though the backing had disappeared) by the first deadline of May 1751, then 36 pounds more that June, and then you'd be in: you'd receive Volume 1. Twenty-four pounds more in December, please, for Volume 2. An additional 36 by June again, and Volume 3. Thirty-six more in December, Volume 4; and so on. Ten volumes in all by December 1755, and all for a total of 280 pounds—this at a time when your work would bring you 2 (for unskilled labor) to 6 (skilled labor) pounds a day.[27]

Le Breton publishers printed eight thousand elegant brochures to sell it. The *Encyclopédie* would be printed on the same paper (in the 1700s, this was a thing; watch a family comparison shop today for a television at Best Buy, weighing screen sizes and resolutions, and imagine . . .) as the brochure you were holding, they promised, and in the same classic folio

---

26 For the best time line, see "General Chronology of the Encyclopédie," ARTFL Encyclopédie, University of Chicago, accessed October 13, 2020, http://encyclopedie.uchicago.edu/node/82. For the prospectus in French, see "Prospectus," ARTFL Encyclopédie, University of Chicago, accessed October 13, 2020, http://encyclopedie.uchicago.edu/node/174. The heroism of the American academic institutions below involved in keeping this eighteenth-century work alive in the twenty-first cannot be overstated. The full French text from all volumes and plates, thanks to the University of Chicago, is online: "The ARTFL Encyclopédie," ARTFL Encyclopédie, University of Chicago, accessed October 13, 2020, http://encyclopedie.uchicago.edu/. The most authoritative and complete English translation, thanks to the University of Michigan, is here: "The Encyclopedia of Diderot and d'Alembert," Michigan Publishing, University of Michigan Library, accessed October 13, 2020, https://quod.lib.umich.edu/d/did/. John Lough calls the prospectus flat-out a lie. See Lough, *The Encyclopédie*, 20. I am grateful to MIT's Vice President for Open Learning Sanjay Sarma for applying the term "truth engine" to our work at MIT—and by extension to this work of our forebears.

27 Gerry Lalonde, "Monetary Values in 1650–1750 in New France Compared to Today," Rootsweb.com, accessed October 13, 2020, http://freepages.rootsweb.com/~unclefred/genealogy/MONETARY.htm.

design. Each volume would contain some 240 pages. The notes and indices would come last.

Moreover, they said:

> *L'OUVRAGE que nous annonçons, n'est plus un Ouvrage à faire. Le Manuscrit & les Desseins en sont complets. Nous pouvons assurer qu'il n'aura pas moins de huit Volumes, & de six cens Planches, & que les Volumes se succéderont sans interruption.*[28]

But in fact the manuscript wasn't in. The designs hadn't been commissioned. What became, through the force of will of hundreds of Enlightenment personalities, some money, and some luck, a project (initially) of 22 million words, 74,000 articles, 18,000 pages of text, and 28 volumes in all (17 of them text, 11 of them engraved illustrations)—what became right up there, after William Tyndale's and then others' work with the books of the Bible, the greatest project of knowledge assembly, compilation, and distribution then yet exercised—was still on the drawing board, its writers and editors, its business plan, its creative team, and, not least, its finances still far from established. Denis Diderot, one of its masterminds (and fresh out of jail, to boot), was huckstering with his sales language during that November of 1750, hoping against hope—"*Le Manuscrit & les Desseins en sont complets*," indeed!—that capital might accumulate in a form sufficient to launch the project.

The original, less ambitious plan that Le Breton had conceived—and announced—was to publish a translation of a more basic English encyclopedia—a dictionary, really—com-

---

28 "Prospectus," ARTFL Encyclopédie.

piled by Ephraim Chambers and published in England in 1728. But the plan, for a shorter five-volume set, changed—and grew.[29]

Funny, that a project we shall describe as such a sterling contribution to knowledge and fact should have been conceived in language so false and untrue. And ironic, that the sales brochure would carry on it a legend that it had been published by a printer licensed by the king, under the required royal permission—the permission, in other words, of the power that its merchandise was, ultimately, to destroy.

░ ░ ░

The prospectus was not that radical a document. It set forth to "inform the public" about the work that the Enlightenment team—the *Encyclopédistes*, as they would come to be known—was "presenting." Diderot hailed the contribution of the modest dictionary, as a form, to art and science, praised the major dictionaries and plans for encyclopedias that had been published up to then, and then called for a bigger kind of mega-dictionary, much larger than any dictionary or encyclopedia that had been published to date. In the name of the editorial team (which, again, was still to be assembled), he called for (and promised) a new scope for the new reference work: addressing and embracing, cataloging and presenting knowledge across all of the sciences, the liberal arts, and the mechanical arts.

To accomplish this, the *Encyclopédistes* had assembled artisans and scholars, he said, and assigned appropriate articles

---

29 For the most helpful history of encyclopedia work preceding this one, see Philipp Blom, *Enlightening the World:* Encyclopédie, *The Book That Changed the Course of History* (New York: Palgrave Macmillan, 2006).

to all of them.[30] "The different writers whose talents we have employed have put the stamp of their particular styles on each article, as well as that of the style proper to the subject matter and the object of their part," he wrote. They paid particular attention to the "mechanical arts," as he called them—saying that their writing "impelled us to go directly to the workers."

> We approached the most capable of them in Paris and in the realm. We took the trouble of going into their shops, of questioning them, or writing at their dictation, of developing their thoughts and of drawing therefrom the terms peculiar to their professions. . . . [S]everal times we had to get possession of the machines, to construct them, and to put a hand to the work. It was necessary to become apprentices, so to speak, and to manufacture some poor objects ourselves in order to learn how to teach others the way good specimens are made.[31]

The writing of the *Encyclopédie* was eventually to span almost twenty thousand articles over more than twenty years (1751–1777)—but even at the start the editors could foresee some of the challenges:

---

30 For more information on the *Encyclopédistes*, see "The Encyclopédistes," ARTFL Encyclopédie, University of Chicago, accessed October 13, 2020, https://encyclopedie.uchicago.edu/node/168; Frank A. Kafker and Serena L. Kafker, *The Encyclopedists as Individuals* (Liverpool: Liverpool University Press, 1988), http://www.voltaire.ox.ac.uk/book/encyclopedists-individuals; "The Encyclopédistes," Wikimedia Foundation, last modified July 1, 2020, 20:25; https://en.wikipedia.org/wiki/Encyclop%C3%A9distes; Electronic Enlightenment Project, Bodleian Libraries, University of Oxford, 2008–2019, http://www.e-enlightenment.com/.

31 "The Encyclopedia of Diderot and d'Alembert," Michigan Publishing, University of Michigan Library, accessed October 13, 2020, https://quod.lib.umich.edu/d/did/did2222.0001.083/1:4/--preliminary-discourse?rgn=div1;view=fulltext;q1=preliminary+discourse. All the English quotations of Diderot in this chapter derive from this University of Michigan project.

A technique of chemistry will not have the same tone as the description of ancient baths and theaters; the operations of a locksmith will not be set forth in the same way as the studies of a theologian on a point of dogma or discipline. Each thing has its coloration, and the various branches of knowledge would become indistinct if they were reduced to a certain uniformity.

When it was reproduced in full, as part of the encyclopedia proper, the prospectus would carry a folded map of knowledge as the *Encyclopédistes* conceived it—and it was this majestic, comprehensive vision, based on and inspired by works of Francis Bacon, Gottfried Wilhelm Leibniz, and others, that pointed, in 1750, to the incendiary. This was a genealogical tree, a diagram of knowledge phylogenesis showing where and how forms of knowledge grow, sprung from the three human faculties of memory (wherefrom history is derived), reason (philosophy), and imagination (poetry and fine arts). But it also suggested that new understandings of the human condition could be created by interrogating philosophy, religion, politics, and society all together, and not one (say, for example, religion) singly, or one more so than the others. There was a seedling sense, under this tree, that a social order needed to grow more—dare one say it— logical, reasonable, reasoned: in a word, rational. Diderot considered Bacon the originator of the empirical method, and in one of the articles—"Baconisme"—that he contributed to the *Encyclopédie* he praised the man as the project's intellectual forefather. And why not, as Bacon had hoped in his time to assemble a sweeping encyclopedia, too, with the modest-enough title of *The Phenomena of the Universe;*

or a Natural and Experimental History for the Foundation of Philosophy.[32]

The prospectus announced that this new work would be, as we say today, "fact-based"; there would be an underlying and overarching commitment on the part of all contributors and the work as a whole to the verification of its source materials. This commitment to reference—what Princeton scholar Anthony Grafton has called the "curious history" of the footnote—is the foundation of modern scholarly communication. It's the foundation of what today's Wikipedia terms verifiability, and in many ways the foundation for truth in knowledge and society.[33]

Verification is potentially "a long and painful process," Diderot declared.

> We have tried as much as possible to avoid this inconvenience by citing directly, in the body of the articles, the authors on whose evidence we have relied and by quoting their own text when it is necessary.
>
> We have everywhere compared opinions, weighed reasons, and proposed means of doubting or of escaping from doubt; at times we have even settled contested matters. . . . Facts are cited, experiments compared, and methods elaborated . . . in order to excite genius to open unknown routes, and to advance onward to new discoveries, using the place where great men have ended their careers as the first step.

---

32 Lough, *The Encyclopédie*, 63; Michael W. Twomey, "Inventing the Encyclopedia," in *Schooling and Society: The Ordering and Reordering of Knowledge in the Western Middle Ages*, ed. Alasdair A. MacDonald and Michael W. Twomey (Groningen: Peeters Publishers, 2004).

33 Anthony Grafton, *The Footnote: A Curious History* (Cambridge, MA: Harvard University Press, 1999). It's funny to footnote a book about the footnote in a section of this book discussing the footnote.

What this meant in practice was revolutionary: there would be no accepted truths but for those that could be proven and cited.

Fact-based versus faith- and belief-based—the start and spark of the Enlightenment.

Diderot also addressed the scope of the project in one other dimension—that of time, and of the *Encyclopédistes'* commitment to rendering something that would take a lot of it and last for all the rest. "It took centuries to make a beginning," he wrote, referring to the time it had taken to prepare the foundation for the work, "and it will take centuries to bring it to an end." "What an advantage it would have been for our fathers and for us, if the works of the ancient peoples, the Egyptians, the Chaldeans, the Greeks, the Romans, etc., had been transmitted in an encyclopedic work, which had also set forth the true principles of their languages." He expressed the hope that he and his team were making that contribution for us today; he speaks to us, quite directly, from centuries ago. "May the Encyclopedia become a sanctuary," he wrote, "where the knowledge of many is protected from time and from revolutions. *Will we not be more than flattered to have laid its foundations?*"

The prospectus was not a radical document. But it became something radical. Indeed, when its text, edited some and added to, was published the following year as the grand opening essay in the first one-thousand-page volume of the *Encyclopédie*, the text of that initial discourse, taken altogether, became the first colossal manifesto of human progress (in an . . . encyclopedia!), the greatest single undertaking of the Enlightenment; indeed, as one scholar as written: "It *is* the Enlightenment, insofar as one can make a claim for any single work."[34] This *Preliminary Discourse* (1751) is now compared to the Declaration of Independence (1776), the Declaration of the Rights of Man and of the Citizen (1789), and *The Communist Manifesto* (1848). It is— it instantly became—"one of the great victories for the human spirit and the printed word."[35] The *Encyclopédie* would present to the world 17 volumes of text, each volume containing on average 900 pages, each page (in two columns) containing roughly 1,200 words—some 20 million words in all. But it was through the Preliminary Discourse, itself 45 pages long, that "for the first time large numbers of people were coming to the bracing conclusion that the progress of humanity could be carried forward indefinitely in this world, and men of letters felt they were the prime movers of that progress."[36]

Volume I (*A–Azymites*) appeared in 1751, as did II (*B–Cézimbra*). Volume III (*Cha–Consécration*) appeared in 1753; IV (*Conseil–Dizier, Saint*) in 1754; V (*Do–Esymnete*) in 1755; VI (*Et–Fné*) in 1756; and VII (*Foang–Gythium*) in 1757, all in Paris; and Volumes VIII through XVII (H–Z) in 1765. The eleven volumes of plates appeared between 1762 and 1772.

And the articles: oh!

A sampling:

---

34 Richard N. Schwab, "Translator's Introduction," in *The Encyclopedia of Diderot & d'Alembert Collaborative Translation Project* (Ann Arbor: Scholarly Publishing Office of the University of Michigan Library, 2009), http://quod.lib.umich.edu/d/did/schwabintro.html, accessed October 13, 2020. Originally published in Jean Le Rond d'Alembert, *Preliminary Discourse to the Encyclopedia of Diderot*, trans. Richard N. Schwab with the collaboration of Walter E. Rex (Chicago: University of Chicago Press, 1995), ix-lii.

35 Darnton, *The Business of Enlightenment*, 13.

36 Schwab, "Translator's Introduction." See also Lough, *The Encyclopédie*, ix, 64.

ADORER.
AGNUS SCYTHICUS.
AUTORITÉ POLITIQUE.
BELBUCH & ZEOMBUCH.
BRAMINES.
CAPUCHON.
CAUCASE.
CHEF D'OEUVRE.
COLLEGE.
COPERNIC.
CORDELIER.
DAMNATION.
ECCLÉSIASTIQUE.
ÉCOLE.
ÉGALITÉ NATURELLE.
ENCYCLOPÉDIE.
EXPERIMENTAL.
FORMULAIRE.
GENÈVE.
IDOLE, IDOLÂTRE,
    IDOLÂTRIE.
IMPÔT.
INTENDANTS ET COM-
    MISSAIRES.
INTOLERANCE.
LABOREUR.
LIBELLE.

LIBERTÉ NATURELLE.
LIBERTÉ CIVILE.
LIBERTÉ POLITIQUE.
LOI FUNDAMENTALE.
MAGES.
MAGIE.
MALFAISANT.
MANES.
MASSACRE.
MENACE.
MILICE.
MODIFICATION, MODI-
    FIER, MODIFICATIF,
    MODIFIABLE.
MONARCHIE. (Are we
    getting it?)
MONARCHIE ABSOLUE.
MONARCHIE ÉLECTIVE.
MONARCHIE LIMITÉE.
    (Good!)
MONARQUE.
NOMMER.
OBEISSANCE. (Work
    with me here!)
OFFENSE.
ORIGINE.
PACIFIQUE.

PARDONNER.
PARTISAN.
PERTURBATEUR.
PEUPLE, LE.
POUVOIR.
PRESSE.
PRÊTRES.
PRIVILÈGE.
PROMISSION.
PROPAGATION DE
    L'EVANGILE.
PROPRIÉTÉ.
PROSTITUER, PROSTI-
    TUTION.
QUESTION.
REPRESENTANTS.
SCANDALEUX.
SEL.
SPINOSISTE.
SUPERSTITION.
TAILLE A VOLONTÉ.
THÉOCRATIE.
TRAITE DES NEGRES.
VICE.
VOLUPTUEUX.[37]

The text of the *Encyclopédie* included thousands of articles, on everything from asparagus to the zodiac, as the leading translation effort into English has described it. As a historian

---

37 Lough, *The Encyclopédie.* For the full chronology, see "General Chronology of the Ency-clopédie," ARTFL Encyclopédie. Ultimately more than one hundred printers would get involved with the production of the work; see Melvyn Bragg, "The *Encyclopédie*," *In Our Time,* BBC Radio 4, 45:00, http://www.bbc.co.uk/radio4/history/inourtime/inourtime_20061026.shtml.

of the project has explained, by organizing the work's articles alphabetically—as opposed to thematically—the editors
"implicitly rejected the long-standing separation of monarchic,
aristocratic, and religious values" from "those associated with
bourgeois culture and the country's trades."[38] And at the core
of the work were pages, even lines, that rocked and cracked the
eighteenth-century intellectual seismograph.

▩ ▩ ▩

The words and phrases—single words!—that William Tyndale
had newly translated in the Bible had likewise rocked the sixteenth-century establishment—church, state, and especially
Thomas More—a hundred ways to Sunday. The Bible's texts
before Tyndale spoke of the priest, the Church, charity, and
doing penance; Tyndale swept all that away.

> He translated the Greek word *presbuteros* as "elder,"
> whereas the church had always translated it as "priest";
> he translated *agape* as "love," where the church had
> always had it as "charity"; he translated *ekklesia* as "con-
> gregation," whereas the church had had it as "church";
> and he translated *exomologeo* as "acknowledge," where
> the church used "confess." Above all, he translated the
> Greek word *metanoeo* as "repent." *Metanoeo* is a classical
> and New Testament Greek word meaning "a change in
> the mind." It means that sort of complete change that
> can come over people's minds and change the direction
> of their lives. The Latin church had always translated

---

38 Andrew S. Curran, *Diderot and the Art of Thinking Freely* (New York: Other Press, 2019), 118.

that as *paenitentiam agite*, meaning "do penance." Now, to do penance involves paying money, so they didn't want the New Testament to be saying "repent." But if you look in Luke 17:3–4, Christ says "repent." In Acts 2:37, the people asked Peter and the apostles, "What shall we do?" The Greek in verse 38 says "repent." The church, however, says "do penance."[39]

The bravado is extraordinary. Tyndale said of the church and to it:

> Penance is a word of their own forging, to deceive us withal, as many others are. In the scripture we find *poenitentia*, "repentance;" *agite poenitentiam*, "do repent;" *poeniteat vos*, "let it repent you." . . . Of repentance they have made penance, to blind the people, and to make them think that they must take pains, and do some holy deeds, to make satisfaction for their sins; name such as they enjoin them. As thou mayest see in the chronicles, when great kings and tyrants came to themselves, and had conscience of their wicked deeds; then the bishops coupled them, not to Christ, but unto the pope, and preached the pope unto them; and made

---

39 David Daniell, *The Bible in English: Its History and Influence* (New Haven, CT: Yale University Press, 2003), 149. For Tyndale's work with the Greek, see Robyn Page, "Tyndale's Crucible," *Vision*, Summer 2003, https://www.vision.org/tyndales-crucible-331; Robyn Page, "William Tyndale: A Bible for the People," *Vision*, Summer 2003, https://www.vision.org/william-tyndale-bible-people-453. For more on the Hebrew, and the history, see Michael Weitzman, "On Translating the Old Testament: The Achievement of William Tyndale," *Reformation* 1 (1996): 165–180, consulted online at http://www.tyndale.org/reformjo1/weitzman.html. The depth of exegesis required is extraordinary: "Our knowledge of biblical Hebrew is far from perfect even today. The proper method of deciding what a word means is to examine its usage in a good number of contexts. However, the Bible is brief, and very little else has survived in Hebrew from ancient times. As a result, of the different words attested in biblical Hebrew, four out of five occur fewer than twenty times in the Old Testament. Indeed, about a thousand occur just once."

them to submit themselves, and also their realms, unto the holy father the pope, and to take penance, as they call it; that is to say, such injunctions as the pope and bishops would command them to do, to build abbeys, to endote them with livelihood, to be prayed for for ever, and to give them exemptions and privilege and license to do whatever they lust unpunished. . . .

The mother church, and the high altar, must have somewhat in every testament. Offerings at priests' first masses. Item, no man professed, of whatsoever religion it be, but he must bring somewhat. The hallowing, or rather conjuring of churches, chapels, altars, super-altars, chalice, vestments, and bells. Then book, bell, candlestick, organs, chalice, vestments, copes, altarcloths, surplices, towels, basins, ewers, ship. Censer, and all manner ornament must be found them freely; they will not give a mite thereunto. Last of all, what swarms of begging friars are there! The parson sheareth, the vicar shaveth, the parish priest polleth, the friar scrapeth, and the pardoner pareth; we lack but a butcher to pull off the skin.[40]

He gave people the wherewithal to challenge the church's "vain superstition," "false doctrine," "filthy lusts," "proud ambition," and "unsatiable covetousness." We thus can speak of what one of Tyndale's great modern interpreters has described as the "power of articulate contention" that Tyndale's trans-

---

40 William Tyndale, *Doctrinal Treatises and Introductions to Different Portions of the Holy Scriptures* (Cambridge: Cambridge University Press, 1848), 238. Quoted in David Ginsberg, "Ploughboys versus Prelates: Tyndale and More and the Politics of Biblical Translation," *Sixteenth Century Journal* 19, no. 1 (Spring 1988), 45–61, online (behind a paywall) at https://doi.org/10.2307/2540960.

lation work "induced in the common man." By creating "an intimate appeal to the single reader, each and every one," by "removing the encrustations of centuries of turgid and stagnant religious doctrine," and by "freeing the original prisoner-text from an expropriatory Church," Tyndale's texts as well as the very act of assembling and publishing them produced nothing less than a superpower, a moral force, amazingly, that would be "enough to uphold individuals in daring acts of dissent against overwhelming spiritual and political authority and to sustain these individuals during the sufferings that would follow such acts." He also knew that the Bible, for the most part, did not have readers; it had *listeners*; he knew that for the original writers of the Bible, it was "clearly of paramount importance to show people relating to each other through speech," and so he focused on the power of that speech; and he knew that "the dimension of sound would have been all the more urgent for the first audiences to whom these texts were addressed, who would of course not have read them silently but rather would have listened to them."

> Tyndale opened the door to a Scripture that could belong to Everyman, that could be fashioned and refashioned to suit mundane needs and wants. It was now possible to entertain the idea of a book as something other than monolithic granite, as something as pliable, and yet coherent, as mercury. A Word-to-person symmetry had been proposed, one that would put man on equal footing with his book, in contradistinction to the mother Church, a tome hidden away for prelatical eyes only.

"Scripture," moreover, "now spoke not only to the individual, but more importantly to the new society of individuals who were beginning to be united through their common access to Scripture in the vernacular. . . . The democratization of the Bible is precisely what Tyndale was after."[41]

▨ ▨ ▨

The *Encyclopédie* did the same—in ways that seem subtle today, but it smote orthodoxy with steel sledgehammers. Key articles in among the thousands—on topics that can be grouped under "religion," say, or "philosophy," or "politics and society," challenged the government and the church, even as the censors watched. The article on "Reason," for example, told us that

> No proposition can be accepted as divine revelation if it contradicts what is known to us, either by immediate intuition, as in the case of self-evident propositions, or by obvious deductions of reason, as in demonstrations.

—and the clerics were not fans. An equally impassioned condemnation of the slave trade made few friends among any who had a hand in the business:

> Slave trade is the purchase of Negroes made by Europeans on the coasts of Africa, who then employ these unfortunate men as slaves in their colonies. This pur-

---

41 "The Church was being edged out as the focal point, the common rallying ground, of man's ambition." Ginsberg, "Ploughboys versus Prelates"; Robert Alter, *The Art of Bible Translation* (Princeton, NJ: Princeton University Press, 2019), 102–103. See also Stephen Greenblatt, *Renaissance Self-Fashioning: From More to Shakespeare* (Chicago: University of Chicago Press, 1980).

chase of Negroes to reduce them into slavery is a negotiation that violates all religion, morals, natural law, and human rights.[42]

Swipes at the monarchy and the church appeared where you might expect—articles on CONSCIENCE, LIBERTÉ DE; FANATISME; TOLÉRANCE; CROISADES—but further, the article on CHAOS contained Enlightenment swipes at the Biblical myth, and FORTUNE on the gross inequalities of wealth in eighteenth-century Europe. Diderot and his colleagues— the most progressive of them, anyway—could be found "putting their bolder thoughts into short and relatively out of the way articles or quite often simply by working them into longer and more prominent ones."[43] Thus, in articles on XENXUS and XOXODINS—about Japanese religion—punches at the Jesuits and the Jansenists, and in explanations of Indian and Mexican religious experiences—SHAVVARKA, YPAINA— potshots at the pope.[44] "The learned article 'Cannibals' ended with the mischievous cross-reference: 'See Eucharist, Communion, Altar, etc.'" Diderot's modern biographer explains that approximately twenty-three thousand articles, or about one-third of the total, had at least one cross-reference. "The

---

42 Drew Armstrong, "Knowledge Reconfigured," *Constellations*, University of Pittsburgh, accessed October 13, 2020, https://constellations.pitt.edu/article/knowledge-reconfigured.

43 One Diderot biographer put it this way: "The public soon learned to identify, whether with alarm or delight, the manifold contrivances of editorial guile." Arthur M. Wilson, *Diderot: The Testing Years, 1713–1759* (New York: Oxford University Press, 1957), 131.

44 Lough, *The Encyclopédie*, 103, 112; Robert Darnton, *Censors at Work: How States Shaped Literature* (New York: W. W. Norton, 2015). The main printer would also censor the work himself from time to time—enraging not a few of the key contributors. See "André le Breton," Wikimedia Foundation, last modified April 18, 2020, 11:58, https://en.wikipedia.org/wiki/Andr%C3%A9_le_Breton; Rose Miyatsu, "A Revolutionary Encyclopedia," blog post, University Libraries, Washington University in St. Louis, November 14, 2017, https://library.wustl.edu/a-revolutionary-encyclopedia/.

total number of links—some articles had five or six—reached almost 62,000."[45]

"The ambition of the *Encyclopédie*," as one history tells us, "was to change the way people thought."

> The audacity of this project is brought into focus when considered in relation to the very limited nature of formal education available in eighteenth-century Europe. Universities were accessible only to a privileged elite and their curricula—inherited from the Middle Ages—remained devoted largely to the study of ancient Greek and Latin authors, law, medicine and, most important, theology. The *Encyclopédie*, by contrast, reached a European-wide audience. By 1789, it is estimated that *24,000* complete sets in various formats and editions had been printed, more than half of which were distributed outside France.[46]

It wasn't only the words and ideas inside the volumes that effected this change. It was the process of taking advantage of print, of commerce, of networks of contributors, printers, and distributors, to situate a major locus of knowledge and authority outside existing power institutions. Not only were

---

45 David A. Bell, "What We've Lost with the Demise of Print Encyclopedias," *New Republic*, March 19, 2012, https://newrepublic.com/article/101795/encyclopedia-britannica-publish-information; for the *Encyclopédie* article itself, see Edme-François Mallet, "Cannibals," *The Encyclopedia of Diderot & d'Alembert Collaborative Translation Project*, trans. Dena Goodman (Ann Arbor: Michigan Publishing, University of Michigan Library, 2009), http://hdl.handle.net/2027/spo.did2222.0001.094, accessed October 13, 2020. Originally published as "Anthropophages," *Encyclopédie ou Dictionnaire raisonné des sciences, des arts et des métiers*, 1:498 (Paris, 1751). See also Curran, *Diderot*, 118. Curran maintains that the editors planned out every article—"tens of thousands of possible entries"—in advance of commissioning the first one, for "fear of missing a cross-reference"; Curran, *Diderot*, 110.

46 Armstrong, "Knowledge Reconfigured," emphasis added.

contributors and editors and printers and purveyors critical of these power institutions, but they became, by the force of their interrogations and example, a stronger and stronger power institution themselves. Publishing itself was strictly censored—book publishers and pamphleteers were required to have a publishing license, or *privilège*, from the state, or some kind of *permission tacite*; licenses could be, and often were, revoked at any minute.[47] Indeed, the *Encyclopédie*'s license was pulled several times, and its permission to publish was always under threat.[48] The very idea that knowledge could be so established—and further, published with cross-references to other knowledge within the same emerging institution!—was itself a remarkable thing. In an age when "to follow one's reason wherever it led was a crime in the eyes of the orthodox," here "was a work which breathed a new spirit, one which was hostile to tradition and authority, which sought to subject all beliefs and institutions to a searching examination."[49]

---

47 On the *permission tacite*: "The curious and very common practice constitutes an excellent example of the sort of paradoxical and illogical procedure that the anomalies of the *ancien regime* brought into being. A tacit permission was an official connivance of an infringement of the regulations. The process was so general and so regularized that a register of most tacit permissions was kept on file by the syndic of the corporation of booksellers. Other tacit permissions, however, were accorded orally and without registration, the author and printer merely being given private and non-documentary assurance that they might publish a particular manuscript without molestation from the police. In every case, however, the censors previously read the manuscripts in the usual way and the director of publications knew perfectly well what was going on. [A]ll these numerous books were printed anonymously, with misleading places of publication printed on their title pages, the point being that they should bear every mark of being illicit and clandestine in order to save the government from being officially embarrassed by any statements they might contain." Wilson, *Diderot*, 131–132. Indeed, *Encyclopédie* biographer Philipp Blom goes so far as to say that "the majority of books that appeared during the *ancien regime* were clandestine editions, smuggled into the city in bales of hay and the false bottoms of barrels of salted herring, or printed inside wood piles and on boats, in the alcoves of bourgeois houses and the huts in the gardens around Paris, and hawked in the streets and inns by specialized colporteurs, constantly on the lookout for police." See Blom, *Enlightening the World*, 10–11.

48 Lough, *The Encyclopédie*, 94, 233–236.

49 Lough, *The Encyclopédie*, 139, 398.

The *Encyclopédie* project, in a word, shifted the giant spotlights of knowledge storage and distribution away from monolithic religious orders and behemoths of state-run and state-controlled institutions and shined them on something new—something that looked, in the bright glare, like something that we the people could, one day, control.[50] Remember, as one scholar tells us,

> [t]he scholarly societies of the seventeenth and early eighteenth centuries, while hoping to contribute to material progress, were concerned primarily with the erudite and professional activities of closeted savants and did not dream of transforming the conditions of the world in a fundamental way.[51]

The 1750 prospectus had been run off with a foldout of a chart of knowledge—a diagram of understanding, a topic map or XML schema, a summary of the principles, the *Principia*, of human knowledge—composed and drawn by Francis Bacon and printed as a bonus takeaway, like a pennant or a decal you received free with your mid-eighteenth-century direct-mail solicitation.[52] Much as Google would be developed by two gentlemen fixated—coming, as they did, out of the informa-

---

50 For a positive take on the teleology of all of this, see John Willinsky, *The Intellectual Properties of Learning: A Prehistory from Saint Jerome to John Locke* (Chicago: University of Chicago Press, 2017). See also Michael Jensen, "The New Metrics of Scholarly Authority," *Chronicle of Higher Education*, June 15, 2007, online (behind a paywall) at https://www.chronicle.com/article/The-New-Metrics-of-Scholarly/5449.

51 Schwab, "Translator's Introduction."

52 For more on its inspiration, Francis Bacon, see "*New Atlantis*," Wikimedia Foundation, last modified April 16, 2020, 16:14, https://en.wikipedia.org/wiki/New_Atlantis; https://www.fbrt.org.uk/bacon/; and the website Six Degrees of Francis Bacon, http://www.sixdegreesoffrancisbacon.com.

tion-science world—on the value and reference of citation for ranking the verifiability of published information, the *Encyclopédie*, too, was built from a reference mindset. Articles across the enormous project *cited one another*—further solidifying the status of the collected volumes as themselves an ultimate and independent reference. Furthermore, the contributors were identified—by name, initials, codes. Not all of the contributors were major figures like Voltaire or Rousseau; indeed, an annoyed Diderot would write in 1768 that

> [i]n addition to some excellent people, there were others who were weak, mediocre, and totally incompetent. A jumbled work resulted, where a schoolboy's rough draft is found next to a masterpiece, a stupidity alongside something sublime, a page written with force, purity, passion, judgment, reason, and elegance on the back of a page that is poor, trivial, dull, and wretched.[53]

But their contributions—many of them, anyway—were attributed, sourced, verifiable. Of the 140 or so contributors we know about, only 20 or so were paid. And in many ways the most fascinating thing is that in those instances when contributors were not identified, it was often so that their contributions actually could be more pointed; in those instances where the citation framework was not so clear, it was often so that pre-

---

53 Quoted in Frank A. Kafker, "The Recruitment of the Encyclopedists," *Eighteenth-Century Studies* 6, no. 4 (Summer 1973): 452–61, online (behind a paywall) at https://doi.org/10.2307/3031579. And Diderot could sling it in hot French: "L'Encyclopédie fut un gouffre, où ces espèces de chiffonniers jetèrent pêle-mêle une infinité de choses mal vues, mal digérées, bonnes, mauvaises, détestables, vraies, fausses, incertaines, et toujours incohérentes et disparates." See Lough, *The Encyclopédie*, 82.

viously banned books and other works could be quoted, and even excerpted, more freely.[54] The whole damn thing was such a triumph!

The prospectus was not that radical a document. But it became something radical. It became the manifesto of the *Encyclopédie*, the *Encyclopédie* became the manifesto of the Enlightenment—and the Enlightenment became the manifesto of the call to action for freedom and justice and equality that still motivates us today.

The Monsterverse would come for it, of course—but that's for later.

※ ※ ※

As William Tyndale had Aaron Swartz, Diderot, too, had his successor, a modern cognate: act of freedom to act of freedom. The prospectus that would follow Diderot's in importance would actually follow in 1999.

That year, MIT's free-software activist and hacker Richard M. Stallman called for a universal *online* encyclopedia, covering all areas of knowledge, and a complete library of instructional courses—and, equally important, as a parallel to what we have been reading and as an inspiration to us today, a movement (quite literally, he says a "movement") to develop it, "much as the Free Software Movement gave us the free operating system GNU/Linux."

---

54 Dan Edelstein, Robert Morrissey, and Glenn Roe, "To Quote or Not to Quote: Citation Strategies in the *Encyclopédie*," *Journal of the History of Ideas* 74, no. 2 (April 2013): 213–36, online (behind a paywall) at https://www.jstor.org/stable/43291299; and Curran, *Diderot*. See also Darnton, *The Business of Enlightenment*; Robert Darnton, *The Literary Underground of the Old Regime* (Cambridge, MA: Harvard University Press, 1982); Robert Darnton, *George Washington's False Teeth: An Unconventional Guide to the Eighteenth Century* (New York: W. W. Norton, 2001).

The free encyclopedia will provide an alternative to the restricted ones that media corporations will write.

Stallman published a list of what that the encyclopedia would need to do, what sort of freedoms it would need to give to the public, and how it could get started. This was in 1999. It was to take advantage of the new century's newest connective technology—so it would be online. It would be

An encyclopedia located everywhere.

An encyclopedia open to anyone—but, most promisingly, to teachers and students.

An encyclopedia built of small steps.

An encyclopedia built on the long view: "If it takes twenty years to complete the free encyclopedia, that will be but an instant in the history of literature and civilization."

An encyclopedia built with evangelists: "Let's present . . . examples systematically to the academic community."

An encyclopedia containing one or more articles for any topic you would expect to find in another encyclopedia—"for example, bird watchers might eventually contribute an article on each species of bird, along with pictures and recordings of its calls"—and "courses for all academic subjects."

1999.

An encyclopedia with criteria of freeness.

An encyclopedia that permits universal access.

An encyclopedia that permits mirror sites and verbatim copies.

An encyclopedia that permits translation into other languages.

An encyclopedia that permits quotation with attribution.

An encyclopedia that permits modified versions of pictures and videos, for courses.

An encyclopedia built on only free software.

An encyclopedia without central control.

An encyclopedia that encourages peer review.

An encyclopedia with no catalogue—at least not yet.

An encyclopedia where pages inside link to other pages—but with no links to web pages that are restricted.

An encyclopedia that upholds the freedom of everyone, but especially teachers, to contribute.

An encyclopedia built by people who will spread the word.[55]

The licensing nonprofit Creative Commons would soon after declare Stallman to be its intellectual forebear. "In December 2002," the organization's website notes, Creative Commons "released its first set of copyright licenses for free to the public . . . inspired in part by [Stallman's] Free Software Foundation's GNU General Public License."

---

55 Richard Stallman, "The Free Universal Encyclopedia and Learning Resource," Gnu.org, https://www.gnu.org/encyclopedia/anencyc.txt. See also "GNE (encyclopedia)," Wikimedia Foundation, last modified June 24, 2020, 12:51, https://en.wikipedia.org/wiki/GNE_(encyclopedia); "The Free Encyclopedia Project," GNU Project Web Server, accessed October 13, 2020, https://www.gnu.msn.by/encyclopedia/; and "History of Wikipedia," McGill School of Computer Science, accessed October 13, 2020, https://www.cs.mcgill.ca/~rwest/wikispeedia/ wpcd/wp/h/History_of_Wikipedia.htm. Stallman's essay is reprinted as this book's Appendix.

More to the point, Wikipedia to this day attributes its founding to Stallman, too, having based its "technological and conceptual underpinnings," it says, on the "free-as-in-freedom online encyclopedia . . . proposed by Richard Stallman in December 2000."[56]

Actually, 1999.

56 https://creativecommons.org/about/history/; "About the Licenses," Creative Commons, accessed October 13, 2020, https://creativecommons.org/licenses/; "History of Wikipedia," Wikimedia Foundation, last modified July 7, 2020, 6:32, https://en.wikipedia.org/wiki/History_of_Wikipedia. Edward Snowden claims inspiration from Stallman, too; see Snowden and Daniel Ellsberg in conversation at HOPE 2014: "HOPE X (2014:): A Conversation with Edward Snowden," Channel 2600, YouTube, July 22, 2014, video, 1:26:20, https://www.youtube.com/watch?v=6PHFjLkwOZE. (Snowden's remarks begin at 41:11.) As Lawrence Lessig has written, "[W]hen our world finally comes to understand the power and danger of code—when it finally sees that code, like laws, or like government, must be transparent to be free—then we will look back at this uncompromising and persistent programmer and realize the vision he has fought to make real: the vision of a world where freedom and knowledge survives the compiler. And we will come to see that no man, through his deeds or words, has done as much to make possible the freedom that this next society could have." Lawrence Lessig, introduction to Joshua Gay, ed., *Free Software, Free Society: Selected Essays of Richard M. Stallman*, 3rd ed. (Boston: Free Software Foundation, 2012), ix.

3. The Commissariat

1989. November. As the Berlin Wall started to come down, we in the West who didn't live (yet, anyway) under a system of mass surveillance began to recognize more fully than we ever had before just what a nefarious, ostensibly absolute system had been established to restrict the freedoms of people in the eastern part of Europe—from East Germany and the Baltic states through Hungary, Poland, and Czechoslovakia, down through Romania, Yugoslavia, Albania, and then across all eleven time zones and fifteen republics of the Soviet Union. That system was odious. It crushed the souls of generations, killed millions, and distorted reality for hundreds of millions more. The damage is still being undone.

And for what? Without it, perhaps, we might never have had worlds of art and culture created under these particular eastern tyrannies, including especially those by the writers—Witold Gombrowicz, Tadeusz Konwicki, Bruno Schulz, Václav Havel, Bohumil Hrabal; Nobel laureates such as Czeslaw Milosz, Svetlana Alexievich, Aleksandr Solzhenitsyn, and Boris Pasternak—who have had so much to teach us about beauty, morality, absurdity, and truth. But maybe it existed then to show us now what a system designed and imposed upon us without our consent could actually do to us as people. That system—the Monsterverse, *à la Russe*—was designed and built in the name of the very same Enlightenment that brought us the *Encyclopédie* and Rousseau's *Social Contract* and the American and French revolutions; indeed, it was first installed by a Soviet Commissar of Enlightenment in the 1920s. The Enlightenment that this commissar—Anatoly Lunacharsky, a Russian revolutionary and confidant of Vladimir Lenin—was supposed to preside over never, in fact, materialized. Its last nominal vestige today is the Russian, formerly Soviet, state monopoly publishing house for Russian school textbooks, Prosveshcheniye ("Enlightenment"), headquartered in Moscow. ("Eight generations of Russian people grew up and learned using our books," its website says.)[57] But the Soviet model, and its Central and Eastern European knock-offs, dominated the intellectual and cultural landscape of all of these countries—in the Soviet Union from 1917, and in the Eastern bloc from after World War II—thanks to the power of a military, security, intelligence, and police apparatus that was able to suppress dissent, alternatives, and opposition. It governed all media and information, from newspapers and book publishing to radio and film. It was designed to produce a new type of Soviet socialist man, a socially engineered human being who, in theory, fed a certain diet of information while being controlled, in body and mind, by a governmental system, would behave according to socialist principles and build post–Soviet revolutionary society: a society, in practice and theory, no longer focused on perpetuating private gain, injustice, inequity, and worse.

In reality, of course, the Soviet system became one of the most heinous and oppressive ever built. Any system that leads to the requirement to register every typewriter with the state, as the Soviet-imposed system did in communist Romania, and every Xerox machine and mimeograph with the government, as it did in postwar Poland, is fairly likely to be biased against freedom of thought. Media and communication, as a monopoly busi-

---

57 "Prosveshcheniye: The Way for Over 87 Years," Prosveshcheniye, accessed October 13, 2020, https://prosv.ru/eng.

ness run by the state, becomes an engine, we can see now, that exerts—for systemic reasons, and independent of the personalities involved in stewarding it—a nefarious impact on liberty, equality, and justice.[58] Indeed, monopolies of any kind, state or private, determining a society's media and information landscape will exert a largely nefarious effect on society, wherever that society may be and at whatever time in human history.

The Soviet architecture of totalitarian thought control was built, to be sure, upon earlier imperial systems of censorship and information policies from the Russian, Hapsburg, and Ottoman empires. But the Soviet architects who designed it in Moscow and Saint Petersburg and exported it westward brought it to a whole new level. For the printing press, the dominant media at the time, the plan's draught was clear. Step one: bring all book-production equipment and materials—typesetting, printing, binding, and packaging machinery, as well as paper production—under state control. Step two: control all publishers' access to outside information and manuscripts. Step three: control the distribution of all printed materials—books, journals, newspapers, and magazines. Step four: control the access of national publishers to foreign readers (and hard currency) and of national readers to foreign literature. Step five: place control of every publisher's finances under the state.

❊ ❊ ❊

Saturday, January 27, 1990, four thirty in the afternoon: as the Polish United Workers' Party was meeting in Warsaw's Palace of Culture to formally disband after forty-one years of rule, the cur-

---

58 See Peter B. Kaufman, "Central and Eastern Europe," in *International Book Publishing: An Encyclopedia,* Philip G. Altbach and Edith S. Hoshino, eds. (New York: Garland Publishing, 1995).

tain rose on Richard Wagner's six-hour opera *Götterdämmerung* ("The Twilight of the Gods") in Warsaw's famous Teatr Wielki. Around five o'clock Warsaw time, as the three Fates watched the golden thread of the future get clipped in two, signaling the end of the eternal rule of the gods on the stage, delegates to the last Communist Party meeting in Poland were singing the "Internationale" together for the last time (a scene televised on the evening news), and hundreds of protesters, in a small and rather cathartic riot, were hurling bottles, rocks, and invective at the ring of blue and white militia vans guarding the Palace. Outside the gates of Warsaw University, on Nowy Świat, the winter sun was setting over makeshift tables where vendors were displaying books and pamphlets by, among other writers, Raymond Aron, Václav Havel, and Jeane Kirkpatrick, and whiskered students were selling little pins that read, "No more communism." One student was selling a sticker of the same Mount Rushmore–type portrait of the four heads of Marx, Engels, Lenin, and Stalin that had graced billboards all over the Soviet Union in the late 1940s. Without a caption, the image conveyed a simple indictment in 1990 Poland: that all systems that begin with Marx lead inevitably to the savagery of Stalin.

Sticker for sale in Warsaw, 1990.

This was a day of carnival in a season of change for Poland—in many ways representative of the situation in Central and Eastern Europe at large. The economic reform program of the new Polish prime minister, Tadeusz Mazowiecki, was at the end of its fourth week of slashing subsidies and eliminating cheap credits and tax concessions, after having already devalued the zloty. According to Polish state television, inflation was at 68 percent that month; prices on basic goods had risen on average 45 to 50 percent since the start of the year four weeks earlier; food prices had skyrocketed 755 percent. Real income had dropped some 40 percent. Mazowiecki's chief spokesperson, Małgorzata Niezabitowska, stated that 55,800 people were registered as unemployed in January (as against 9,600 in December). The country had begun setting up soup kitchens. On Krakowskie Przedmieście, a graffito scrawled in thick red ink provided strollers with one citizen's verdict on the reform and its champion, Leszek Balcerowicz. "Balcerowicz," it read, "is a Mengele of the economy." The clutches of protestors who used to congregate, before the water cannons came, in front of the enormous former Central Committee headquarters on Nowy Świat had already moved on to chant in front of the finance ministry on Świętokrzyska.

Nowhere was the strain of Polish austerity measures more evident than in the field of culture. That year the new culture minister was Izabella Cywińska, a former theater director and Solidarity member, who had been imprisoned for a period during martial law. Under pressure from both her enemies and her friends to preserve state subsidies for various cultural programs and institutions, she had in fact appeared quite ruthless in withdrawing government funding, in line with the Balcerowicz reform program. As a result, some 160 theaters had had to close, 130 weeklies had failed, and 300 journalists were already out of work in Warsaw. Acknowledging herself, on the record, to be "*la donna mobile*," Cywińska reversed herself on earlier promises to keep down the state price of Polish newsprint and book paper and to keep up subsidies to important literary journals. As a result, the price of paper—2.8 million zlotys (US $300) per ton in December and 12 million zlotys (US $1,280) per ton in January—had risen as high as the world price, and book publishers had begun to turn to the better-quality and more readily available paper of Finland.

Cywińska, like other post-communist culture ministers in the region, had surrounded herself with advisors who had been close colleagues from the literary and theater underground. In her view, those who knew how to economize on a microscale to obtain supplies and services on the black market would be able to find ways of economizing on the macro—given the free market that had started to emerge. It is true that the black market seemed to be regulated by the same laws of supply and demand that had begun to exert their effect on the unregulated general economy. But the rules of these two economies were not identical, and so Cywińska and her top advisors found them-selves being criticized on two fronts. On the one hand, there were those who charged that the ministry was not using enough nonmarket mechanisms to prop up valuable institutions during the difficult transition period of shock therapy. (As an example, this group was demanding reform of the absurd tax laws in Poland that made the costs of private philanthropy—the dona-tion of cash, equipment, or services to publishers—prohibitive.) On the other hand, there were those who blamed the new gov-ernment for not yet having created purer market conditions for culture—a sort of natural-selection environment in which only the economically fittest would survive. In a November 1989 con-fidential report, as the austerity measures were being planned, the ministry's Department of Books put these two views together in a sort of dialectical unity. Pure market conditions, the report stated, would be the most ideal environment for book publishing in Poland. But it blamed a recession in the book industry in late 1989 on the sudden *urynkowienie*, or marketization, of the general economy, and it went on to recommend continued select government intervention in the industry.[59]

Poland's conflicted approach concerning the government and the economy—representative, in a number of ways, of attitudes throughout the region—dated back to the consolidation of totalitarian thought control and the command economy, both established in the late 1940s and early 1950s. For forty years in the countries of Central and Eastern Europe, the state controlled the fields of culture, education, and media with an iron fist—much more severely than in even the harshest traditions of the Russian, Hapsburg, and Ottoman empires. Over these decades, the communists of Eastern Europe, basing their efforts in a bastard social-science jargon born with the Bolshevik Revolution of 1917, tried to perfect the totalitarian control of media and communication. Russian political philosophers, some of whom had become Soviet ones, developed blueprints for control that seemed to them a part of the great experiment that was the revolution. The leading exponents of this social engineering saw print as a key instrument in the transformative educational process that would bring into the world a qualitatively "new" society of socialists. In *The ABC of Communism: A Popular Explanation of the Program of the Communist Party of Russia* (1922)—among the best known and most widely circulated of all the pre-Stalinist explanations of communism—Nikolai Bukharin and Evgenii Preobrazhenskii wrote that

---

59 For more, see Peter B. Kaufman, "Polish Publishing Goes to Market," *The Nation*, May 20, 1991.

The most powerful method of state communist propaganda is the state publishing activity. The nationalization of all the reserves of paper and of all the printing establishments, makes it possible for the proletarian state, despite the great scarcity of paper, to publish by the million any literature which is particularly important for the masses at a given moment. Everything issued from the state presses is made available to the generality of the people by publication at a very low price, and by degrees it is possible to issue books, pamphlets, newspapers, and posters for free. The state propaganda of communism becomes in the long run a means for the eradication of the last traces of bourgeois propaganda dating from the old regime; and it is a powerful instrument for the creation of a new ideology, of new modes of thought, of a new outlook on the world.[60]

Russian philosophers from the nineteenth and early twentieth century, such as Vissarion Belinsky, Alexander Herzen, and Nikolai Chernyshevsky, embodying both wittingly and unwittingly various Russian imperial traditions, no doubt helped to lay the groundwork for this approach—to state, to state and society, to revolution.[61] But it was the early Soviet minister Anatoly Lunacharsky, who served in the USSR's government for twelve years, from 1917 to 1929, as Commissar of Enlightenment, who was given the brief. Considered (at least in

---

60 N. Bukharin and E. Preobrazhenskii, *The ABC of Communism: A Popular Explanation of the Program of the Communist Party of Russia* trans. Eden and Cedar Paul (London: Communist Party of Great Britain, 1922), 245.

61 Jeffrey Brooks, *When Russia Learned to Read: Literacy and Popular Literature, 1861–1917* (Princeton, NJ: Princeton University Press, 1985). See also James H. Billington, *The Icon and the Axe: An Interpretive History of Russian Culture* (New York: Alfred A. Knopf, 1966); James H.

his own words) "a Bolshevik among intellectuals and an intellectual among Bolsheviks," Lunacharsky took as his mandate
to remake the new state's education system and the arts—and
had a heavy hand in the design of its media control.[62] It was
his planning that built the Soviet Monsterverse—but it owed
much to the longstanding fascination in Russia for the French
Enlightenment. Let us remember that Russia's empress Catherine the Great had been so enamored of Voltaire that she
invited him to the Russian capital to consult with him on the
design of Russian cultural and educational institutions. She had
been so enamored of Diderot that she invited him to Russia so
he could publish the *Encyclopédie* there. She asked Diderot to
submit to her a plan for fundamentally remaking the education system she had inherited—it was only in Russia, she said,
that he could put the values of the French Enlightenment into
practice—and she offered to pay him his entire salary for doing
so, for fifty years, in advance (which he accepted).[63] Indeed, the

Billington, *The Face of Russia: Anguish, Aspiration, and Achievement in Russian Culture* (New York: TV Books, 1998); "Russian Enlightenment," Wikimedia Foundation, last modified June 10, 2020, 7:33, https://en.wikipedia.org/wiki/Russian_Enlightenment; Marc Raeff, *Origins of the Russian Intelligentsia: The Eighteenth-Century Nobility* (New York: Houghton Mifflin, 1966); and the nicely titled work of Lesley Chamberlain, *Ministry of Darkness: How Sergei Uvarov Created Conservative Modern Russia* (London: Bloomsbury Academic, 2019).

62 Sheila Fitzpatrick, *The Commissariat of Enlightenment: Soviet Organization of Education and the Arts under Lunacharsky, October 1917–1921*, Cambridge Russian, Soviet and Post-Soviet Studies (Cambridge: Cambridge University Press, 1970); and A. L. Tait, "Lunacharsky, the 'Poet-Commissar,'" *Slavonic and East European Review* 52, no. 127 (April 1974): 234–251, online (behind a paywall) at https://www.jstor.org/stable/4206869. See also "Narkompros," Monoskop, last modified October 21, 2016, 23:09, https://monoskop.org/Narkompros.

63 For more on the Soviet approach to the original Enlightenment—still a young field of study—see Peter H. Kaufman, "Soviet Perspectives on the French Enlightenment and Rev-olution," *Studies in Eighteenth-Century Culture* 20 (1991): 115–29, online (behind a paywall) at https://doi.org/10.1353/sec.2010.0149; Philip Moran, "Leninism and the Enlightenment," *Studies in Soviet Thought* 30, no. 2 (August 1985): 109–30, online (behind a paywall) at https://www.jstor.org/stable/20100034; and Arnold Miller, "The Annexation of a Philosophe: Diderot in Soviet Criticism, 1917–1960," *Diderot Studies* 15 (1971): 5–464, online (behind a paywall) at https://www.jstor.org/stable/40372415.

empress bought the libraries of Voltaire and other Enlighten-ment luminaries and brought them to Russia, where they are still ensconced in Russian state libraries to this day.[64]

This pseudoscience of creating "a new ideology, of new modes of thought, of a new outlook on the world"—again, the Soviet Monsterverse—involved much more than an oppres-sive system of censorship. After World War II, every state in postwar Central and Eastern Europe took a basic series of steps to quash any possibility of free thought that could be construed as challenging to the regime. Together, these steps, adumbrated below, constituted one of the more damaging, enduring experi-ments in thought control that modern Europe has ever known.

Step one was to bring all book production equipment and materials—typesetting, printing, binding, and packaging machinery, as well as paper production—under state control throughout the Soviet-controlled Eastern bloc. When, for example, the Czechoslovak Communist Party seized power in 1948, publishing houses were ransacked, their typecases and let-terpresses removed, and paper mills nationalized. Printing was made a state monopoly industry and centralized to such a degree that from 1948 to early 1990 there were only five legal book printers in Bohemia and Moravia. The largest of these, Poli-grafický Prumysl, employed an astonishing seventeen thousand

---

64 Home page, Voltaire Library, accessed October 13, 2020, http://nlr.ru/voltaire; "The Vol-taire Library Project: Using Digital Humanities to Understand Voltaire's Influences," Voltaire Foundation blog, July 24, 2018, https://voltairefoundation.wordpress.com/2018/07/24/the-vol-taire-library-project-using-digital-humanities-to-understand-voltaires-influences/; Gillian Pink, "Voltaire in St Petersburg: The Voltaire Library and the Marginalia Project," December 3, 2012, in Oxford University Podcasts, MP3 audio, 30:45, https://podcasts.ox.ac.uk/voltaire-st-pe-tersburg-voltaire-library-and-marginalia-project; various contributors, "Was There a Russian Enlightenment?" December 3, 2012, Oxford University Podcasts, MP3 audio, https://podcasts.ox.ac.uk/series/was-there-russian-enlightenment; Alex Shashkevich, "Stanford Senior Digi-tally Documents Voltaire's Research Process," *Stanford News*, September 26, 2018, https://news.stanford.edu/2018/09/26/new-stanford-project-gets-inside-voltaires-mind/. See also Andrew S. Curran, *Diderot and the Art of Thinking Freely* (New York: Other Press, 2019), 316–350.

workers in 1989. These printing houses maintained a vertical as well as horizontal monopoly on the entire book production cycle. They controlled its every aspect, from typesetting and printing through trimming, binding, and packaging. And only a certain number of publishers—usually one for each sector (textbooks, science, history, literature, children's books)— received legal licenses from the regime. That said, editors and publishers in the region have always been forthright about the fact that this kind of state control predated Communist power in the region. Státní Pedagogické Nakladatelství, the state publishing house for textbooks in Czechoslovakia, for example, was founded by Empress Maria Theresa in 1775, originally as a branch of the empire's *Bundesverlag*. And then, as under Communist rule, state representatives read every manuscript before it went to press. The editors' stake in explaining that tradition is a major one: they wish for new visitors to understand that eradicating the idea of state control from Czech publishing involved pulling out roots that had grown into the soil not for three generations but for ten.

Step two was to control the publishers' access to outside information and manuscripts. DILIA, the state copyright agency, was created in 1950 under the control of the Czech ministry of culture. Before the revolution, DILIA represented all Czech publishers seeking to buy foreign rights and all Czech authors who were allowed by the writers union to sell their rights abroad—except the signatories of Charter 77, who were forbidden by the state from publishing or selling their rights at all. The ministries of culture and finance also controlled the hard-currency receipts and expenditures of all publishing houses, so that no editor or publisher could acquire foreign manuscripts abroad and circumvent DILIA.

The royalty laws that DILIA dealt with day to day were designed to repress creativity and reward servility to the state. Czech authors were paid royalties according to the number of signatures (pages) they had in their printed book and the number of copies the publisher printed. This encouraged cronies of publishing chieftains to write long books about nothing important and ask for six-figure print runs. For works from abroad, DILIA used to pay Western authors a flat fee for their rights—say, a thousand US dollars for the right to print a medical text in a run of ten thousand copies, and a pro rata fee for whatever exceeded ten thousand copies. And needless to say, no publisher in the Soviet Monsterverse had legal access to information sources that are standard international reference works in Western publishing—resources, for example, such as *Literary Market Place* or *Books in Print*.

Step three was to control the distribution of all printed materials—books, journals, newspapers, and magazines. It became clear that distribution was the single largest problem plaguing publishers throughout the region. In Czechoslovakia, control was exercised through two state-run distribution agencies: Knižní Velkoobchod (KV) for books and První Novinová Společnost (PNS) for journals, magazines, and newspapers. A few publishing houses were allowed to keep their own prewar bookshops after 1948, but book wholesaling was, without exception, nationalized. Year after year, book publishers grew used to believing KV's market surveys, to printing the number of copies stipulated by KV, and to setting the prices on their books according to national guidelines from a government institute. Publishers abstained from any duties that might resemble Western-style publicity and marketing. After the collapse of communism, most of the formerly exclusive, legal publishers had no idea who exactly was "end-using" their books.

Yet every week, about thirty to forty new titles, or 1 million copies, were delivered by KV to the 1,200 bookselling establishments in Bohemia and Moravia. The deliveries were based on a three-stage planning process stretched out over two years. In the first stage, some eighteen months before D-Day (always a Thursday), publishers sent three hundred to four hundred copies of their list of forthcoming titles (the *edicni plan*) to KV headquarters; KV would collate them and send a package by post to the eight district headquarters of Knižní Maloobchod (KM), its regional subsidiaries. KM was responsible for conducting surveys to determine the book market in each district and for sending the numbers back to Prague. Most of the time the numbers were computed by "experience," in the words of the staff—easier in specialty literature ("as the market is known"); more difficult in children's literature and belles lettres. A publisher could also send its *edicni plan* directly to bookstores to publicize its list of new and forthcoming books, but that was not a common practice.

This step concluded, representatives from the eight KM headquarters, plus a representative from Slovakia, would come to an inn outside of Prague for one week (usually in the spring) in order to hear presentations by the leading publishers about the books these publishers were most interested in promoting (about ten such presentations per day). But, of course, these meetings could not result in changed price structures for single books or series, significant advertising campaigns in magazines or on television, or major changes in projected print runs. Book prices were set by tamper-proof state guidelines, established by a single pricing institute. Advertising and all promotional gimmickry, so very necessary in Western publishing, were absent or primitive throughout the Eastern bloc. The allocation of paper was controlled by an immovable state apparatus in the ministry of culture. Indeed, as these meetings had almost nothing to do with the interplay between actual demand for literature and real possibilities for satisfying that demand, they usually took on an existential air—helpless retailers and wholesalers meeting with powerless publishers—and ultimately degenerated (or perhaps evolved) into a free-flowing beer festival.

The second phase of publication would begin when the publisher would send a book into production at the typesetting/printing house (books were most often typeset and printed by the same establishment). At this point the publisher would send KV a synopsis of the final product and the exact estimated production schedule. KV would contact KM directly or through its monthly bulletin, *Co nového vyjde* (What's Newly Published), to adjust the delivery numbers if necessary, and then conclude a wholesale purchase order from the publisher. (KV would pay 70 percent of the cover price of a book to the publisher and sell it to KM at 77 percent, the 7 percent net representing KV's take on the book trade. The figure is not dissimilar to the net margin of book-trade wholesalers elsewhere in Central and Eastern Europe; Romania's Întreprindera de Diffuzare i Cărţii, for example, took 8 percent.[65])

At this stage, three possibilities existed: One, the publisher might want to circulate more copies of a given book than KV agreed to market; KV would take them if the publisher bore the

---

65 Peter B. Kaufman, "Publishing: Romanian Remainders," *Times Literary Supplement*, London, July 6–12, 1990.

cost of publicizing the extra copies. Two, the number of copies ordered would match the number scheduled for printing—in which case, there was no problem. Three, the number that the publisher would print might be less than the number KV would order (this occurred all the time). In this case, KV would alert the retail centers. The book dealers would agree to divide the actual print run among themselves, often basing the division on district population figures, with no consideration paid to actual demand.

In the third phase of publication, the publisher would notify KV that the book was about to be issued. Through its other weekly newsletter, *Nové knihy* (New Books), KV would alert stores, roughly a month in advance, as to the week in which the book would be delivered. *Nové knihy*, though produced for the book trade, actually sold briskly at PNS kiosks because people had no other way of knowing which new books would be appearing in the shops on Thursday (books rarely being reviewed in advance of publication). About a week after the announcement, KV would begin loading its trucks and cars for shipment to stores and weigh-station warehouses. The shipping process would take about a fortnight before a title reached the remotest of bookshops; critics used to say that the books, wrapped in unprotective paper (not plastic), would sit for months in rattletrap warehouses with leaky roofs. Bookshops that received their books ahead of the announced publication date were obliged to keep them out of customer reach until the designated date of delivery. This system lasted until March 1990—four months after the revolution—when it was breached by émigré publishers who, carrying formerly banned books in trucks, vans, and cars, rumbled across fallen border checkpoints from West Germany, Austria, France, and

Switzerland, and also from Canada, the United States, and the United Kingdom, bringing their produce to market directly to the bookstores.

Step four was to control the access of national publishers to foreign readers (and hard currency) and of national readers to foreign literature. In Czechoslovakia, Artia was established in the 1950s as the state trading monopoly for the import and export of cultural products such as sheet music, violins, and books. Virtually every Czech publishing house that wanted to sell its books abroad, and every institution and individual that sought to buy foreign books, had to proceed at some point through this enormous bureaucratic apparatus. Knižní Velkoobchod was Artia's leading supplier of books for export; Zahraniční Literatura, a small network of foreign-literature (mainly Soviet literature) bookstores, was its biggest client for books imported from abroad. Bloated for forty years by sinecure staff positions and an unfair, artificial monopoly that restricted the access of Czech publishers to markets in the West, Artia, like DILIA, lost its monopoly once the Berlin Wall came down.

Step five, easily the most important, was to put control of every publishing house's finances under the state. The state monitored publishers' expenditures, taxed them heavily, and tithed all of the income. An elaborate subsidy-and-tax system of pipes and funnels was built among the houses, printing plants, state book-trade organs, and relevant ministries to directly subsidize certain houses, indirectly subsidize printing plants and distributors (so that they could not function without state support), tax and reward authors, and control the profits earned by any and all publishers. The consequent fiscal helplessness—"pauperization," as some put it, in translation—of many publishers after the revolutions of 1989 became one of the sorest sources of concern.[66]

The United Nations Universal Declaration on Human Rights, a touchstone charter for human freedom, set forth in 1948 that "everyone has the right to freedom of opinion and expression; this right includes freedom to hold opinions without interference and to seek, receive and impart information and ideas through any media and regardless of frontiers."[67] In Article 19 of the International Covenant on Civil and Political Rights, part of the Universal Declaration, it is written:

> Everyone shall have the right to freedom of expression; this right shall include freedom to seek, receive and impart information and ideas of all kinds, regardless of frontiers, either orally, in writing or in print, in the form of art, or through any other media of his choice.[68]

This covenant was adopted by the United Nations General Assembly in 1948 (after May, when the Communists in Prague staged their bloodless coup) by a vote of 48 to 0, with eight

---

66 For more, see: Peter B. Kaufman, "Publishing in Budapest," *Scholarly Publishing* 21, no. 4 (July 1990): 195–204; Peter B. Kaufman, "Coming Up for Air," *Publishers Weekly*, September 7, 1990; Peter B. Kaufman, "Two Prague Publishers: Academia and SPN," *Scholarly Publishing* 22, no. 31 (April 1991): 143–154; Peter B. Kaufman and Gleb Uspensky, "50 Million Agatha Christies Can't Be Wrong," *Publishers Weekly*, November 9, 1992. See also Peter B. Kaufman, "A Profile of Prosveshcheniye Publishing House: State-Administered Textbook Publishing in the Russian Federation," prepared for the World Bank, Washington, DC, 1994, unpublished.

67 "Universal Declaration of Human Rights," United Nations, accessed July 10, 2020, https://www.un.org/en/universal-declaration-human-rights/.

68 "International Covenant on Civil and Political Rights," United Nations Human Rights, Office of the High Commissioner, accessed July 10, 2020, https://www.ohchr.org/en/professionalinterest/pages/ccpr.aspx.

abstentions; Czechoslovakia was one of the eight. International jurists maintain that the covenant has acquired, through its "cumulative and pervasive effect," among other reasons, the force of international law. The communist states of Europe accepted the Universal Declaration when they signed the Final Act of the Conference on Security and Cooperation in Europe in Helsinki in 1975, but they violated the spirit and letter of the law until 1989. UNESCO's mandate to "promote the free flow of ideas by word and image" followed.[69] The United Nations (through the UN Human Rights Council) passed a resolution affirming "that the same rights that people have offline must also be protected online, in particular freedom of expression, which is applicable regardless of frontiers and through any media of one's choice,"[70] and condemning "unequivocally measures to intentionally prevent or disrupt access to or dissemination of information online."[71] Of course, these multilateral initiatives did not arise in a vacuum; they were part of a Cold War world, an emerging bipolar world, pitting what was once the freer

---

69 "Fostering Freedom of Expression," UNESCO, accessed October 13, 2020, https://en.un-esco.org/themes/fostering-freedom-expression; and "About Us," UNESCO, last modified June 30, 2020, http://www.unesco.org/new/en/communication-and-information/about-us/.

70 Wendy Zeldin, "U.N. Human Rights Council: First Resolution on Internet Free Speech," Global Legal Monitor (blog), Library of Congress, July 12, 2012, http://www.loc.gov/law/for-eign-news/article/u-n-human-rights-council-first-resolution-on-internet-free-speech/; Somini Sengupta, "U.N. Affirms Internet Freedom as a Basic Right," *New York Times*, July 6, 2012, https://bits.blogs.nytimes.com/2012/07/06/so-the-united-nations-affirms-internet-freedom-as-a-basic-right-now-what/.

71 "The Special Rapporteur's 2017 Report to the United Nations Human Rights Council Is Now Online," United Nations Human Rights, Office of the High Commissioner, accessed October 13, 2020, http://www.ohchr.org/EN/Issues/FreedomOpinion/Pages/SR2017Report-toHRC.aspx; "UNHRC: Reject Attempts to Weaken Resolution on Human Rights and the Internet," Article 19, June 30, 2016, https://www.article19.org/resources/unhrc-reject-attempts-to-weaken-resolution-on-human-rights-and-the-internet/. See also "Development and Access to Information 2019," International Federation of Library Associations and Institutions, accessed October 13, 2020, https://da2i.ifla.org/.

West against the East under totalitarianism.[72] But the written commitments of state signatories notwithstanding, every one of the state actors in the Soviet Monsterverse restricted the access of its citizens to ideas, limited the "free flow of information"—and, by doing so, malformed millions of members of the generations that would follow.

▨ ▨ ▨

In *Too Loud a Solitude*, Bohumil Hrabal's comic allegory about the life of the printed word in Czechoslovakia, the wise fool Hanta—Hrabal's hero—works at a pulping press, forced to destroy the two tons of old books that are recycled each month. But Hanta has such a deep love for the book that he cannot bring himself to pulp all of the tomes that the garbage men bring to him. He rescues so many each week— old philosophy volumes, lives of the saints, first editions of novels—that all the shelves and cupboards of his little apartment gradually become stuffed with Schiller, Lao Tzu, and Nietzsche.

Early on in the novel, Hanta describes how horrified he was as a youth by the physical destruction of books—before his senses were deadened by thirty-five years working the compactor. He had chanced across a cache of thousands of gilt-edged, leather-bound volumes from the Royal Prussian Academy, stowed in some barns near Prague just after World

---

72　See Karl R. Popper, *The Open Society and Its Enemies*, 2 vols. (Princeton, NJ: Princeton University Press, 1966); Miklós Haraszti, *The Velvet Prison: Artists Under State Socialism* (New York: Basic Books, 1987); Václav Havel, *Living in Truth: Twenty-Two Essays Published on the Occasion of the Award of the Erasmus Prize to Václav Havel*, ed. Jan Vladislav (London: Faber and Faber, 1987); and Czeslaw Milosz, *The Captive Mind* (New York: Vintage Books, 1981).

War II. With a librarian friend, he had arranged to bring the books to the ministry of foreign affairs, just "until things simmered down," when they could be returned to Germany. But someone snitched, the Soviet army found out, and they declared the books spoils of war. Hrabal describes Hanta's shock at what the soldiers did:

> So the column of military vehicles started transporting all the leather-bound tomes with their gilt edges and titles over to the railroad station, where they were loaded on flatcars in the rain, and since it poured the whole week, what I saw when the last load of books pulled up was a constant flow of gold water and soot and printer's ink coming from the train. Well, I just stood there, leaning against a lamppost, flabbergasted, and as the last car disappeared into the mist, I felt the rain on my face merging with the tears, so when on my way out of the station I saw a policeman in uniform, I crossed my wrists and begged him with the utmost sincerity to take out his handcuffs, his bracelets, as we used to call them, and take me in—I'd committed a crime, a crime against humanity.

This was Hanta's first brush with the postwar destruction of the printed word. "A few more years of the same, though," writes Hrabal, "and I got used to it."[73]

In reality, most of the book lovers, intellectuals, lovers of ideas, and citizens of Central and Eastern Europe never did. Indeed, for all of those decades, an independent "second

---

73 Bohumil Hrabal, *Too Loud a Solitude* trans. Michael Henry Heim (New York: Harcourt, 1990), 11.

society" battled Stalinist strictures and censors with whatever communications equipment could be found and put to use: carbon paper, mimeograph machines, and makeshift printers and binderies, as well as radio, television, audiocassette recorders, and VCRs. Tens of thousands of people were regularly involved in the production of illicit publications in Central and Eastern Europe and in the Soviet underground, and millions read and disseminated them. Václav Havel, speaking as one of the dissidents in 1975, explained why. He spoke of censorship producing a loss that is "infinitely deeper and more significant than might appear from the numbers involved."

> The forcible liquidation of [. . .] a journal—a theoretical review concerned with the theatre, say—is not just an impoverishment of its particular readers. It is not even merely a severe blow to theatrical culture. It is simultaneously, and above all, the liquidation of a particular organ of society's self-awareness and, hence, an interference, hard to describe in exact terms, in the complex system of circulation, exchange and conversion of nutrients that maintain life in that many-layered organism which is society today; a blow against the natural dynamic of the processes going on within that organism; a disturbance of the balanced interplay of all its various functions, an interplay reflecting the level of complexity reached by society's anatomy. And just as a chronic deficiency of a given vitamin (amounting in quantitative terms only to a negligible fraction of the human diet) can make a man ill, so, in the long run, the loss of a single periodical can cause the social

organism much more damage than would appear at first sight.[74]

Samizdat—from the Russian, to self- (*sam*) publish (*izdat*)—is credited for helping to end totalitarian thought control in Central and Eastern Europe and the former Soviet Union, bringing freer expression and more democratic institutions to hundreds of millions of people. With typewriters, carbon paper, and the copy machine, dissident writers and thinkers in the East bloc created a parallel communications culture, even a parallel political culture, and they managed to outflank official media and its state-controlled messages. The ideas shared across samizdat's so-called second society or second culture became the backbone of the human rights movement and freedom and free expression. Future Nobel Prize Laureates Boris Pasternak, Alexander Solzhenitsyn, and Andrei Sakharov, among others, first published much of their work this way—as did world leaders including Havel and Lech Wałęsa who emerged from the underground dissident movement. Indeed, Solzhenitsyn, Havel, and others maintained that the liberation of the Soviet Union and the East bloc would not have happened without it.[75]

Today it might be worth thinking about creating a parallel samizdat culture of our own here at home, as we scan the

---

74 See Havel's inspirational "Letter to Dr. Gustáv Husák, General Secretary of the Czechoslovak Communist Party," in Václav Havel, *Living in Truth*, 3–35, and quoted at greater length in Kaufman, "Two Prague Publishers." Jan Vladislav's edited collection, sad to say, is not yet available online in its entirety—neither at the Internet Archive (https://archive.org/details/vaclavhavellivinoohave) nor in the HathiTrust Digital Library (https://catalog.hathitrust.org/Record/002471389).

75 Václav Havel, "The Power of the Powerless" and "Six Asides about Culture," in Havel, *Living in Truth*, 36–122, 123–135, and Peter B. Kaufman, "Eastern Europe is Out of Print," *New York Times*, April 6, 1991, http://www.nytimes.com/1991/04/06/opinion/eastern-europe-is-out-of-print.html. See also H. Gordon Skilling, *Samizdat and an Independent Society in Central and Eastern Europe* (Columbus: Ohio State Press, 1989), 8.

American communications landscape and solemnly realize how our media elites keep failing us over and over again. The fact is, our mainstream television networks, radio broadcasters, newspapers, press agencies, and magazines have missed and/or avoided essentially every critical story for the last thirty years. Our mainstream media has failed to help Americans focus on, understand, predict, or explain the roots of Donald Trump's 2016 election (and the Americans who voted for him), the rise of Bernie Sanders (and the Americans who supported him), the real estate and banking crisis of 2008 (and the Americans who suffered so profoundly from it), the invasion and occupation of Iraq (and the Americans and Iraqis and others who have been killed and wounded there), the earlier rise of al-Qaeda—indeed, even the collapse of the Soviet bloc and Berlin Wall brought about in part by the underground press. Our coastal media elites live in a bubble. Issues that are key to millions of voters in the heartland—and issues that are vital for Americans to discuss moving forward—are systematically ignored.[76]

What if now were the time for a new self-publishing here at home—a new samizdat? The time to create a new, parallel communications network and a fresh system for information sharing? A parallel network and a fresh system owned not by commercial interests—so Twitter, Facebook, Medium, and other seemingly "self-publishing" platforms can't factor in here—nor by the state or the government, but by the very people who create and maintain them, part of a widening non-profit, noncommercial ecosystem. Václav Havel spoke of the battle of first and second cultures as an epic contest between "an anonymous, soulless, immobilizing ('entropic') power," on the

---

76 "Do You Live in a Bubble? A Quiz," PBS, March 24, 2016, http://www.pbs.org/newshour/making-sense/do-you-live-in-a-bubble-a-quiz-2/.

one hand, and "life, humanity, being, and its mystery," on the other.[77] Fellow dissidents spoke of samizdat's second culture as "the *only* meaningful construction" people could create if they did not want "to remain passive appendices of the political and social structures created by the ruling power."[78] They signaled each other as they wrote, distributed, and published—from the smallest codes, of the kinds that the *Encyclopédistes* used, to the largest and, also like the *Encyclopédie*, most earth-shattering.[79] Solzhenitsyn spoke of the mystical wisdom of a process in which information that is urgent somehow rises to the top. Samizdat, Solzhenitsyn wrote, "knows what is what."[80]

This may be the moment for media that politics enjoyed 2,600 years ago, when democracy—*dēmos* (people) plus *kratia* (power, rule)—took hold in Greece. Indeed this may be the moment when the Internet could bring to media what our Periclean forbears brought to government more than twenty centuries ago—the power of the people.[81] Havel wrote of truth—relevant enough today—as a "virus," something that can "slowly spread through the tissue of the life of lies, gradually causing it to disintegrate." Hard to read that now, for sure, but back then he was referring to a society—Czechoslovakia,

---

77 Havel, "Six Asides about Culture," in Havel, *Living in Truth*, 133.

78 Skilling, *Samizdat and an Independent Society in Central and Eastern Europe*, 221 (emphasis added).

79 Historian Anthony Grafton tells us how certain East German historians would make special "statements of intellectual centrality and allegiance" by putting the works of Marx and Engels out of alphabetical order at the start of their lists of citations. Coded, indeed. Anthony Grafton, *The Footnote: A Curious History* (Cambridge, MA: Harvard University Press, 1999), 11.

80 Aleksandr I. Solzhenitsyn, *The Oak and the Calf: Sketches of a Literary Life in the Soviet Union* (New York: Harper & Row, 1975), 284. See also Michael Scammell, *Solzhenitsyn: A Biography* (New York: W. W. Norton & Co., 1984).

81 Peter B. Kaufman, "Toward a New Samizdat," *Medium*, December 19, 2016, https://medium.com/@pbkauf/toward-a-new-samizdat-2af60f506d54.

Poland, Russia, the whole bloc—in which everyone was living the lie, rather than living in truth. The "crust presented by the life of lies is made of strange stuff," Havel wrote.

> As long as it seals off hermetically the entire society, it appears to be made of stone. But the moment someone breaks through in one place, when one person cries out, "The emperor is naked!"—when a single person breaks the rules of the game, thus exposing it as a game— everything suddenly appears in another light and the whole crust seems then to be made of a tissue on the point of tearing and disintegrating uncontrollably.

Havel wrote of truth as a "bacteriological weapon" that a single civilian can use "to disarm an entire division."[82] Much as Diderot and the *Encyclopédistes* described their project as a "war machine"—*machine de guerre*—designed to defeat church and state back in their day as well.[83]

▦ ▦ ▦

The battles over the future of the past in this part of the world were real[84]—and were not fought only over print and paper;

---

82 Havel, "The Power of the Powerless," in Havel, *Living in Truth*, 58–60.

83 Henry C. Clark, "How Radical Was the Political Thought of the *Encyclopédie?*" Online Library of Liberty, https://oll.libertyfund.org/pages/lm-diderot; and Veronique Le Ru, *Subversive Lumières: L'Encyclopédie comme machine de guerre* (Paris: Centre national de la recherche scientifique, 2007). The *Encyclopédie* did have as its frontispiece an engraving of Truth radiating light, and Reason and Philosophy trying to catch it. It was the Age of Reason, after all. https://en.wikipedia.org/wiki/Lumi%C3%A8res#/media/File:Encyclopedie_frontispice_section_256px.jpg.

84 István Rév, *Retroactive Justice: Prehistory of Post-Communism* (Stanford, CA: Stanford University Press, 2005).

control over the screen, and indeed the network of screens and sounds that cinema and television made manifest, was a key tenet of the early Soviet social architects.[85] The Polish writer Tadeusz Konwicki, looking with me at the monstrous television tower in Warsaw thirty years ago, likened the structure to a hypodermic needle shooting "narcotic shit" into the body politic of the Polish nation. Withdrawal from that kind of dependence—on a national scale—brought with it paroxysms of junkie violence.[86] Let us remember that in the so-called bloodless or "velvet" revolutions that erupted as these and other countries burst out of this suffocation, the blood that *was* shed, in the main, ran from the corpses of protesters that army tanks and gunshots scattered at the feet of the television towers in Bucharest, Vilnius, and Moscow. They were protesting the lies lived, purveyed, and broadcast by the totalitarian state.

These were the first real and physical battles for control over our screens, battles of freethinkers versus . . . the Monsterverse.[87]

---

85 See Dziga Vertov, *Kino-Eye: The Writings of Dziga Vertov*, ed. Annette Michelson and trans. Kevin O'Brien (Berkeley: University of California Press, 1984); Christina Kiaer, *Imagine No Possessions: The Socialist Objects of Russian Constructivism* (Cambridge, MA: MIT Press, 2005); V. S. Listov, *Lenin i Kinematograph, 1917–1924* (Moscow: Isskustvo, 1986); Susan Tumarkin Goodman and Jens Hoffmann, *The Power of Pictures: Early Soviet Photography, Early Soviet Film*, trans. Galya Korovina (New Haven, CT: Yale University Press, 2015); Richard Taylor, ed. and trans., *The Film Factory: Russian and Soviet Cinema in Documents, 1896–1939* (London: Routledge & Kegan Paul, 1988); Sergei Eisenstein, *S. M. Eisenstein: Selected Works Volume III: Writings, 1934–1947*, ed. Richard Taylor and trans. William Powell (London: British Film Institute, 1996); and Jamie Miller, *Soviet Cinema: Politics and Persuasion under Stalin, KINO: The Russian and Soviet Cinema* (London: I. B. Tauris, 2010); and Ellen Mickiewicz, *Split Signals: Television and Politics in the Soviet Union* (New York: Oxford University Press, 1988). See also Velimir Khlebnikov, *Collected Works of Velimir Khlebnikov, Volume I: Letters and Theoretical Writings*, ed. Charlotte Douglas and trans. Paul Schmidt (Cambridge, MA: Harvard University Press, 1987).

86 Author interview with Tadeusz Konwicki, January 29, 1990, Warsaw, Poland. See also Konwicki, *A Minor Apocalypse*, trans. Richard Lourie (New York: Vintage Books, 1984).

87 For a comparison of the Velvet Revolution to the 1905 revolution and Russia's Bloody Sunday, see Peter B. Kaufman, introduction to *Russia and Its Crisis*, by Paul Miliukov (New York: Barnes & Noble, 2005).

4. The New Network

Indeed, when we look at the *original* Enlightenment, it is the printers and their books and their pamphlets and broadsides, and the ideas they brought forth in them, that formed the networks—communication networks, social networks—of the time.[88] Modern historians—and it is spellbinding to consider how historians will look back at *us*, a hundred, two hundred, three hundred years from now—speak explicitly about our "networks of enlightenment" and "republics of letters" across Europe, Asia, and the rest of the world, and the forces of state and corporate censorship arrayed against them. The data on the European readers of early modernity, book- and print buyers, printers, and distributors—is now only beginning to emerge as a field of proper study. Who had access to printing licenses then? Access to the means of production? Who had a hand in the distribution of publications, and thus the diffusion of ideas? Some have begun to map out the "six degrees of Francis Bacon" connecting all the freethinkers across the said "republic."[89] And where did the money come from? As to the contributors to the great Enlightenment encyclopedia project, ultimately the writers—which is to say the writers only, not including here printing-shop workers, people who milled the trees

88 Robert Darnton, *The Literary Underground of the Old Regime* (Cambridge, MA: Harvard University Press, 1982).

89 "Mapping the Republic of Letters," Stanford University, accessed October 13, 2020, http://republicofletters.stanford.edu/; "Networks of European Enlightenment," Stanford University, accessed October 13, 2020, https://networksofenlightenment.stanford.edu/; Six Degrees of Francis Bacon, http://www.sixdegreesoffrancisbacon.com/.

and made the paper, horsemen with their wagonloads of literature and boat captains who brought packages of books through the oceans, seas, rivers, canals—would number about three hundred.[90] Their overwhelmingly male, overwhelmingly elite composition has suggested to some modern historians that these networks had a stake in propping up the existing statist order, and vice versa—a system that, based on the rich, landed, European noble, would come crashing down doubly hard in a new and revolutionary age of democratic politics that would follow.[91] And the philosophers behind them perhaps were no different.

> Despite the leveling tendency inherent in their faith in reason, they aimed to take over the commanding heights of culture and to enlighten from above. This strategy led them to concentrate on the conquest of salons and academies, journals and theaters, Masonic lodges and key cafes, where they could win the rich and powerful to their cause and even gain access, by back doors and boudoirs, to the throne.[92]

The battleground of ideas of the original Enlightenment—perhaps, the "Enwhitenment"—was the battleground of text, of words, of print—paper and ink being the weapons of choice. Today we need to study a new kind of network—really the network of networks, of television networks, of online communities, of social networks. The battleground of and for the

---

90 Robert Darnton, *The Business of Enlightenment: A Publishing History of the Encyclopédie, 1775–1800* (Cambridge, MA: Harvard University Press, 1979), 512.

91 Maria Teodora Comsa et al., "The French Enlightenment Network," *Journal of Modern History* 88, no. 3 (September 2016), 495–534.

92 Robert Darnton, *George Washington's False Teeth: An Unconventional Guide to the Eighteenth Century* (New York: W. W. Norton, 2001), 5.

twenty-first century is the battleground of another kind of rectangle: not the book, the journal, the pamphlet, or the newspaper, but the rectangle of the screen. Indeed, today, when we interrogate our moment and attempt to understand its true potential, the first aspect to remark upon is that transformational power today will rely, first and foremost, on video culture. Look at YouTube, for one example. Five billion videos watched each day. Two billion active monthly users. Thirty million active daily users. Five hundred million views per day on mobile platforms. Fifty million users have created content they have shared. In an average minute in 2019, we uploaded to our network some three hundred hours' worth of video—five hours of video per second. It still skews male, this audience, but it's global—80 percent of users are outside of the United States, and this platform, a vast archive of video, open to anyone, anytime, anywhere, operates in eighty-eight countries and in seventy-eight languages. And that's just YouTube.[93]

Screen culture more generally is linking many of us to one another in a broader network. Wikipedia provides usage statistics about itself that (not incidentally, as we'll see) are much more transparent than YouTube's. English Wikipedia has 35.8 million users (those who have registered a user name), 141,000 of whom are classed as active users (those who have edited the encyclopedia in the past thirty days); under the eye of 1,184 administrators, some 572 new articles go up each day. Edits—the favorite measure of this collective publishing operation—concatenate today

---

93 "YouTube for Press," YouTube.com, accessed October 13, 2020, https://www.youtube.com/yt/about/press/; "YouTube by the Numbers: Stats, Demographics, and Fun Facts," Omnicore, accessed October 13, 2020, https://www.omnicoreagency.com/youtube-statistics/; Ben Gilbert, "YouTube Now Has Over 1.8 Billion Users Every Month, Within Spitting Distance of Facebook's 2 Billion," *Business Insider*, May 14, 2018, https://www.businessinsider.com/youtube-user-statistics-2018-5.

at 1.8 per second.[94] Wikipedia's editors are now spread out around the world and multilingual, but also are still overwhelmingly male, and probably white.[95] All of Wikipedia's edits can be seen (and heard!) live on Hatnote, a website developed by two free-culture activists that is replete with celestas and clavichords, violins, and more, all to help us hear and visualize the encyclopedia's text being written and edited, in real time.[96]

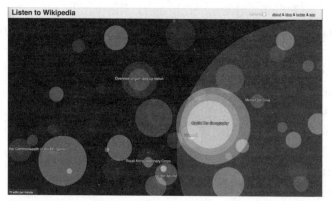

Hatnote. Listen to Wikipedia, at: http://listen.hatnote.com/.

The world of knowledge is in many ways morphing toward a screen world—and it may be that this, more than any other single thing, is facilitating what we can now call our "*new* Enlighten-

---

94 And 880 million edits so far. "Wikipedia:Wikipedians," Wikimedia Foundation, last modified June 29, 2020, 20:40, https://en.wikipedia.org/wiki/Wikipedia:Wikipedians; "Wikipedia:Statistics," Wikimedia Foundation, last modified July 15, 2020, 17:37, https://en.wikipedia.org/wiki/Wikipedia:Statistics.

95 The data on the top editors is extraordinary: "Wikipedia:List of Wikipedians by Number of Edits," Wikimedia Foundation, last modified July 2, 2020, 1:32, https://en.wikipedia.org/wiki/Wikipedia:List_of_Wikipedians_by_number_of_edits. See also Eric Zachte, "Just How Many People Are Reading Wikipedia in Your Country, and What Language Are They Using?" Diff (blog), Wikimedia Foundation, October 27, 2017, https://blog.wikimedia.org/2017/10/27/new-interactive-visualization-wikipedia/.

96 "Listen to Wikipedia," Wikimedia Foundation, last modified June 27, 2020, 12:31, https://en.wikipedia.org/wiki/Listen_to_Wikipedia.

ment."[97] Picture an airplane flight across an ocean at night: As the sky darkens, dinner is served, and then the most noticeable thing about the plane is that almost everyone is sitting lit by the video screens in front of them. One or two out of every ten people may be reading—whether on a tablet or from a printed book—but the rest are *watching*. In many ways we are all the passengers on this plane, relying no longer on speech or the printed page but on the screen and its moving images for much of the information we receive about our world.[98] Video is the key to that networked world. The company Cisco Systems—which makes many of the devices that connect us—deploys a forecasting tool it calls the Visual Networking Index (VNI). The latest VNI—which, yes, sometimes overreaches—tells us that there were 3.4 billion Internet users on the planet in 2017—almost half of the planet's current population of 7.7 billion people. By 2022, there will be 4.8 billion Internet users—60 percent of the planet. Sometime during the early life of this book, more people in the world will be connected to the Internet than not. By 2022, more than 28 billion "devices and connections" will be online. And—here's the kicker—video will make up 82 percent of global Internet traffic.[99] Video.

Video!

Video!

It's dominant already. During peak evening hours in the

97 For more, see Peter B. Kaufman, *A Manual of Video Style: A Guide to the Use of Moving Images in Scholarly Communication* (Cambridge, MA: MIT Press, forthcoming).

98 Peter B. Kaufman, "Oral History in the Video Age," *Oral History Review* 40, no. 1 (January 2013), online (behind a paywall) at https://www.tandfonline.com/doi/full/10.1093/ohr/ohto33?scroll=top&needAccess=true.

99 "Cisco Annual Internet Report (2018–2023) White Paper," Cisco.com, last updated November 2018, https://www.cisco.com/c/en/us/solutions/collateral/service-provider/visual-networking-index-vni/white-paper-c11-741490.html and "Cisco Annual Internet Report," Cisco, accessed October 13, 2020, https://www.cisco.com/c/en/us/solutions/service-provider/visual-networking-index-vni/index.html. See also "Current World Population," Worldometer, http://www.worldometers.info/world-population/.

Americas, Netflix can account for as much as 40 percent of downstream Internet traffic, and Netflix—Netflix alone—constitutes 15 percent of Internet traffic worldwide.[100]

Video. Its primacy has deep roots as well. In contrast to what we might believe, which is to say, that society and its rules are based upon what seems to be the primacy of print, our lives as humans have featured a visual and sound culture—with pictures and sounds, as opposed to written words and texts—for much longer than they have a textual one. For most of our time on the planet we have been an aural people, an oral culture. We began that way. "Homo sapiens," as the teacher, priest, and scholar Walter J. Ong has written, "has been in existence for between 30,000 and 50,000 years. The earliest script dates from only 6,000 years ago." For most of the years in between, it was sound and picture that we used to communicate. And as Ong reminds us, "Written texts all have to be related somehow, directly or indirectly, to the world of sound, the natural habitat of language, to yield their meanings. 'Reading' a text means converting it to sound, aloud or in the imagination. . . . Writing can never dispense with orality."[101] Likewise, MIT linguistics professor emeritus Shigeru Miyagawa and his colleagues have suggested that the cave paintings of early modern man were situated where they were—deep within the caves—not for protection from enemies or as the best place for a fire

---

100 Todd Spangler, "Netflix Eats Up 15% of All Internet Downstream Traffic Worldwide (Study)," *Variety*, October 2, 2018, https://variety.com/2018/digital/news/netflix-15-percent-internet-bandwidth-worldwide-study-1202963207/; Matt Binder, "Netflix Consumes 15 Percent of the World's Internet Traffic," Mashable, October 4, 2018, https://mashable.com/article/netflix-15-percent-worlds-internet-traffic/#6Ua7.DtxGGqT.

101 Walter J. Ong, *Orality and Literacy: The Technologizing of the Word*, 2nd ed. (New York: Routledge, 2002), 2, 8, 82–83. As Jared Diamond puts it, "History before the emergence of writing . . . constitutes 99.9. percent of the five-million-year history of the human species." Diamond, *Guns, Germs, and Steel: The Fates of Human Societies* (New York: W. W. Norton, 1999), 9.

but because the auditory properties of these spots would facilitate the proper echoes and volume necessary for performance
storytelling about the animals drawn on the wall. Sound and
picture in the Pleistocene—the movie.[102]

In many ways we are now returning to this world of a sound-
and-picture audience, after a detour among the letters. And
who controls our access to these screens? Google once declared,
during its march to digitize them all, that we in the world had
published 129,864,880 books—identifying, in essence, the
world's print archive that had at one time or another been manufactured as codices.[103] What is the equivalent tally for what's
in the world's moving image and sound libraries? In 2010,
UNESCO estimated world audiovisual holdings at a lofty 200
million hours. The sources for that number always seemed
somewhat unclear, and by now of course the total is completely

---

102 Shigeru Miyagawa, Cora Lesure, Vitor A. Nóbrega, "Cross-Modality Information
Transfer: A Hypothesis about the Relationship among Prehistoric Cave Paintings, Symbolic
Thinking, and the Emergence of Language," *Frontiers in Psychology* 9, no.115 (February 20,
2018), https://doi.org/10.3389/fpsyg.2018.00115. See also Rock Art Acoustics, last updated
August 24, 2016, https://sites.google.com/site/rockartacoustics/.

103 This was in 2010. Leonid Taycher, "Books of the World, Stand Up and Be Counted! All
129,864,880 of You," Google Books Search (blog), August 5, 2010, http://booksearch.blogspot.
com/2010/08/books-of-world-stand-up-and-be-counted.html; "Google's Tally of World's
Book Titles: 129,864,880," *All Things Considered*, NPR, August 12, 2010, https://www.npr.org/
templates/story/story.php?storyId=129160859?storyId=129160859. The Comité des Sages of the
European Commission attempted to quantify all media to digitize on the European continent
in its 2011 report *The New Renaissance*; see European Commission, "Digital Agenda: 'Comité
des Sages' Calls for a 'New Renaissance' by Bringing Europe's Cultural Heritage Online," news
release, January 10, 2011, http://europa.eu/rapid/press-release_IP-11-17_en.htm?locale=en.
The two-hundred-page report called for an investment of 100 billion Euros to digitize all
of Europe's cultural heritage—including its audiovisual collections. "The figure," noted the
authors, "includes the digitisation of 77 million books, 24 million hours of audiovisual pro-
grammes, 358 million photographs, 75.43 million works of art, 10.45 billion pages of archives"
and so on. See the full report: Elisabeth Niggemann, Jacques De Decker, Maurice Lévy, *The
New Renaissance: Report of the "Comité des Sages" on Bringing Europe's Cultural Heritage Online*
(Luxembourg: Publications Office of the European Union, 2011), http://www.eurosfaire.prd.
fr/7pc/doc/1302102400_kk7911109enc_002.pdf.

out of date.[104] Although there have been some attempts at surveys, no one really knows.[105] And who controls our access to the libraries of content developed and produced and archived over the last hundred-plus years? Who controls—or tries to control—our search across these screens and servers for the moving pictures and sounds we are looking for? Some answers, in our new Republic of Images, are all too familiar already.

▓ ▓ ▓

Far from the caves of Lascaux, from the renderings on stone of animals in flight, we are all witness now to sustained, systematic attacks against fact—against traditional sources of knowledge, evidence, and truth.

---

104 See Peter B. Kaufman, *Assessing the Audiovisual Archive Market: Models and Approaches for Audiovisual Content Exploitation* (Hilversum: PrestoCentre, 2013), https://publications.beeldenge-luid.nl/pub/1818/. Recently, however, one scholar pinpointed the original calculation behind that number, beginning with a 2001 PrestoCentre project that found 4.8 million hours in ten broadcast archives. That scholar rounded the number to 5 million, and then multiplied it by ten to form an estimate for Europe. The same scholar then doubled that total to benchmark an estimate for the entire world. Another scholar thought 100 million hours was too small and doubled it again. Such is how UNESCO published its figure! "Sic semper scientas," as the original scholar wrote to me. Should major national archives wish to conduct some proper inventories, that would be welcome. A masterpiece of the genre is *Guide to the BBC's Archives 2012: What's in the Archives, and How to Use Them*, edited by Jake Berger ("BBC Archives," Wikimedia Foundation, last modified May 28, 2020, 19:06, https://en.wikipedia.org/wiki/BBC_Archives (fn. 4), which should actually be here: "BBC Archive Services," BBC.com, accessed October 13, 2020, http://www.bbc.co.uk/information-andarchives/access_archives. See also the Library of Congress MIC project: "MIC: Moving Image Collections," Library of Congress, accessed October 13, 2020, https://www.loc.gov/today/cyberlc/feature_wdesc.php?rec=4321. Exemplary private efforts include Rick Prelinger's *The Field Guide to Sponsored Films* (San Francisco: National Film Preservation Foundation, 2006), now online, along with many of the cataloged films: "Online Field Guide to Sponsored Films," National Film Preservation Foundation, accessed October 13, 2020, https://www.filmpreservation.org/sponsored-films. It has been suggested that UNESCO and multilateral organizations like the Co-ordinating Council of Audiovisual Archives Associations (CCAAA) could play a role in compiling new statistics and some kind of new international inventory.

105 On quantifying the rush of new non-television and non-film audiovisual content coming at us now—an astronomical number of moving images and sounds from billions of devices, users, and platforms—see Richard Wright, "Television Archives in a Post-Television World," presentation at the 2017 FIAT/IFTA World Conference, Mexico City, October 21, 2017, https://www.slideshare.net/fiatifta/television-archives-in-a-posttelevision-world-wright.

There is a strong sense that we are in what one set of scholars calls an "epistemic crisis."[106] Our media and information ecosystem—television, radio, the Internet—is now flooded, often purposefully, with falsehoods, bad information, and errors.[107] The RAND Corporation has given a name to this phenomenon, one marked by "increasing disagreement about facts and analytical interpretations of facts and data; a blurring of the line between opinion and fact; the increasing relative volume, and resulting influence, of opinion and personal experience over fact; [and] declining trust in formerly respected sources of factual information"; they call it "truth decay."[108] And the crisis presents open dangers. "The violation and despoiling of truth," writes one expert—alongside cynicism, weariness, and fear—can "make people susceptible to the lies and false promises of leaders bent on unconditional power." And as Hannah Arendt reminded us, when she explored the depravity of the twentieth-century Monsterverse, the "ideal subject of totalitarian rule . . . is not the convinced Nazi or the convinced Communist, but people for whom the distinction between fact and fiction (i.e., the reality of experience) and the distinction between true and false (i.e., standards of thought) no longer exist."[109]

---

106 Yochai Benkler, Robert Faris, and Hal Roberts, *Network Propaganda: Manipulation, Disinformation, and Radicalization in American Politics* (New York: Oxford University Press, 2018), https://doi.org/10.1093/oso/9780190923624.001.0001.

107 Soroush Vosoughi, Deb Roy, and Sinan Aral, "The Spread of True and False News Online," *Science* 359, no. 6380 (March 9, 2018): 1146–51, https://doi.org/10.1126/science.aap9559; Robert Faris et al., "Partisanship, Propaganda, and Disinformation: Online Media and the 2016 U.S. Presidential Election," Berkman Klein Center for Internet & Society Research Paper (Cambridge: Harvard University, 2017), http://nrs.harvard.edu/urn-3:HUL.InstRepos:33759251; Yochai Benkler, Robert Faris, Hal Roberts, and Ethan Zuckerman, "Study: Breitbart-Led Right-Wing Media Ecosystem Altered Broader Media Agenda," *Columbia Journalism Review*, March 3, 2017, https://www.cjr.org/analysis/breitbart-media-trump-harvard-study.php; and David M. J. Lazer et al., "The Science of Fake News," *Science* 359, no. 6380 (March 9, 2018): 1094–1096, https://doi.org/10.1126/science.aao2998.

108 Jennifer Kavanagh and Michael D. Rich, *Truth Decay: An Initial Exploration of the Diminishing Role of Facts and Analysis in American Public Life* (Santa Monica, CA: RAND Corporation, 2018), https://www.rand.org/pubs/research_reports/RR2314.html.

109 Quoted in Michiko Kakutani, *The Death of Truth: Notes on Falsehood in the Age of Trump* (New York: Tim Duggan Books, 2018), 11. See also Lee McIntyre, *Post-Truth* (Cambridge, MA: MIT Press, 2018).

The current moment is marked also by a general assault on expertise—including most especially the kind of leadership proofs that universities exist to generate, espouse, disseminate, and preserve. The denial of science, the denial of basic evidence, has been called "depraved" and even criminal, given how it affects the climate and the world economy and society.[110] Massive, sustained, and systematic efforts are under way now at all levels of society to discredit experts and professionals, and especially the media and institutions of higher education.[111]

At the same time, consolidation of and control over the publishing of facts and data that come from the knowledge industry—universities, libraries, museums, archives—is tightening into oligopolies.[112] As historian, philanthropist, and open access advocate Peter Baldwin tells us, more than half of "all natural science and medical research is now published by the largest five academic publishing houses: Reed-Elsevier, Wiley-Blackwell, Springer, Taylor & Francis, and, depending

---

110 Paul Krugman, "The Depravity of Climate-Change Denial," *New York Times,* November 26, 2018, https://www.nytimes.com/2018/11/26/opinion/climate-change-denial-republican.html.

111 The literature is vast. See, for example, Tom Nichols, *The Death of Expertise: The Campaign Against Established Knowledge and Why It Matters* (Oxford: Oxford University Press, 2017). See also Recode Staff, "Full Transcript: New York University Journalism Professor Jay Rosen," *Recode,* February 3, 2017, https://www.recode.net/2017/2/3/14503050/full-transcript-new-york-university-journalism-professor-jay-rosen-trump-facts.

112 Vincent Larivière, Stefanie Haustein, and Philippe Mongeon, "The Oligopoly of Academic Publishers in the Digital Era," *PLoS ONE* 10, no. 6 (June 10, 2015): e0127502, https://doi.org/10.1371/journal.pone.0127502; Stephen Buranyi, "Is the Staggeringly Profitable Business of Scientific Publishing Bad for Science?" *Guardian,* London, June 27, 2017, https://www.theguardian.com/science/2017/jun/27/profitable-business-scientific-publishing-bad-for-science. See also Jon Tennant, "Academic Publishing Is Broken. Here's How to Redesign It," *Fast Company,* July 9, 2018, https://www.fastcompany.com/90180552/academic-publishing-is-broken-heres-how-to-redesign-it; Hans De Wit, Phillip G. Altbach, and Betty Leask, "Addressing the Crisis in Academic Publishing," *Inside Higher Ed,* November 5, 2018, https://www.insidehighered.com/blogs/world-view/addressing-crisis-academic-publishing; and Fiona Macdonald, "These Five Companies Control More Than Half of Academic Publishing," *Science Alert,* June 12, 2015, https://www.sciencealert.com/these-five-companies-control-more-than-half-of-academic-publishing.

on the metric, either the American Chemical Society or Sage Publishing. The social sciences are even worse off. In 1973, one in ten articles were published by the big five, now it is more than half. 71% of all psychology papers are published by them."[113] When publishing houses in the knowledge business can clear $270 million in profit in a single year—as Wiley did in 2017—do we think universities and scholars and libraries and audiences are being fundamentally well served?[114] The situation is akin to the movie business, where the so-called "Big Six" studios—20th Century Fox, Warner Bros., Paramount Pictures, Columbia Pictures, Universal Pictures, and Walt Disney Studios—collectively command approximately 80 to 85 percent of U.S. and Canadian box office revenue.[115] Or akin to the music business, where there is an equally powerful force gathered, recently around six music companies, then (after some consolidation) five, then four, now—Warner Music Group, Universal Music Group, Sony Corporation—three.[116]

113 Peter Baldwin, "Why Are Universities Open Access Laggards?" *Bulletin of the German Historical Institute* 63 (Fall 2018): 67–80, https://www.arcadiafund.org.uk/wp-content/uploads/2018/11/why-are-universities-open-access-laggers.pdf. See also Claudio Aspesi et al., "SPARC Landscape Analysis," March 29, 2019, https://doi.org/10.31229/osf.io/58yhb.

114 A. Townsend Peterson et al., "Open Access Solutions for Biodiversity Journals: Do Not Replace One Problem with Another," *Diversity and Distributions* 25, no. 1 (January 2019):5–8, https://doi.org/10.1111/ddi.12885. See also Jonathan Tennant, *Democratizing Knowledge: A Report on the Scholarly Publisher, Elsevier* (Brussels: Educational International, October 2018), https://www.ei-ie.org/en/detail/16061/elsevier-putting-a-price-on-knowledge; David Matthews, "Is It Time to Nationalise Academic Publishers?" *Times Higher Education*, March 2, 2018, https://www.timeshighereducation.com/blog/it-time-nationalise-academic-publishers.

115 Georg Szalai, "Studio-by-Studio Profitability Ranking: Disney Surges, Sony Sputters," *Hollywood Reporter*, February 20, 2017, https://www.hollywoodreporter.com/lists/studio-by-studio-profitability-ranking-disney-surges-sony-sputters-977497.

116 Will Meyer, "Taking the Music Industry Monopoly Seriously," *Hypebot*, March 26, 2018, https://www.hypebot.com/hypebot/2018/03/taking-monopoly-power-seriously-.html; "Music Industry," Wikimedia Foundation, last modified June 8, 2020, 04:57, https://en.wikipedia.org/wiki/Music_industry; and Jodie Griffin, "Copyright, Consolidation, and the Music Licensing Marketplace," *Public Knowledge*, August 2, 2013, https://www.publicknowledge.org/blog/copyright-consolidation-and-the-music-licensing-marketplace/.

The trade book publishing economy has its Big Five as well: Penguin Random House, HarperCollins, Simon & Schuster, Hachette, and Holtzbrinck. In each of these knowledge industries, as the core group shrinks from six to five, and from five to fewer, you wind up heading toward the models of knowledge industries in other countries, like those in the previous chapter, that imposed totalitarian models of thought control—and whose regimes were defeated in part by the purposeful spread of, and never-slaking thirst for, information worldwide.[117]

Where we could have a robust alternative to these tightening grips on the throat of our discourse, we just don't. Public and non-profit media's role in our domestic media and communications landscape is not what it could be or should be—or what it was; as we explore further on, it has changed mightily since receiving its original mandate, as has the media ecosystem in which it operates.[118] Today, public broadcasting is really but an ember of its former blaze—its original intent almost burnt out; its reformist hopes flickering; its content, occasional glow notwithstanding, all but irrelevant in a communications landscape where the public pays more attention to everything else. Financial challenges are affecting the viability of publishing companies and the ability of many to report as they once did, and also to edit and fact-check—commercial news organizations and information providers are

---

117 Peter B. Kaufman, "Central and Eastern Europe," in *International Book Publishing: An Encyclopedia*, Philip G. Altbach and Edith S. Hoshino, eds. (New York: Garland Publishing, 1995); Kaufman, "Publishing in Budapest," *Scholarly Publishing* 21, no. 4 (July 1990), 195–204; Kaufman, "Publishing: Romanian Remainders," *Times Literary Supplement*, London, July 6–12, 1990; and Kaufman, "Two Prague Publishers: Academia and SPN," *Scholarly Publishing* 22, no. 31 (April 1991), 143–154. Everything that is old may one day be new again.

118 The literature is vast. See, for example, Laurie Ouellette, *Viewers Like You?: How Public TV Failed the People* (New York: Columbia University Press, 2002).

now part of the tottering precariat.[119] We rely on ad-supported, far-from-value-neutral search engines for most information classification and retrieval. The public today is "increasingly reliant on search engines for getting information, instead of libraries, librarians, teachers, researchers, and other knowledge keepers and resources"—and the consequences of depending on "algorithms (such as those that power search and recommendation engines) may include deeper social inequality."[120] These search engines— and the main and most powerful sources of our news, information, sound, and moving images now—are commercially owned and driven. "Is it a problem," one author asks, "that our mental representation of the world is the product of a for-profit entertainment industry?" His immediate answer: yes.[121]

There is, at bottom, a fresh culture of division and violence and disrespect in our modern discourse—in the media, and online in particular. Although the Trump administration has not, per se, been a singular focus of this work, the stink was remarkably strong at the head. Many commentators would agree that, as one distinguished journalist has put it, "no modern president has adopted and weaponized such malevolent rhetoric as a lingua franca."[122]

---

119 The financial crisis of publishing is described at every turn in the literature. See especially Micah Altman and Chris Bourg, "A Grand Challenges-Based Research Agenda for Scholarly Communication and Information Science," final report, MIT Grand Challenges Summit, December 17, 2018, https://doi.org/10.21428/62b3421f.

120 Safiya Umoja Noble, *Algorithms of Oppression: How Search Engines Reinforce Racism* (New York: NYU Press, 2018). See also Safiya U. Noble, "Google and the Misinformed Public," *Chronicle of Higher Education*, January 15, 2017, https://www.chronicle.com/article/Google-the-Misinformed/238868?cid=cp84.

121 Greg Jackson, "Vicious Cycles," *Harper's Magazine*, January 2020, https://harpers.org/archive/2020/01/vicious-cycles-theses-on-a-philosophy-of-news/.

122 David Remnick, "The Stakes," Comment, *New Yorker*, November 5, 2018, https://www.newyorker.com/magazine/2018/11/05/the-midterm-elections-are-a-referendum-on-donald-trump. For more on the dangerous ecosphere President Trump managed to cultivate on Twitter, see Peter B. Kaufman, "45's 45," *Medium*, February 12, 2018, https://medium.com/@pbkauf/45s-45-553bef55fco5. For more on the lower depths of the Internet, including the hateful language on festering sites on

Weaponized malevolence: violence is in the air; the same blood-lusts we saw centuries ago, in Tyndale's time, and maybe even in the cave. And it isn't so much that they have returned as that they never went away.

▓ ▓ ▓

We are only beginning now to step up. Catalyzing alternatives is, in large part, the urgent purpose of this book. As this current crisis is exacerbated, the need for collective action becomes more and more evident to all who consider themselves stakeholders, however modestly, in the Enlightenment project of liberty, equality, fraternity—and peace. Some progressive government officials and public initiatives are addressing the problem and uniting in recognition of the dangers.[123] Media professionals are uniting and calling for change, with additional proposals for new models and new movements.[124] Technology gurus—MIT's Tim Berners-Lee, founder of the Internet (if there is one such person) among them—are uniting as well.[125] But sweeping new visions for action, and

---

the dark web like 4chan, 8chan, and Endchan, see Andrew Marantz, "Election Night with the Meme Debunkers," Daily Digest, *New Yorker*, November 19, 2018, https://www.newyorker.com/magazine/2018/11/19/election-night-with-the-meme-debunkers.

123 Maegan Vazquez, "175 Former US Officials Added to List Denouncing Trump for Revoking Brennan's Security Clearance," CNN.com, August 20, 2018, https://www.cnn.com/2018/08/20/politics/john-brennan-more-intelligence-officials-statement/index.html; Veronica Stracqualursi, "Former Intelligence Leaders: Trump Attempting to 'Stifle Free Speech' by Revoking Brennan's Clearance," CNN.com, August 17, 2018, https://www.cnn.com/2018/08/17/politics/brennan-security-clearance-former-intel-officials/index.html; Eli Stokols, "13 Former U.S. Spy Chiefs Accuse Trump of Trying to Stifle Free Speech and Politicize Intelligence," *Los Angeles Times*, August 16, 2018, http://www.latimes.com/politics/la-na-pol-trump-intel-chiefs-20180816-story.html.

124 See, for example, *The Correspondent*, an online platform "for unbreaking news": Home page, *The Correspondent*, accessed October 13, 2020, https://thecorrespondent.com/.

125 Ian Sample, "Tim Berners-Lee Launches Campaign to Save the Web from Abuse," *Guardian*, London, November 5, 2018, https://www.theguardian.com/technology/2018/nov/05/tim-berners-lee-launches-campaign-to-save-the-web-from-abuse.

collective action at that, will need to be summoned by universities and across the horizon of all knowledge institutions—museums, libraries, public broadcasters, archives—involving any and every organization with a mission or mandate to educate.

The good news is that the impact extension and brand extension opportunities online for us as educators and publishers now are almost limitless. And the public—in the United States and world-wide—is often broadly and deeply invested in the ways our media is published and regulated, and in the impact of current, poorly fashioned controls over that media upon society.[126] Coming at us orthogonally, perhaps, is yet another pressure: Sci-Hub, Library Genesis (Libgen), and ResearchGate—global pirate hubs—are providing access to knowledge in new ways, via curating risk takers who operate outside currently legal and normative bounds. As scholars have dared to report, "as of March 2017, Sci-Hub's data-base contains 68.9% of the 81.6 million scholarly articles registered with Crossref and *85.1%* of articles published in toll access jour-nals." In other words, most recently published scholarly research is now available online for free.[127]

The numbers do not lie. There are billions of Internet users—18 billion Wikipedia page views per month; 2.32 billion

126 Jon Brodkin, "FCC Explains Why Public Support for Net Neutrality Won't Stop Repeal," *Ars Technica*, November 22, 2017, https://arstechnica.com/tech-policy/2017/11/why-the-fcc-ignored-public-opinion-in-its-push-to-kill-net-neutrality/; Dawn C. Chmielewski, "Internet Whipped Into Frenzy Over FCC's Proposal To Wipe Out Net Neutrality Rules – Reactions," *Deadline*, November 21, 2017, https://deadline.com/2017/11/internet-outrage-fcc-repeal-net-neutrality-1202213217/; Jon Brodkin, "'No Secret Instructions' from Obama to FCC, Wheeler Tells Congress," *Ars Technica*, March 17, 2015, https://arstechnica.com/tech-policy/2015/03/no-secret-instructions-from-obama-to-fcc-wheeler-tells-congress/.

127 Daniel S. Himmelstein et al., "Sci-Hub Provides Access to Nearly All Scholarly Litera-ture," *eLife* 7 (March 1, 2018), https://doi.org/10.7554/eLife.32822 (emphasis added). See also Joe Karaganis, ed., *Shadow Libraries: Access to Knowledge in Global Higher Education* (Cam-bridge, MA: MIT Press, 2018), online at https://mitpress.mit.edu/books/shadow-libraries; and John Bohannon, "Who's Downloading Pirated Papers? Everyone." *Science*, April 28, 2016, https://www.sciencemag.org/news/2016/04/whos-downloading-pirated-papers-everyone.

people active on Facebook—and we are networked.[128] What is our duty in this age—the digital age, the age of Facebook, Trump, post-truth, and truth decay—to share knowledge with the world? Preparing answers for these questions, engaging in meaningful discussion and debate, seeing the world we've inherited through fresh eyes—in such ways can we understand best how we ourselves are positioned for this new Enlightenment. Struggle will be necessary. No outcome is assured or predestined.

The future is something we each can affect. I am not a religious man, not yet anyway, but almost any fool can see how powerful a force the Bible has been (and not the Bible alone, but the Koran and various holy scriptures and texts) throughout the world. Any fool with eyes to see can appreciate the power of grand cathedrals or great art. Of hearing great music. Of reading literature from Milton and Dostoevsky to Faulkner and Morrison and beyond.

Yet "we must remember," as Bible historians tell us, "when we hold a modern English Bible in our hands that the English Bible was made in blood."[129]

It may be, as a man once said, that all property is theft, and maybe all knowledge is spread in blood. Blood—and fire.

And from fire, light.

---

128 "Company Info," Facebook, accessed October 13, 2020, https://newsroom.fb.com/company-info/; "Wikimedia Statistics," Wikimedia Foundation, accessed October 13, 2020, https://stats.wikimedia.org/v2/#/all-projects; Monica Anderson, Paul Hitlin, and Michelle Atkinson, "Wikipedia at 15: Millions of Readers in Scores of Languages," FactTank (blog), Pew Research Center, January 14, 2016, http://www.pewresearch.org/fact-tank/2016/01/14/wikipedia-at-15/.

129 "William Tyndale: Man with a Mission," extended video-recorded interview with David Daniell, Vision Video, MP4 video, 42:00, https://www.visionvideo.com/mp4/500884V/man-with-a-mission-mp4-digital-download. An abridged transcript may be viewed online at https://www.visionvideo.com/files/manwmission.pdf.

5. *Visual Education—(I)*

Our age is known for violence. It has been marked by alienation. It has spawned bureaucracy. It has embraced cynicism.

Yet human beings long for alternatives; they long to matter.

They hunger for a community of shared values reflecting the triumph of intelligence and the life of the spirit.

—From *A Public Trust: The Report of the Carnegie Commission on the Future of Public Broadcasting (New York: Bantam Books, 1979)*

The Carnegie Commission that MIT's former president James Rhyne Killian assembled in 1966 was extraordinary by any measure. More than half a century ago, it included fifteen members—current and former university presidents, a novelist, a pianist, media titans, labor activists, government officials, businesspeople and inventors—on a roster that privileged white men but not only; women, people of color, foreign-born individuals, and religious denominations were represented. Strong—for 1967. And in the space of a year, the commission and its members held eight formal meetings over some twenty-eight meeting days and sought input from more than 225 people; its members visited ninety-two sites in thirty-five states and also seven foreign countries; and as a group they issued, at the end, twelve recommendations, all of them geared, as the landmark 1967 report stated, toward more firmly establishing what they called "an instrument for the free communication of ideas in a free society."

"We have become aware of technology as an immense power," their report stated. "What confronts our society is the obligation to bring that technology into the full service of man, so that its power to move image and sound is consistently coupled with a power to move mind and spirit." The report went on: "Television should enable us not only to see and hear more vividly, but to understand more deeply." And on: "Public television, elevating its own sights and those of its public, can help provide for the university a resource not unlike the university press, making its own contribution in terms it can freely honor. It is not merely a matter of calling upon the scholar for an account of his accomplishments, but of making for him a place within television to which he can repair as he is accustomed to turn to the printing press. . . . Great teachers should have opportunities to interpret the new math, the new physics, the new social sciences. . . . The unique opportunity is to bring before those who seek to understand, those who understand deeply."

And—up.

For its ending:

> If we were to sum up our proposal with all the brevity at our command, we would say that what we recommend is freedom. We seek freedom from the constraints, however necessary in their contexts, of commercial television. We seek for educational television freedom from the pressures of inadequate funds. We seek for the artist, the technician, the journalist, the scholar, and the public servant freedom to create, freedom to innovate, freedom to be heard in this most far-reaching medium. We seek for the citizen freedom to view, to

see programs that the present system, by its incompleteness, denies him.

Because this freedom is its principal burden, we submit our Report with confidence: to rally the American people in the name of freedom is to ask no more of them than they have always been willing to provide.[130]

The work of the commission resulted almost immediately in a bill (S. 1160) that quickly in turn became Public Law 90-129 (81 Stat. 365): the Public Broadcasting Act of 1967. The funding of the commission, the political ability of the commissioners, the timing of its establishment—all resulted in a perfect flight that allowed for a bill and then a law and then a presidential signature.

At the signing ceremony, President Johnson spoke to say:

It was in 1844 that Congress authorized $30,000 for the first telegraph line between Washington and Baltimore. Soon afterward, Samuel Morse sent a stream of dots and dashes over that line to a friend who was waiting. His message was brief and prophetic and it read: "What hath God wrought?"

---

130 Carnegie Commission on Educational Television, *Public Television: A Program for Action: The Report of the Carnegie Commission on Educational Television* (New York: Bantam Books, 1967), 8, 13, 17, 94, 99. *New York Times* columnist James Reston wrote in 1967 that Killian's Carnegie Commission's report would be recognized as "one of the transforming occasions in American life"; see Vesna Jaksic Lowe, "The Breakthrough Commission Behind PBS and NPR," News, Carnegie Corporation of New York, November 3, 2017, https://www.carnegie.org/news/articles/public-broadcasting-turns-50/. The MIT Library Archives hold President Killian's papers from the commission; see "James R. Killian Papers," MIT Archives Space, MIT Libraries, accessed October 13, 2020, https://archivesspace.mit.edu/repositories/2/resources/916; "Carnegie I," *Current*, accessed October 13, 2020, https://current.org/tag/carnegie-i/. Killian later wrote that "helping to design and launch public television and public radio was one of the most rewarding undertakings" of his career. See "James R. Killian, or How Sputnik Paid for College Educations," Engineering and Technology History Wiki, last modified September 17, 2015, 15:18, https://ethw.org/James_R._Killian,_or_how_Sputnik_paid_for_college_educations.

Every one of us should feel the same awe and wonderment here today.

For today, miracles in communication are our daily routine. Every minute, billions of telegraph messages chatter around the world. They interrupt law enforcement conferences and discussions of morality. Billions of signals rush over the ocean floor and fly above the clouds. Radio and television fill the air with sound. Satellites hurl messages thousands of miles in a matter of seconds.

Today our problem is not making miracles—but managing miracles. We might well ponder a different question: What hath man wrought—and how will man use his inventions?

Today, he said, "we rededicate a part of the airwaves—which belong to all the people—and we dedicate them for the enlightenment of all the people."

"We must consider," he said, "new ways to build a great network for knowledge—not just a broadcast system, but one that employs every means of sending and storing information that the individual can use."

Johnson continued:

Think of the lives that this would change:

The student in a small college could tap the resources of a great university. . . .

Yes, the student in a small college tapping the resources of the greatest university in the hemisphere.

The country doctor getting help from a distant laboratory or a teaching hospital;

A scholar in Atlanta might draw instantly on a library in New York;

A famous teacher could reach with ideas and inspirations into some far-off classroom, so that no child need be neglected.

Eventually, I think this electronic knowledge bank could be as valuable as the Federal Reserve Bank.

And such a system could involve other nations, too—it could involve them in a partnership to share knowledge and to thus enrich all mankind.

A wild and visionary idea? Not at all. Yesterday's strangest dreams are today's headlines and change is getting swifter every moment.

I have already asked my advisers to begin to explore the possibility of a network for knowledge—and then to draw up a suggested blueprint for it.[131]

The system he was signing into law, he said, "will be free, and it will be independent—and it will belong to all of our people."

But today, scan the dial, the grid, the web. Where has this vision gone?

A more inspiring question: What brought us to this point of eloquence in 1967?

The answer to the second question—the prehistory of public media—is as extraordinary as the backstory of the Carnegie Commission itself.

131 "President Johnson's Remarks," Corporation for Public Broadcasting, accessed October 13, 2020, https://www.cpb.org/aboutpb/act/remarks; "President Lyndon Johnson and The Public Broadcasting Act of 1967," Thirteen, YouTube, November 9, 2017, video, 2:53, https://www.youtube.com/watch?v=GCHZR46LCeA; Joseph Califano Jr., "How President Johnson Set the Stage for Passage of the Public Broadcasting Act," *Current*, May 5, 2017, https://current.org/2017/05/how-president-johnson-set-the-stage-for-passage-of-the-public-broadcasting-act/?wallit_nosession=1.

The answer to the first is: the Monsterverse.

▩ ▩ ▩

The founding "Constitution" of the Boston Society for the Diffusion of Useful Knowledge, published in 1829, reads:

> A number of gentlemen who feel interested in the promotion and diffusion of useful knowledge, have held several meetings to consider the expediency of forming an Association for the purpose of advancing these objects; and the undersigned have been appointed a Committee to form such an Association, and to recommend it to the patronage of the friends of popular education.
>
> From infancy to the age of seventeen, the means provided in this city by public munificence and private enterprise, are ample. From seventeen to the age when young men enter on the more active and responsible duties of their several stations, sufficient opportunity does not appear to be afforded for mental and moral cultivation.
>
> At this period of life, when the mind is active and the passions urgent, and when the invitations to profitless amusements are strongest and most numerous, it is desirable that means should be provided for furnishing at a cheap rate, and in an inviting form, such useful information as will not only add to the general intelligence of the young men referred to, but at the same time will prepare them to engage more understandingly, with a deeper interest, and with better prospect

of success, in the pursuits to which their lives are to be devoted.

The existing deficiency of such means is clearly a subject of regret; and the undersigned are of opinion that this deficiency may most easily and fully supplied by courses of Lectures delivered in different parts of the city, under the auspices of a Society, whose sanction may secure to the Lecturers employed, the confidence and resort of the public. . . .

The Association shall be called the "Boston Society for the Diffusion of Useful Knowledge." And its object shall be to promote and direct popular education by lectures and other means.[132]

In March 1836, the lead founder of the society, John Lowell Jr., passed away in India. He had been on a world tour to recover his senses after the death of his wife and only two children from scarlet fever. Lowell was the scion of a Boston-based textile fortune, and his will made provisions to establish— with, it is said, half of his entire estate, some $250,000 in 1836 dollars—a trust dedicated to the maintenance and support of free public lectures and public classes or courses, much in line with the Boston Society's ambition, and stipulated they be free to all the citizens of Boston, regardless of their race or gender.[133]

From this extraordinary bequest the Lowell Institute was established. And beginning in 1840, prominent minds from around the country and the world were invited by the Lowell

132 "Boston Society for the Diffusion of Useful Knowledge," *Intelligence, American Journal of Education* 4, no. 2 (March/April 1829): 176–179.

133 Kelly J. Conn and Mya M. Mangawang, *The Lowell Institute School at Northeastern University* (Boston: Northeastern University, 2015), http://hdl.handle.net/2047/D20196863.

Institute's new trustees to come to Boston and lecture on any number of topics—geology, ornithology, theology, botany—and at any number of meeting places the Lowell Institute would rent for the purpose. One hundred talks were offered in its first year alone. At the time, Lowell's gift was the largest such individual bequest ever seen, and no less a personality than Oliver Wendell Holmes Jr. said, "No nobler or more helpful institution exists in America than Boston's Lowell Institute." And the gyre widened. The institute began to sponsor free courses, its first a series of fine arts lectures at what would become Boston's new Museum of Fine Arts,[134] and then—even though Lowell's will expressly forbade his funds to be spent on bricks and mortar—underwrote a project that brothers Henry Darwin Rogers and William Barton Rogers had presented to John Amory Lowell (cousin to John Lowell Jr. and executor of his estate): the polytechnic institute that would become MIT.

> The School of Industrial Sciences, which was to become the Massachusetts Institute of Technology, was opened in February 1865 in leased rooms in the building of the Mercantile Library Association on Summer Street and in the dwelling of Judge Jackson. The objectives of the school and the courses that it offered were, as described in the First Annual Catalogue. First. To provide a full course of scientific studies and practical exercises for students seeking to qualify themselves for the profession of the Mechanical Engineer, Civil Engineer, Practical Chemist, Engineer of Mines, and Builder and

---

134 It's still going strong: "Lectures and Courses," Museum of Fine Arts, Boston, accessed October 13, 2020, https://www.mfa.org/programs/lectures-and-courses.

Architect. Second. To furnish such a general education, founded upon the Mathematical, Physical and Natural Sciences, English and other Modern Languages, and Mental and Political Sciences, as shall form a fitting preparation for any of the departments of active life. Third. To provide courses of Evening Instruction in the main branches of knowledge above referred to, for persons . . . who are prevented by occupation or other causes, from devoting themselves to scientific study during the day, but who desire to avail themselves of systematic evening lessons or lectures.

The support for these free evening classes at MIT spurred gifts extending Harvard's educational mission under its new president (as it happened, fellow Lowell descendant A. Lawrence Lowell) to offer further free classes, and then—quick decades thereafter—moved into a new area in which to deliver "useful information" to "add to the general intelligence": that being broadcasting. The institute supported the Lowell Institute Cooperative Broadcasting Council, established in 1946 by the presidents of Boston College, Boston University, Harvard, MIT, Northeastern, and Tufts, together with the leadership of the Boston Symphony Orchestra, Brandeis University, the Museum of Fine Arts, the Museum of Science, and the New England Conservatory of Music.[135] Programming featuring courses and concerts started being produced for Boston's commercial radio stations, but then—in 1951—the council applied

---

135 "The Lowell Institute Cooperative Broadcasting Council and WGBH Program Guides, 1949–1969," Digital Commonwealth, accessed October 13, 2020, https://www.digitalcommonwealth.org/collections/commonwealth:6h4428405; "WGBH," American Archive of Public Broadcasting, accessed October 13, 2020, https://americanarchive.org/participating-orgs/1784.2.

for its own license and radio frequency. A radio tower was built—on a great blue hill, so W-GBH—and then a television tower, and then a network of educational stations, and all, as Lowell had envisioned, with the public weal in mind.[136] The founder and first president of WGBH radio would become one of the first presidents of the public broadcasting system described by President Johnson above.[137]

But that wasn't all. Fast forward: On December 17, 1965, the Lowell Institute's trustee Ralph Lowell is invited to deliver remarks to James Killian's Carnegie Commission meeting in New York. He describes his pride in the Lowell Institute Cooperative Broadcasting Council's work and the membership fees that the partner institutions—expanded from

---

136 "Lowell Institute Puts Culture on Air," *Harvard Crimson*, October 10, 1951, https://www.thecrimson.com/article/1951/10/10/lowell-institute-puts-culture-on-air/; "Lowell Institute's WGBH Takes Air," *Harvard Crimson*, October 6, 1951, https://www.thecrimson.com/article/1951/10/6/lowell-institutes-wgbh-takes-air-ptonight/. And WGBH would build its first television studio in the middle of what is now the MIT campus. "TV at MIT," MIT 2016: Celebrating a Century in Cambridge, http://mit2016.mit.edu/video#lg=1&slide=11; "Announcement from Hartford Gunn and David Ives about a fire at WGBH," October 14, 1961, American Archive of Public Broadcasting, https://americanarchive.org/catalog/cpb-aacip_15-19s1rwtr.

137 Larry Creshkoff, "Hartford N. Gunn, Jr.—1927–1986," WGBH Alumni, March 20, 2000, https://wgbhalumni.org/profiles/g/gunn-hartford/. The Lowells and the visual-education movement spawned a whole series of initiatives across the country—disparate, sometimes hankering to be federated—that at one point wore the great mantle of the "university of the air." For more, see Susan Matt and Luke Fernandez, "Before MOOCs, 'Colleges of the Air,'" *Chronicle of Higher Education*, April 23, 2013, https://www.chronicle.com/blogs/conversation/2013/04/23/before-moocs-colleges-of-the-air/; "History (1934)," University of Southern California, accessed October 13, 2020, https://about.usc.edu/history/. See also Peter B. Kaufman, "Visual Education and the University of the Air," presentation at the Content in Motion 2015 EUscreen annual meeting, Warsaw, Poland, December 4, 2015, http://blog.euscreen.eu/events/warsaw-conference-2015/; Moys Schuttert, "Archives in the Digital Era—an Interview with Anna Sobczak," EUscreen Blog, June 26, 2017, http://blog.euscreen.eu/archives/8207. More than one effort before PBS started to build a subsidized national production center; see Victoria Cain, "An Indirect Influence Upon Industry: Rockefeller Philanthropies and the Development of Educational Film in the United States, 1935–1953," in *Learning with the Lights Off: Educational Film in the United States*, ed. Devin Orgeron, Marsha Orgeron, and Dan Streible (New York: Oxford University Press, 2012), 230–248.

the original list—contribute to match Lowell's charity. He reminds the commission of television's unique importance "as the only medium capable of combining sight, sound, color, and immediacy, it is an information and educative force without equal."

In our country right now, he says, we have

two systems for using television. One, the commercial, is huge, powerful, enormously well financed. It has vast technical capacity, superb equipment, endless energy. The other, the educational, is relatively puny, ineffectual, and financially undernourished. It is all too often lacking in people, in leadership, and in drive.

But we have to fund it, he says, in large part because of

the spreading feeling that what is transmitted over television will inevitably make a difference in the kind of society we produce. Behind the 111 or more educational television stations stand the nation's greatest educational and cultural institutions. Through the 111 ETV stations, the highest aspirations of our society are expressed—albeit imperfectly. In their general, non-classroom programming, the ETV stations are reaching out to receptive minds—wherever they may be—with programming that strives to present the widest possible range of human experience and to show the best that mankind has to offer.[138]

---

138 Lowell's written presentation is in the James R. Killian papers at MIT Libraries. He still felt compelled—perhaps in the spirit of time—to establish his and his family's neoliberal cre-

The lineage from John Lowell to Ralph Lowell takes us through lectures to public education to broadcasting and back again. It is the same promise that motivates the collective force of hope against the worst that mankind has to offer.

Which is, for lack of a better term, the Monsterverse.

▩ ▩ ▩

The whole grand story is one of what early on in American life was called "visual education"—a beautiful term if there ever was one. The story dates from the very start of the moving-image medium, on the cusp of the twentieth century, and it continues right up to the present second. For as you are reading these words, someone, somewhere, is watching an educational video online, and someone else (perhaps even me) is producing one. Huzzas about the importance of visual education have been loud at times—and certain patches from our history might be identified as boon times for our highest hopes and dreams for the concept. The start of the 1920s was one such period; the early 1950s, another; the decade of the 1960s, with the Killian Carnegie Commission and the extraordinary founding of American public media, yet another; and now the present moment, again another, what with the web, the commitment of powerful educators to teach all the people in the world, and the promise of online learning still so tantalizing and still so unfulfilled. Yet notwithstanding the soaring

---

dentials. "No one," he told the commission, "is more deeply committed to the system of free private enterprise than I am. The Lowells have produced merchants, bankers, and manufacturers for generations. But we have also produced poets, artists, and educators and I am very much aware that neither group can long exist without the other." See "James R. Killian papers," MIT Archives Space, MIT Library, accessed October 13, 2020, https://archivesspace.mit.edu/repositories/2/resources/916.

language of Lyndon Johnson, above, at the launch of what may have been our best effort, these ambitions have been—have always been, every time—battered, dashed, and crushed, the search for knowledge and methods of knowledge distribution always smothered, it would seem, by the larger, more popular, more powerful, and much more lucrative leviathan of entertainment, and within that innocuous concept, misinformation, and within that an even greater monstrousness: efforts to purposely stupefy our population and render it unable, as a result, to act in concert and in its own best interests.

The story of the progress of visual education, then, is as much a story of the opposite of progress—regress—and indeed those who carry the standard of visual education in a progressive march during any of these periods always seem like opposition figures, when it should, quite naturally, be the reverse.[139] It didn't, of course, have to be this way. Our century of film began, roughly, with Thomas Edison in the late 1800s. By 2020 we have reveled in 100, 125 years of film and television—yet, notwithstanding the Carnegie Commission of 1967 and other efforts to bring into our era the Enlightenment's power and passion, we're about to muck it up, fuck it up, muck-it-fuck-it-up again, fuck it up as we have fucked up book publishing, journal publishing, music publishing, and more. We are going to knot up our genius and imagination in the same set of intricate, twisted Laocoönish publishing and distribution and

---

139 For more, see Michele Hilmes, *Radio Voices: American Broadcasting, 1922–1952* (Minneapolis: University of Minnesota Press, 1997); Thomas Streeter, *Selling the Air: A Critique of the Policy of Commercial Broadcasting in the United States* (Chicago: University of Chicago Press, 1996); Michele Hilmes, ed., *The Television History Book* (London: British Film Institute, 2003); Laurie Ouellette, *Viewers Like You?: How Public TV Failed the People* (New York: Columbia University Press, 2002); Eugenia Williamson, "PBS Self-Destructs," *Harper's Magazine,* October 2014, https://harpers.org/archive/2014/10/pbs-self-destructs/; and Peter Decherney, *Hollywood's Copyright Wars: From Edison to the Internet* (New York: Columbia University Press, 2012).

sales models; the same almost completely (now) unregulated environment; the same type of uninspired and uninspiring leadership; the same huge and trivial contracts devoid of essential liberties and freedoms; and the same hangdog public attitude—a purely toxic combination that together with our failure as a republic to defend other basic societal freedoms will obligate us to stay deformed, upside down, and inside out. It will obligate us precisely *not* to share knowledge and *not* to make the world better by all our actions and investments, no matter how benevolent, in the field.

Lord, as Tyndale might have said, how counterintuitive!

▓ ▓ ▓

Vachel Lindsay, one of the first American film critics—someone profoundly attuned to and hopeful about the power of the moving image—spotted the parallels and the linkages between print culture and screen culture: between film, just bursting vitally onto the world scene, and ancient languages long dead; between libraries, on the one hand, and dictionaries and encyclopedias on the other. "Edison is the new Gutenberg," Lindsay wrote in 1915. "He invented the new printing." The Egyptian "Book of the Dead," he wrote, with its treasury of hieroglyphs and pictographs, is "certainly the greatest motion picture I ever attended." As such, "American civilization grows more hieroglyphic every day."[140] "The art museums of America should rule the universities, and the photoplay studios as well. In the art

---

140 Early filmmakers also and often compared movies to books. And why not? See Sergei Eisenstein, "Dickens, Griffith, and Ourselves," in S. M. Eisenstein: *Selected Works Volume III: Writings, 1934–1947*, ed. Richard Taylor and trans. William Powell (London: British Film Institute, 1996), 193–239.

museums should be set the final standards of civic life, rather than in any museum libraries or routine classrooms. And the great weapon of the art museums of all the land should be the hieroglyphic of the future, the truly artistic photoplay." And the makers of those photoplays—especially the professional photoplay newswriters? "They should take the business of guidance in this new world as a sacred trust, knowing they have the power to influence an enormous democracy."

Lindsay asked, then, almost as a voice from the future:

> Why did the millionaires who owned such a magnificent instrument descent [sic] to such silliness and impose it on the people? . . . This American invention, the kinetoscope, which affects or will affect as many people as the guns of Europe [1915!], is not yet understood in its powers.

He predicted that

> The motion pictures will be in the . . . schools. . . . Textbooks in geography, history, zoology, botany, physiology, and other sciences will be illustrated by standardized films. Along with these changes, there will be available at certain centres collections of films equivalent to the Standard Dictionary and the Encyclopedia of Britannica. . . .
>
> Photoplay libraries are inevitable, as active if not as multitudinous as the book-circulating libraries. The oncoming machinery and expense of the motion picture is immense. . . . Every considerable effort to develop a noble idiom will count in the final result, as the writers of early English made possible the lan-

guage of the Bible, Shakespeare, and Milton. We are perfecting a medium to be used as long as Chinese ideographs have been. It will, no doubt, like the Chinese language, record in the end massive and classical treatises, imperial chronicles, law-codes, traditions, and religious admonitions.

Presaging debates at MIT and elsewhere in 2020, Lindsay continued:

When men work for high degrees in the universities, they labor on a piece of literary conspiracy called a thesis which no one outside the university hears of again. The gist of this research work that is dead to the democracy, through the university merits of thoroughness, moderation of statement, and final touch of discovery, would have a chance to live and grip the people in a motion picture transcript, if not a photoplay. It would be University Extension. The relentless fire of criticism which the heads of the departments would pour on the production before they allowed it to pass would result in a standardization of the sense of scientific fact over the land. Suppose the film has the coat of arms of the University of Chicago along with the name of the young graduate whose thesis it is. He would have a chance to reflect credit on the university even as much as a football player.[141]

---

141 Vachel Lindsay, *The Art of the Moving Picture* (New York: Modern Library, 2000), 14, 15, 17, 135, 149, 150, 151. The full text of the original 1915 edition may be consulted online at the Internet Archive (https://archive.org/details/artofmovingpictu00lind/page/n5); a 1922 edition may be viewed via Project Gutenberg (http://www.gutenberg.org/files/13029/13029-h/13029-h.htm). Dissertations, government documents, scientific demonstrations: all could be adapted into films, Lindsay posited, and so rescued from their otherwise inevitable destiny of "innocuous desuetude" (154).

But we get ahead of ourselves.

▩ ▩ ▩

Thomas Edison, for his part, fervently believed in the power of the moving picture to educate. With cinema, he said, "education can be manufactured wholesale," like any other product of the factory.[142] He found film a key educational tool—full of promise, "almost the same as bringing that object itself before the child or taking the child to that object," and "the closest possible approximation to reality."[143] "Virtually deified in the scholarly press," as one scholar has written, "as the father of electricity, the phonograph, and the cinema," the genius inventor of the twentieth century repeatedly and often fervently spoke of the power of the screen to uplift, to inspire, and above all, to educate. It was a time—almost exactly a century before YouTube—when efforts were being marshalled by hundreds of people and companies across the United States and the world to bring that power into theaters, but also into meeting rooms, homes, offices, and schools. Projectors and playback machines, with names like the Homograph, the Ikonograph, the Projectoscope, the Panoptikon, the Muto-

---

142 Quoted in Alison Griffiths, "Film Education in the Natural History Museum: Cinema Lights Up the Gallery in the 1920s," in *Learning with the Lights Off*, Orgeron, Orgeron, and Streible, eds., 145. Numerous examples of educational film efforts may be viewed online at "Online Videos," Learning with the Lights Off Companion Website, Oxford University Press, accessed October 13, 2020, https://global.oup.com/us/companion.websites/9780195383836/examples/; "Educational Films," Internet Archive, accessed October 13, 2020, https://archive.org/details/educationalfilms; and "Collection Items," American Archives of the Factual Film Collection, Library of Congress, accessed October 13, 2020, https://www.loc.gov/collections/national-screening-room/?fa=partof:american+archives+of+the+factual+film+collection.

143 Quoted in Jennifer Peterson, "Glimpses of Animal Life: Nature Films and the Emergence of Classroom Cinema," in *Learning with the Lights Off*, Orgeron, Orgeron, and Streible, eds., 141.

scope, the Cosmograph, the Biograph, the Edengraph, the Power Cameragraph, the Kineclair, the Phantoscope, the Photophone, the Ernemann Kinox, the Optiscope, the Pathescope, the Veriscope, the Kinetograph, the Kinetoscope, the Kinetophonograph, the Synchronoscope, the Animatograph, the Spirograph, the Vitascope, and more, all were competing for a share of a burgeoning market, attention, and investment. Edison said, "I can teach more accurate geography in half an hour to a class of young pupils by moving pictures than a pedagogue can in a month." "The moving picture art," he went on, "will largely supplement the art of printing for the transmission and diffusion of knowledge."[144]

These early years—right before the 1910s, in the 1910s, and in the 1920s, much the same as today, a century later, with the Internet—saw a rush of new organizations, some commercial, some noncommercial, being formed to produce, distribute, analyze, and help coordinate efforts to deploy the moving picture for teaching and learning. Among them were the National Academy of Visual Instruction, the Visual Instruction Association of America, the Society for Visual Education, the National Education Association Division of Visual Instruction, and more. The editors of the inaugural issue of *Visual Education* wrote, "We believe that the future awaiting the present efforts

---

144 Quoted in Ben Singer, "Early Home Cinema and the Edison Home Projecting Kinetoscope," *Film History* 2, no. 1 (Winter 1988): 37–69, online (behind a paywall) at https://www.jstor.org/stable/3814949. Singer makes the point that the new trade journals *The Moving Picture World* and *The Show World* published discussions of educational applications for film in 1907, their first year of publication. See also Devin Orgeron, Marsha Orgeron, and Dan Streible, "A History of Learning with the Lights Off," in *Learning with the Lights Off*, Orgeron, Orgeron, and Streible, eds., 1–66. It was Edison's invention—starting with the 1889 Kinetoscope—that won the day, and the specifications he designed for film size, image dimensions, even the arrangement of sprockets and sprocket holes for film reels, remained the world standard until only a few years ago. See Paul Saettler, *The Evolution of Educational Technology* (Greenwich, CT: Information Age Publishing, 2004), especially 92–93.

toward visual education will be more brilliant than the dreams of its most ardent devotees."[145] The French film producer and distributor Charles Pathé, addressing the whole world as his market, declared, "The cinema is the newspaper, the school, and the theater of tomorrow." One professor of education declared that "the motion picture is the single most potent educational factor in our present-day civilization."[146] Edison, meanwhile, was, as usual, backing up his words with actions, producing educational films not only for theatrical release but also for classroom projection with such titles in history as "The Minute Men," about the American Revolution, and in science as "Cecropia Moth," "Magnetism," and "The Life History of the Silkworm."[147]

These were years when the explosion of cinema and screen culture was astronomical; a new universe was being formed.[148] As one scholar has written, in these "take-off" years, "cinema industrialized entertainment by standardizing it, automating it and making it tradable." The average length of films released in these years, measured in feet of film, soared by orders of magnitude—from 80 feet in 1897 to 700 in 1910 to 3,000 in 1920,

145 "Foreword," *Visual Education* 1, no. 1 (1920): 6. "Undoubtedly," though, the editorial went on, "much of the prophecy now being uttered so freely on all sides will prove to have been either false or gravely misdirected. But the future will come—as the future always does—and it will bring to American education great benefit or untold harm to us according as it is moulded by the sound judgments of educational experts or by the bungling hands of enthusiastic tyros."

146 Orgeron, Orgeron, and Streible, "A History of Learning with the Lights Off," in *Learning with the Lights Off*, Orgeron, Orgeron, and Streible, eds., 22.

147 Saettler, *Evolution of Educational Technology*, 96.

148 Charles Musser, *The Emergence of Cinema: The American Screen to 1907* (Berkeley: University of California Press, 1990); Eileen Bowser, *The Transformation of American Cinema 1907–1915* (Berkeley: University of California Press, 1990); Richard Koszarski, *An Evening's Entertainment: The Age of the Silent Feature Picture, 1915–1928* (Berkeley: University of California Press, 1990); Paul Starr, *The Creation of the Media: Political Origins of Modern Communications* (New York: Basic Books, 2004).

at a time when a reel of film held 1,500 feet and each reel would play for about fifteen minutes.[149]

It was in the 1920s that cinema—and thus screen culture, in its own twenties or late teens—first became a mass medium in terms of production and distribution.[150] The impulse to dedicate the new medium, this new industry, to good purposes—in fact to bring out its innate goodness, to develop its true promise—was strong. Edison's film studio associate W. K. L. Dickson had predicted as much, writing that "the advantages to students and historians will be immeasurable. Instead of dry and misleading accounts, tinged with the exaggerations of the chroniclers' minds, our archives will be enriched by the vitalized pictures of great national scenes, instinct with all the glowing personalities which characterized them."[151] Edison himself had said that "the substitution of motion pictures for books in the nation's elementary schools would in twenty years bring about an advancement of ten centuries of civilization."[152] "Experiments I have made with school children have convinced me that 85 per cent of all knowledge is received through the eye. . . . I think motion pictures have just started, and it is my opinion that in twenty years children will be taught through

149 Gerben Bakker, "The Economic History of the International Film Industry," EH.Net Encyclopedia, ed. Robert Whaples, February 10, 2008, http://eh.net/encyclopedia/the-economic-history-of-the-international-film-industry/.

150 Douglas Gomery, "Film and Business History: The Development of an American Mass Entertainment Industry," *Journal of Contemporary History* 19, no. 1(1984): 89–103, online (behind a paywall) at https://www.jstor.org/stable/260426. See also Gregory Waller, *Moviegoing in America: A Sourcebook in the History of Film Exhibition* (Malden, MA: Blackwell Publishers Inc, 2001).

151 Quoted in Oliver Gaycken, "The Cinema of the Future: Visions of the Medium as Modern Educator, 1895–1910," in *Learning with the Lights Off*, Orgeron, Orgeron, and Streible, eds., 67–89.

152 Quoted in "Advertisement for the Society for Visual Education," *Visual Education* 2, no. 5 (May 1921): 41.

pictures and not through books."[153] He even went so far as to say for publication that "books will be obsolete for the schools. . . . It is possible to teach every branch of human knowledge with the motion picture."[154]

That impulse to have an entirely new industry—a medium, a method of communication, information archives, professional creativity, and the passions inherent in every production—point straight to social good, early in its process of development, is a familiar one. It happened in print, it happened in radio, it happened in television, and now, after Google, after Amazon, after YouTube, after Facebook, it's happening today with the Internet. We have, as a society, and always among our angels, this latent wish to make our media change the world, bring us our better selves, touch the stars. And yet that impulse almost always gets snuffed by the onslaught of . . .

. . . the Monsterverse.

▨ ▨ ▨

The attitudes of these early film Tyndales, if one can call them that, preaching the potential of the moving image and the prospects of screen culture for social good, were powerful. The call went out for more wholesome fare for the growing number of movie houses, and at the same time for equipping with screens and projectors other places where groups gathered—and for producing beneficial media for them to watch. An advertise-

---

153 Quoted in "Edison and Educators," *Visual Education* 4, no. 6 (June 1923): 171.

154 Quoted in Saettler, *Evolution of Educational Technology*, 98. Vachel Lindsay, for his part, was not a fan. "As long as the photoplays are in the hands of men like Edison they are mere voodooism," he wrote. "It is only in the hands of the prophetic photoplaywright and allied artists that the kinetoscope reels become as mysterious and dazzling to the thinking spirit as the wheels of Ezekiel in the first chapter of his prophecy" (Lindsay, *Art of the Moving Picture*, 174).

ment appealing to investors to buy shares in the young Society for Visual Education, for example, reminded doubters that the country might have 17,000 motion picture theaters, but that the real opportunity lay in the society's outfitting *226,000* schools, *200,000* churches, and *200,000* meeting lodges, "of which only a *very small number* have projectors" and films.[155] In 1919 and 1920, the frenzy of betterment came to a head: the National Academy for Visual Instruction was incorporated in Washington, DC, in October 1919; the Society for Visual Education was formed in Chicago in November 1919; in 1920, the National Visual Education Association was established in Washington, DC; and in 1921, the Visual Instruction Association of America was founded in New York.

They all were out making their case against the background of an exploding Hollywood—and situating it in the larger and longer history of technology and culture. The new journal *Visual Education*, which billed itself quite forthrightly as "a National Organ of the New Movement in American Education," reminded us in the opening salvo of its first issue that

> when the omnipotent little Printing Press assisted at the birth of the modern world and made effective the power of the human intellect—the most subtle and resistless force in the cosmos—many a learned mind and pious heart grieved at this invention of the devil, for it poured forth so many frivolities which would lead the world inevitably to perdition.

155 "Advertisement," *Visual Education* 2, no. 5 (May 1921): 41. See also Roy Rosenzweig, *Eight Hours for What We Will: Workers and Leisure in an Industrial City, 1870–1920* (Cambridge: Cambridge University Press, 1983).

Hieroglyphics, the editors told us, the alphabet, all of mechanical science, the first boats, trains, bicycles, carriages, airplanes, X-ray machines, telegraphs, and phonographs all had frivolous purposes to which they were first put—and the motion picture was no different. Yet the changes all came—tops were made to spin for children before becoming "gyroscopic governors of modern engines"—and now the motion picture was in the midst of its molt. "Thousands of intellectual men are awake to the existence of this new giant in our midst. Thousands more are stirring in their sleep." And "[t]hinking men [and women] are dimly conscious that something important is being missed." [156]

With these summonses also came a remarkable awareness of the importance of the human record and the contribution of video and screen culture toward it.

> Every day that slips into the past carries significant events of world history into the limbo of the irrevocable. Persons, things, acts, and occasions are seen by a few eyes at the moment of their living actuality, and then must take their place forever in history, imperfectly preserved in the transient memory of witness, in printed words of inadequate description, and in still pictures that record only frozen moments in the march of an event that lived and moved. Yet we have at hand an instrument that will preserve for all time a good fraction of what has occurred since the 20th century began, and practically everything of real significance that will take place throughout the world in all

---

156 "Foreword," *Visual Education* I, no. 1 (January 1920): 2–3.

the years to come. . . . By way of illustration, consider the titles of these old Edison films, made between 1900 and 1905, which George Kleine—a pioneer in modern pictures who never has lost the vision of the serious values obtainable from the great invention—recently had unearthed. These are selected at random from a collection of 179 similar subjects:

- Mount Pelee, smoking before the eruption.
- Eruption of volcano and destruction of St. Pierre.
- President McKinley's funeral.
- Skirmish between Russians and Japs.
- Panorama of Culebra Cut (while canal was building).
- U.S. troops landing at Daiquiri, Cuba.
- Galveston Flood. Search for bodies in ruins.
- The Aeroplane "June Bug."
- Opening of the New York Subway. . . .

What magical possibilities for preserving the past are here suggested! Out of the vast amount of footage taken since 1900, millions of feet still exist containing priceless records. . . . The great record of world activities being made daily by the motion picture is doomed to destruction after its present prescribed course is run, unless steps are taken to preserve it.[157]

Visual Education's editors, contributing writers, and readers were aware of the exponential velocity of information over time.

---

157 "Editorial," *Visual Education* 1, no. 5 (September-October 1920): 8–11. By 1926, even Melvil Dewey himself, forefather of the modern American public library and the organizer

In what may be called "natural education," consider the speed attained since the development of the postal service, the telephone, the telegraph, the modern newspaper, and the mighty motion picture. The man in the street now possesses more real-world knowledge than the learned scholar of 1850 could have amassed in a life time.

There has been "speeding up" somewhere. With the advent of the most enlightening single force since printing—the motion picture—more speed is inevitable. It will come whether we accept, and thereby control it, or refuse and leave it to its headlong and lawless course.[158]

▩ ▩ ▩

The Hebraic lament here is that same recursive refrain we have heard in every industry as it has hit its late teens or early twenties and thus, by our human generational standards, its initial maturity: that commercial ideation and the profit motive put societal needs (let us call it "the public interest") onto the back burner—or indeed onto another stove entirely. When J. W. Shepherd, chairman of the editorial advisory board of *The Educational Screen*, laid into the young motion picture industry in 1923, it was akin to the scathing criticism that Edward R. Murrow, in his 1958 farewell speech, and Newton Minow, in his legendary 1961 "vast wasteland" address, and critics of public

---

of the library and the archive through his innovative and eponymous decimal system, would declare that "the motion picture is . . . one of the greatest agencies for education man has ever devised." Quoted in Elena Rossi-Snook, "Continuing Ed: Educational Film Collections in Libraries and Archives," in *Learning with the Lights Off*, Orgeron, Orgeron, and Streible, eds., 457–477.

158 "Editorial," *Visual Education* 2, no. 1 (January 1921): 8–10.

broadcasting in the late 1970s and early 1980s would deliver of television, and redolent of what critics of the wayward web now deliver to characterize the Internet. Shepherd, a University of Oklahoma professor of education and director of Oklahoma's visual education initiative, believed that the film industry was already out of control. The young regulatory bodies—self-regulatory, really, led by the industry's own Motion Picture Producers and Distributors of America—that had been established to improve the quality of the motion picture had simply failed, he proclaimed.

> *In the first place*, it means that the motion picture theatre, and the motion picture industry for that matter, is fully discredited among the better element. In the *second place*, it means that the motion picture industry and the motion picture theatre have blindly built up a clientele and following of doubtful character and that the only way that they can now hope to remain in the community is to continue a service to the same following. No wonder then that good pictures have no appeal and do not "pay." In the *third place*, it means that large numbers of the population of these communities are not being furnished the recreation and entertainment that the motion picture can furnish, perhaps for cheaply and more satisfactorily than any other agency.
>
> In the *fourth place*, it means that the policies of the motion picture industry and the theatres have been narrow, selfish and too limited with no thought of the communities' welfare and with a complete absence of anything constructive in mind. In the *fifth place*, it means that the motion picture forces have looked

upon the public as logical prey, and even in many cases demanding the right of protection from competition from other community agencies that seek to fill in the breach by giving an occasional moving picture show. This demand for a monopoly on the part of the local motion picture theatre has raised an important far-reaching issue of "rights." Motion picture owners and managers have raised the cry of right to make a living on the one hand but denying on the other any right of the community to protect itself or to control its own destiny. In other words the theatre owners and managers demand for themselves full rights and privileges of protection and monopoly but deny any rights or privileges to the community. The economic fundamental, that only those persons in a community have a right to a living in that community who can serve the community constructively, has no place in the motion picture man's philosophy.

There seems, therefore, to be but one solution. That solution comes from the growing sense of the community's privilege, right and responsibility to govern its own destiny which in the last analysis demands that the community through its *own organization* determine the character and quality of its activities, particularly its entertainment and recreation, very much as it looks after its education, its commercial activities, its religious institutions. No force should be allowed contact with community life which is destructive in its influences. The motion picture certainly should be no exception.[159]

---

159 "Special Editorials," *The Educational Screen* 2, no. 1 (January 1923): 8–10.

It was this exasperation—precisely this exasperation—that would lead, through a few more fits, to the Carnegie Commission and the establishment of American public broadcasting. That exasperation—and precisely that exasperation—arose because men and women of vision sensed promise and danger twinning around something new—an invention, a technology—and sought to alert society to both. In the early and mid-1920s, these voices spoke to us—and their messages are still loud and still clear. Writing for *The Educational Screen* in June 1925, California producer George E. Stone found himself allotted ten full pages to expound upon his solution to the dilemma that no one could create full educational-film catalogs and libraries on a commercial basis. That solution—its chimes ring over almost every page of this book—was to create a nonprofit engine, a "Foundation," to become an "extremely useful center" for "the manufacture, exchange, and distribution of visual material with explanatory texts." As a producer himself of such films—on the origins of life, food, malaria, and diseases more generally—Stone recognized what others saw then and since, namely that "no amount of business organization or efficiency of production will offset the fundamental economic handicaps which confront the producer of educational films." A center that looked like "certain well-established cultural institutions in American life"—public schools, our great symphonies, our libraries, the museums of America, and more—was needed. Stone invoked these models with passion and prescience:

> Visual Education demands a wealth of subject matter comparable to that of a great library or museum. The material must be housed under conditions which will

preserve it indefinitely. It must be organized so as to make available its resources with minimum delay. It must be recognized as in a class with other public institutions and be placed on a free exchange basis for material and publications. It must maintain a highly trained technical staff to be available for all the highly specialized work involved in visual education.[160]

In a word, public broadcast—
But we get ahead of ourselves.

---

160 George E. Stone, "Visual Education—A Retrospect, an Analysis and a Solution," *The Educational Screen* 4, no. 6 (June 1925): 329–348.

6. *Visual Education—(II)*

"[T]he goal we seek is an instrument for the free communication of ideas in a free society."[161] As the Carnegie commissioners called for it, they echoed, even if accidentally, the ambitions of the *Encyclopédie* and its authors and founders in chapter 2, in some places almost verbatim. "Americans will know themselves, their communities, and their world in richer ways [through better, diversified television]. They will gain a fuller awareness of the wonder and variety of the arts, sciences, scholarship, and craftsmanship, and of the many roads along which the product of man's mind and man's hands can be encountered."[162] Diderot could have written the first Carnegie report.[163]

---

161 Carnegie Commission on Educational Television, *Public Television: A Program for Action: The Report of the Carnegie Commission on Educational Television* (New York: Bantam Books, 1967), 8, in one of its twelve recommendations.

162 Carnegie Commission, *Public Television*, 18.

163 In fact, the commission report was drafted largely by Stephen White, Killian's assistant. In a letter to White, E. B. White, the great American writer and arbiter of literary style, lent White number one some lyrics. E. B. White wrote: *The New Yorker* No. 23 West 43rd Street New York, N.Y. 10036 September 26, 1966 Dear Steve: I have a grandson now named Steven White, and I'll bet he can swim faster and stay under longer than you can. As for television, I doubt that I have any ideas or suggestions that would be worth putting on paper. Non-commercial TV should address itself to the ideal of excellence, not the idea of acceptability—which is what keeps commercial TV from climbing the staircase. I think TV should be providing the visual counterpart of the literary essay, should arouse our dreams, satisfy our hunger for beauty, take us on journeys, enable us to participate in events, present great drama and music, explore the sea and the sky and the woods and the hills. It should be our Lyceum, our Chautauqua, our Minsky's, and our Camelot. It should restate and clarify the social dilemma and the political pickle. Once in a while it does, and you get a quick glimpse of its potential. As you see, I have nothing specific to offer and am well supplied with platitudes, every one of them gilt-edged. But thanks for the chance. Yrs, [signature] Andy White E.B. White [addressee] Mr. Stephen White Carnegie Commission on Educational Television 26 New Street Cambridge, Massachusetts See E. B. White, "Carnegie I: E. B. White's Letter to the First Carnegie Commission,"

So how is it that our televisual Enlightenment has never matured?

The founders and supporters of public broadcasting—from the 1960s and also from these earliest years—deserve to celebrate the achievements of the realm, and these are not inconsiderable: flagship programming initiatives, underwritten by philanthropies and government agencies with hundreds of millions of dollars; hours of history, science, business, public affairs, and arts and culture that have gained a place on every television dial, cable box, satellite dish, and streaming menu available to the American public. But there are reasons why television today looks as it does, and why the portrait of our programming grid in 2020 would look so familiar to the figures who critiqued the screen's offerings in the 1910s and 1920s—and in the 1950s, 1960s, 1970s, and since. There's a time line that runs quite steadily through print and film and television and the Internet of media visionaries and reformers speaking and heard, speaking and unheard, speaking and suppressed, not speaking loudly enough—and some, as we have described, reaching the status of prophets and even (as prophets put down by force) martyrs. There is, thus, a time line that runs from *Visual Education* and *The Educational Screen* through to these visions, above, of national solutions in the late 1920s, 1930s, and 1940s; from there through the fights over commercial broadcasting versus public broadcasting as the American model; and from there, with that fight lost, through the Murrows and the Minows; through the Carnegie Commissions, the subsequent reports, the deregulation and weakening of educational and public broadcasting; and now through the gut-

---

Current, September 26, 1966, https://current.org/1966/09/e-b-whites-letter-to-carnegie-i-2/?wallit_nosession=1. 26 New Street in Cambridge, where the Carnegie Commission was headquartered, is now an Enterprise Rent-A-Car.

ting of the mechanisms that had been recommended to govern the Internet and help society—global society, now growing more fully connected—to realize its full promise.[164]

It's the time line, the through line, of the Monsterverse.

Law professor Monroe Price, an expert on Soviet society and methods of thought control, has written that "for any society that seeks to achieve a substantial degree of democratic participation, the structure of the communications system is integrated with the functioning of the political system. That is why it is particularly vital to have meaningful public debate about any law that alters the relationship among principal elements of communications systems and between government and the private systems of communication, or even the balance of power between the makers and distributors of information."[165] As we unfurl in the arguments that follow, cultural and educational institutions are makers and distributors of information today as well, in the digital age, and thus count today among these "principal elements of communications systems" themselves. In the 1920s, not enough of these institutions, not enough key people in government, and not enough of the public recognized the stakes—economic, social, political—

---

164 There was an effort to produce an encyclopedia film company. As an ad for that enterprise put it, "Why Do We Swat That Fly? Why Do Lenses Refract Light? Why Does Iron Rust? Why Does Bread Get Moldy? SHOW THEM WHY! With Encyclopedia Britannica Films!" See Orgeron, Orgeron, and Streible, "A History of Learning," in *Learning with the Lights Off*, Orgeron, Orgeron, and Streible, eds., 49; "Encyclopædia Britannica Films," Wikimedia Foundation, last modified February 23, 2020, 17:51, https://en.wikipedia.org/wiki/Encyclop%C3%A6dia_Britannica_Films; Tim Wagner, "Discoveries within Encyclopaedia Britannica Films," Indiana University Libraries Moving Image Archive (blog), Indiana University Libraries, December 18, 2018, https://blogs.libraries.indiana.edu/filmarch/2018/12/18/discoveries-within-encyclopaedia-britannica-films/; "Encyclopædia Britannica Films," and Internet Archive, accessed October 13, 2020, https://archive.org/search.php?query=creator%3A%22Encyclopaedia+Britannica+Films%22.

165 Monroe E. Price, *Television, the Public Sphere, and National Identity* (Oxford: Clarendon Press, 1995). See also Cass R. Sunstein, "Television and the Public Interest," *California Law Review* 88, no. 2 (2000): 499–564, https://scholarship.law.berkeley.edu/californialawreview/vol88/iss2/9/.

involved, and so the work of the visual education societies evaporated, swallowed up into a larger fight, also lost, for the early control of American broadcasting, which is to say, all these years later, over control of the screens and speakers that today exist in every American home, school, meeting place, desktop, laptop, and phone.

The Carnegie Commission that was to assemble—from its first meeting in New York in December 1965 to its last in Dedham, Massachusetts, in November of the following year[166]—was the product not only of exasperation. When you explore the prehistory of public broadcasting, there's a chill that comes over you—a sense of déjà vu all over again, for two reasons. The first is, as this chapter addresses, that then as now, the hope for enlightenment was—it has always been— there, somewhere prominent, in the American debate over media. The second is that forces back then snookered one of the greatest public trusts out of public control and into private hands, and so ultimately under private control. Then as now, it didn't have to be—it never has to be—that way. Reviewing a masterful history of the early years that followed *Visual Education* and *Educational Screen*, as the country saw "visual education" coopted by those who controlled the screen and then sidelined and often ignored, the greatest historian of the television medium, Erik Barnouw, saw the question to address

---

166 "James R. Killian Papers," MIT Archives Space, MIT Libraries, accessed October 13, 2020, https://archivesspace.mit.edu/repositories/2/resources/916; and "Carnegie I," *Current*, accessed October 13, 2020, https://current.org/tag/carnegie-i/. The papers of the Carnegie Commission are deposited in the Wisconsin Historical Society Mass Communications History Collection; see "About Our Mass Communications History Collection," Wisconsin Historical Society, accessed October 13, 2020, https://www.wisconsinhistory.org/Records/Article/CS4017; "Carnegie Commission on Educational Television Records, 1963-1967," University of Wisconsin Digital Collections, accessed October 13, 2020, http://digicoll.library.wisc.edu/cgi/f/findaid/findaid-idx?c=wiarchives;view=reslist;subview=standard;didno=uw-whs-us0145af;focusrgn=-contentslist;cc=wiarchives;byte=507708481.

as this one: "How [was] our nation ... maneuvered, during pre-television years, into a broadcasting system controlled by and for business[?]"

A glimmer shines from the pool of our tears when we lift our heads from weeping long enough to see that we have one more crack at it with the modern Internet, which has gone far but maybe not too far, which has taken steps and run those steps along the same track as film, as radio, and as television, but maybe not yet past the point of no return.

Philosopher Jürgen Habermas speaks about the new ways in which we are able now to directly affect, for the better, the power structure of the public sphere and deliberative politics worldwide through the production and redistribution of media.[167] This is precisely, one might posit, one reason—the others being greed and money—why the fights over control of the media are so bare-knuckled and brutal and often so violent. As we have noted above, the only blood shed during the most expansive political upheaval in the world since the Second World War—the collapse of communism—was shed at the foot of the television towers in Bucharest, Vilnius, and Moscow, during violent confrontations over the control of the medium, and more specifically as a result of its seizure—for the first time, as it was a medium developed during the Cold War—from the grip of the totalitarian thought-controllers. This struggle, over television, has found several historians and media commentators as its chroniclers, but it's supremely relevant. The dust under which it lives should be blown off as we debate the future of the web.

---

167 Jürgen Habermas, *The Structural Transformation of the Public Sphere: An Inquiry into a Category of Bourgeois Society*, trans. Thomas Burger with Frederick Lawrence (Cambridge, MA: MIT University Press, 1991), and Habermas, "Political Communication in Media Society" (speech delivered to the International Communication Association [ICA], Dresden, Germany, June 6, 2006), http://www.mit.edu/~shaslang/mprg/HabermasPCMS.pdf.

"How was our nation maneuvered?" The urgency of the need to address an even more dangerous behemoth than we have previously confronted—state news and the power of the private sector, now working together—is brand-new. The Fox News empire, which began as an opposition network of principle-free lies and innuendo, under the presidency of Donald Trump became the network of the executive branch, and for the first time in American history we had—de facto, if not de jure—a state television channel, and thriving capillaries of video, radio, images, and print running in and out of the heart and the arteries of the beast. Fox has enjoyed a run of more than two hundred months as the top-rated news network in the country and, in 2018, its highest ratings ever.[168] The attempted evisceration of the idea of a public record, a common and independent source of facts, produced what media critic and historian Jay Rosen calls an "authoritarian news system"—even as in the same breath he indicates that we don't always have the language we need to talk about it.[169] But we do. It's a dress rehearsal for a totalitarian system of thought control, and it's the convergence many have dreamt about—only in a dystopian warp. It's a whiplash twist—not the end of history, as people proclaimed at the end of the Cold War, but the jingle, jangle, tintinnabu-

---

168 Mark Joyella, "Unstoppable: Fox News Hits 200 Months At No. 1," *Forbes*, August 28, 2018, https://www.forbes.com/sites/markjoyella/2018/08/28/unstoppable-fox-news-hits-200-months-at-number-one/#2674a28028cb; Mark Joyella, "Fox News Channel Has Highest Ratings In 22 Years—But MSNBC Is Growing Fast," *Forbes*, December 12, 2018, https://www.forbes.com/sites/markjoyella/2018/12/12/fox-news-channel-has-highest-ratings-in-22-years-but-msnbc-is-growing-fast/#6714e7eb6124; "Cable News Fact Sheet," Journalism and Media, Pew Research Center, June 25, 2019, https://www.journalism.org/fact-sheet/cable-news/.

169 Jay Rosen (@jayrosen_nyu), "We have no language for describing his hate movement against the press—because it is so un-American. But when you try to make that point on television, you have to find the words that can render it properly. This was my attempt with @brianstelter on @CNN," Twitter, April 23, 2019, 7:43 p.m., https://twitter.com/jayrosen_nyu/status/1120835564448690176.

lation of the beginning of the end of our democracy and our many freedoms. Gone now, thanks to Reagan-era deregulation of our communications systems, and generally to deregulation of every aspect of our economy and culture, are the societal standards and norms that protected us in times of quiet from such hideous encroachment.[170] It's what in professional terms might be called a bummer. It's what in New Enlightenment terms we call . . .

. . . the Monsterverse.[171]

▨ ▨ ▨

"*How was our nation maneuvered?*" The book that Barnouw was reviewing was Robert W. McChesney's masterpiece, *Telecommunications, Mass Media, and Democracy*, which chronicles how we lost control of our own broadcasting.[172]

"How did advertising-driven broadcasting," writes another historian, "establish itself as the dominant user of the airwaves in America?"[173]

---

170   "Yochai Benkler: Don't Panic, It's Just the Collapse of Neoliberalism," YouTube, March 4, 2020, https://youtu.be/9tvD2vxAKac.

171   For more on the effect of Reagan-era deregulation on public-interest broadcasting, see "Advisory Committee on Public Interest Obligations of Digital Television Broadcasters: November 9. 1998 Meeting Material," University of North Texas Libraries, last modified November 17, 1998, https://govinfo.library.unt.edu/piac/novmtg/; "Section II: The Public Interest Standard in Television Broadcasting," draft report of the Advisory Committee on Public Interest Obligations of Digital Television Broadcasters, University of North Texas Libraries, accessed October 13, 2020, https://govinfo.library.unt.edu/piac/novmtg/pubint. htm; Richard E. Wiley, Dennis R. Patrick, Laurence A. Tisch, Jonathan D. Blake, and Marshall J. Breger, "Broadcast Deregulation: The Reagan Years and Beyond," *Administrative Law Review* 40, no. 3 (1988): 345–76, https://www.jstor.org/stable/40709586.

172   Robert W. McChesney, *Telecommunications, Mass Media, and Democracy: The Battle for the Control of U.S. Broadcasting, 1928–1935* (New York: Oxford University Press, 1993).

173   Eugene D. Leach, "Tuning Out Education," *Current*, January 14, 1983, https://current. org/1983/01/coop/?wallit_nosession=1.

While what you are reading is not a television-history book, much of our present media and communications infrastructure dilemma is rooted in this history—and in how our commercial system manufactured its present outcome, and how it may always manufacture that same outcome when left untended, unguarded, and unopposed. Attempts to control the structure of our media have produced results that—if not akin to the way our foreign policy works, with trillions of dollars being misdirected at the invasion of the wrong countries—at least might make us uncomfortable enough to insist that Americans take a larger interest and play a larger role in the development of the policies that govern it. Needless to say, perhaps, when you commercialize a medium through advertising, and make almost every media network and media production dependent upon advertising for revenue, you render almost every conceivable piece of media a *commercially valuable* piece of property (witness, say, YouTube), and thus begin to pit, ineluctably, private and commercial interests against public ones.

This means that pressures are put against making media public: against shaping media in and for the public interest, and against sharing media in a timely fashion—in ways that copyright law, introduced prior to advertising, was originally designed to facilitate.

Not surprisingly, then, the history of our national media (and not just ours) is one that presents successive, almost non-stop waves of deregulation efforts wherever there was regulation designed to protect the public interest. McChesney's great contribution to our understanding of this history is his seminal work providing a case study of the cornerstone rollback, and the now ubiquitous commercial interests behind it. His tale is a blow-by-blow account of the lobbying, coopting, filibustering, bribing, and blackmailing by commercial interests of public and educational broadcasting interests in the period immediately following the great calls, discussed above, for film to do better for our citizens, paving the way, as McChesney puts it, "for the emerging dominant paradigm regarding broadcasting in the United States that deemed the control of the ether by commercial broadcasters as inviolable and outside the boundaries of legitimate discussion"—all accompanied by an effort to eliminate from the record the "struggle and debate over the control and structure" of the US broadcasting industry.[174]

And because of this systematic campaign, any meaningful government attempt to regulate the emerging status quo was to be seen as holding "the potential [for our young broadcasting establishment] to degenerate into a heinous state-censored system with the most ignominious implications for democratic rule." "Merely granting the government the right to regulate broadcasting," it was argued by 1936 and 1937, was akin "to 'the erection of a guillotine,' which, were a 'state of national hysteria' to emerge, would almost certainly develop into a situation similar to what had transpired with broadcasting in Nazi Germany."[175] No matter. Reform quashed, the history of efforts at reform excised from the ascendant narrative, we end up with "a dominant 'consensus'

---

174 Dehistoricizing analyses of governing policies serves to delegitimize contemporary efforts to bring about reform and change, and in media and communications policy it's a real problem. "Current debates on global communications policy tend toward ahistorical narratives with a focus on technical issues," one scholar writes. It's a particular problem that media historians and media activists need to address and fix—and fix together—because, as McChesney writes, the "erasure of the broadcast reform movement from broadcasting history" was "expedited by the refusal of important reformers to insist on their place in history." See Victor Pickard, "Neoliberal Visions and Revisions in Global Communications Policy from NWICO to WSIS," *Journal of Communication Inquiry* 31, no. 2 (April 2007): 118–39, https://doi.org/10.1177/0196859906298162; and McChesney, *Telecommunications, Mass Media, and Democracy*, 244.

175 McChesney, *Telecommunications, Mass Media, and Democracy*, 226, 241. In short, as another historian has put it, we've been "snookered." See Leach, "Tuning Out Education."

vision"—as though *it always had to be so*. By 1938, Radio Corporation of America head David Sarnoff would deliver to a national audience over his RCA-owned NBC network a triumphalist vision of commercial American broadcasting, ignoring the struggle of the previous fifteen years, asserting that:

> Our American system of broadcasting is what it is because it operates in the American democracy. It is a free system because this is a free country. It is privately owned because private ownership is one of our national doctrines. It is privately supported, through commercial sponsorship of a portion of the program hours, and at no cost to the listener, because ours is a free economic system. No special laws had to be passed to bring these things about. They were already implicit in the American system, ready and waiting for broadcasting when it came.[176]

For fifteen or twenty years, American progressives and educators went to war in pitched battles against interests that by their nature—by the nature of the generational longevity of capital, and by the human resources that successive generations of capital could and would muster—were built to outlive and outlast them; they engaged in hot battles that were as important to our sense of self as a country as any from the American Revolution, the Civil War, or the civil rights struggle of the 1960s. As we stare at ourselves in the mirror of our screens today, how farcical these false threats from the 1930s seem now! How farcical the threat of fascism from regulating the media, when the

---

176 Quoted in McChesney, *Telecommunications, Mass Media, and Democracy*, 243.

Brett Samuels, "Trump Rally Crowd Chants 'Send Her Back' About Ilhan Omar," *The Hill*, July 17, 2019, https://thehill.com/homenews/administration/453633-trump-rally-crowd-chants-send-her-back-about-omar.

unregulated media we have inherited today broadcasts a live rally led by the most powerful man in the world, with supporters chanting against other races and nations, and does so on the number-one-rated television network, and this broadcast is subsequently redistributed on commercial, largely unregulated social-media platforms! How farcical now, in the light of this history, to have considered the fascist threat to be coming from a regulated media environment, when it is so clearly here, now, having arrived as a result of an unregulated one.

▓▓ ▓▓ ▓▓

The struggle was waged not only outside of the television business. Hopes shone within as well. In the 1950s, NBC executives—led by Sylvester L. "Pat" Weaver, father of actress Sigourney Weaver—carried on full-force efforts within the industry to show, in essence and as they called it, "enlightenment television": art, music, science, things to build the mind and spirit, and in prime time. Weaver wrote long memoranda—there were forty bound volumes of memoranda and manifestos of his in his office at the time he left his job[177]—almost all with invocations like this one: "Let us dare to think and let us think with daring."[178]

For Weaver, the potential of television as a transport of the mind, as one of his biographers put it, was staggering, and he saw it as his mission to extend the vision, experience, and imagination of every viewer in the goal of "upgrading humanity." He wrote, of the viewers he wanted his network to reach:

> Every man will walk the craters of the moon, look into the churning lava of Vesuvius, sit in the ruins of Magna Lepta, be present at tribal dances, and range down the corridors of antland. . . .
>
> A new age of enlightenment is upon us. . . . The articulation of a new positive humanist philosophy is coming in the next five or ten years. The new understanding of the cosmos—the new cosmology—has tremendous implications for all of us. . . . I want to get the writers and producers to shed their cynical hucksterism and think.[179]

---

177 Erik Barnouw, *Tube of Plenty: The Evolution of American Television*, 2nd rev. ed. (New York: Oxford University Press, 1990), 190.

178 Pat Weaver with Thomas M. Coffey, *The Best Seat in the House: The Golden Years of Radio and Television* (New York: Alfred A. Knopf, 1994). See also Pamela Wilson, "NBC Television's 'Operation Frontal Lobes': Cultural Hegemony and Fifties Program Planning," *Historical Journal of Film, Radio, and Television* 15, no. 1 (March 1995): 83–104, https://doi.org/10.1080/01439689500260051; Evan Elkins, "'The Kind of Program Service All the People Want': Pat Weaver's Failed Fourth Network," *Historical Journal of Film, Radio, and Television* 35, no. 1 (2015): 176–94, https://doi.org/10.1080/01439685.2013.858967; and William Boddy, "Operation Frontal Lobes Versus the Living Room Toy: The Battle over Programme Control in Early Television," *Media, Culture, and Society* 9, no. 3 (1987): 347–68, https://doi.org/10.1177/016344387009003006.

179 Wilson, "NBC Television's 'Operation Frontal Lobes.'"

The memos come down to us today in extraordinary detail. Davidson Taylor, the head of public affairs at NBC, helped address the network from within about Weaver's plans. As one of the television historians of the period writes, Taylor and Weaver's September 1951 manifesto on "enlightenment via television" involved "implementing an enlightenment philosophy at three levels":

> The first level involved programs conventionally accepted as public service, which would be overtly informational, educational or cultural. This would include news, documentaries, special events, educational programming, discussions, talks, actuality and religious programming. . . .
>
> The second level of enlightenment programming would involve the inclusion of elements "which are not only entertaining but instructive as well" in regularly scheduled shows primarily devoted to entertainment: This plan requires that producers . . . bear in mind . . . the fact that the real world is fascinating in itself. Examples of such programming would be the Philco Playhouse's presentations of documentary dramas, the incorporation of educational or "cultural" segments in such series as *Kukla, Fran and Ollie* and Milton Berle's *Texaco Star Theater*, and the human interest interview series *We the People*.
>
> The third level of programming represented "the plan formerly referred to by Pat Weaver as Operation Frontal Lobes." (After this point, the entire range of "enlightenment program planning" was referred to as Operation Frontal Lobes.) Anticipated as being the

most controversial among advertisers, the plan for this level proposed that every commercial program in prime time should "once during the months of Fall and Spring present a whole show devoted to enlightenment." NBC proposed that these special shows should be paid for by the regular clients, since "they will see how important their participation . . . is to their own public relations, and to the duty they owe their audience."

In an article the following year, Taylor would stress that Weaver and his colleagues at NBC believed "that commercial television should and must be used for the enlightenment of viewers of the United States . . . that American commercial television, with all its skill to command the attention and to absorb the viewer, must serve the needs of our people to know more about the world in which they live."

We are convinced that the idea of enlightenment, the idea of expansion of horizons, the idea of responsibility, the idea of information and culture must have a part in every program we do . . . . There is no program which cannot from time to time contribute to the enlargement of the minds of those who view television. . . . [Our plan is] based on the conviction that the American appetite for information is immense, that the materials of reality are fascinating, and that the materials of reality are inexhaustible. It is our task to apply the devices of showmanship to the richness of the materials of reality, including not only current affairs, but also history, the sciences, humanities.

As David Sarnoff put it (in a speech that Weaver likely wrote for him before he coopted these ideas, buried them, and drove Weaver out):

> Television can become the greatest force for the enlightenment of a great nation that has ever been known. Our people have an insatiable appetite for self-betterment, for self-improvement. We are not feeding it sufficiently.
>
> The application of the devices of showmanship to the world of fact, of history, of the arts, of the sciences, of the humanities, is the first creative challenge. The network that concentrates first on this task is the network of the future.[180]

Weaver never realized his vision—he and his colleagues in Operation Frontal Lobes were encouraged to leave NBC. That was another watershed moment for the Monsterverse—much as Edward R. Murrow's farewell speech a few years later, in 1958, would point out in ways that were decidedly painful for media industry leaders, many of whom were present in the audience, to hear. Murrow—you can hear him deliver the speech; audio of it still exists today—spoke of his "abiding fear" of what television and radio were "doing to our society, our culture, and our heritage." He spoke of "the evidence of decadence, escapism, and insulation" everywhere—and the fact that in prime-time viewing hours there was "only fleeting and spasmodic reference to the fact that this nation is in mortal danger." Murrow could speak like Lincoln:

---

180 Quoted in Wilson, "NBC Television's Operation Frontal Lobes."

We are engaged in a great experiment to discover whether a free public opinion can devise and direct methods of managing the affairs of the nation. We may fail. But in terms of information, we are handicapping ourselves needlessly.

Let us have a little competition not only in selling soap, cigarettes, and automobiles, but in informing a troubled, apprehensive, but receptive public. Why should not each of the twenty or thirty big corporations—and they dominate radio and television—decide that they will give up one or two of their regularly scheduled programs each year, turn the time over to the networks, and say in effect: "This is a tiny tithe, just a little bit of our profits. On this particular night we aren't going to try to sell cigarettes or automobiles; this is merely a gesture to indicate our belief in the importance of ideas." The networks should, and I think they would, pay for the cost of producing the program. The advertiser, the sponsor, would get name credit but would have nothing to do with the content of the program. Would this blemish the corporate image? Would the stockholders rise up and object? I think not. For if the premise upon which our pluralistic society rests, which as I understand it is that if people are given sufficient undiluted information, they will then somehow, even after long, sober second thoughts, reach the right conclusion—if that premise is wrong, then not only the corporate image but the corporations and the rest of us are done for.

Just once in a while let us exalt the importance of ideas and information. Let us dream to the extent of saying that on a given Sunday night the time normally occupied by Ed Sullivan is given over to a clinical survey of the state of American education, and a week or two later the time normally used by Steve Allen is devoted to a thoroughgoing study of American policy in the Middle East.[181]

And, of course, a few years later would come Newton Minow's speech on the "vast wasteland" of what there was on television for Americans to see, or not.[182]

Weaver, like the generations of Lowells, would have a chance to inform Killian's Carnegie Commission himself. He was invited to speak to the commission's hearing in Boston on March 18, 1966. He set right in. "In our revolutionary times," he said, addressing the commission members, "communications are too important to be handled by response to the status quo vested interests."

Each person can now, technically, be present at all the events, ceremonies, festivals, attractions, museums, universities, lectures, concerts, etc., of the world; may find the audio-visual material to learn from in subjects he wished to pursue; may extend his interest in and knowledge of a vast array of subjects now covered only by books, records, magazines, newspapers in new

181 "RTDNA Speech," PBS, accessed October 13, 2020, https://www.pbs.org/wnet/american-masters/education/lesson39_organizer1.html; "American Rhetoric: Movie Speech: 'good night and good luck' (2005)," American Rhetoric, accessed October 13, 2020, https://americanrhetoric.com/MovieSpeeches/moviespeechgoodnightandgoodluckmurrow.html.

182 Newton N. Minow, *Equal Time: The Private Broadcaster and the Public Interest* (New York: Atheneum, 1964), https://www.americanradiohistory.com/Archive-Bookshelf/Regulatory/Equal-Time-Newton-Minnow.pdf; "Newton N. Minow: Television and the Public Interest," American Rhetoric, accessed October 13, 2020, https://www.americanrhetoric.com/speeches/newtonminow.htm.

audio-visual forms; may attend things never to be available on commercial television because the cost is too high (new plays and movies), the box office effect too great (home games of sports, other box office attractions in the same market), the attraction not suitable to commercial television time and interruption and audience size needs (festivals, cultural coverage shows, educational material, real world coverage in depth, news and information programs in depth), nor affordable by a donation-financed educational system.

What we need to insure, he said, is that

each citizen has access to the total Treasury of Man, the total knowledge of man. The further aim should be that any adult may continue his learning until his deathbed. The use of this material in schools should be accepted, and certainly all children should have attended the presentation of their cultural heritage as part of the basic curriculum; that is, the plays, operas, ballets, concerts, etc., should be recorded by the great artists in the great bastions of culture, and presented through televisions to schools, as well as to adults.[183]

▨ ▨ ▨

The Carnegie Commission assembled the best and the brightest. Killian and his colleagues tapped James B. Conant,

---

183 Weaver's written presentation is also in the Killian Commission Papers at MIT Libraries; see "James R. Killian Papers," MIT Archives Space, MIT Libraries, accessed October 13, 2020, https://archivesspace.mit.edu/repositories/2/resources/916.

former president of Harvard; Lee A. DuBridge, president of the California Institute of Technology; author Ralph Ellison; John S. Hayes, US ambassador to Switzerland; David D. Henry, president of the University of Illinois; Oveta Culp Hobby, chairman of the board of the Houston Post Company; J. C. Kellam, president of the Texas Broadcasting Corporation; Edwin H. Land, the inventor and president of Polaroid; Joseph H. McConnell, president of the Reynolds Metals Company; Franklin Patterson, president of Hampshire College; Terry Sanford, former governor of North Carolina; producer Robert Saudek; pianist Rudolf Serkin; and Leonard Woodcock, vice president of the United Automobile Workers of America.

The commission made twelve recommendations to "extend and strengthen" educational television:

1. Concerted efforts at the federal, state, and local levels to improve the facilities and to provide for adequate support of the individual educational television stations and to increase their number.

2. Congress to act promptly to authorize and to establish a federally chartered, nonprofit, nongovernmental corporation empowered to receive and disburse governmental and private funds in order to extend and improve Public Television programming.

3. Have the above entity "support at least two national production centers," and that it be free to contract with independent producers to prepare Public Television programs for educational television stations.

4. Have the above entity support the production of Production Television programs by local stations for more-than-local use.

5. Support local programming by local stations.
6. Provide the educational television system as expeditiously as possible with facilities for live interconnection.
7. Encourage and support research and development leading to the improvement of programming and program production.
8. Facilitate technical experimentation designed to improve present television technology.
9. Provide the means by which technical, artistic, and specialized personnel may be recruited and trained.
10. Have Congress provide federal funds required by the Corporation through a manufacturers excise tax on televisions sets.
11. Have the U.S. Department of Health, Education, and Welfare provide adequate facilities for stations now in existence and grow the system.
12. Conduct extensive studies intended to develop better insights into the use of television in formal and informal education.

Again, its final report stated:

If we were to sum up our proposal with all the brevity at our command, we would say that what we recommend is freedom. We seek freedom from the constraints, however necessary in its context, of commercial television. We seek for educational television freedom from the pressures of inadequate funds. We seek for the artist, the technician, the journalist, the scholar, and the public servant freedom to create, freedom to innovate, freedom to be heard in this most far-reaching medium.

We seek for the citizen freedom to view, to see programs that the present system, by its incompleteness, denies him.

Because this freedom is its principal burden, we submit our Report with confidence: to rally the American people in the name of freedom is to ask no more of them than they have always been willing to provide."[184]

Other reports would come and go—funded by Carnegie, Sloan, the Twentieth Century Fund, the Carnegie Corporation, the Knight Foundation, the MacArthur Foundation, the Open Society Institute, and more.[185] But the thing that James Killian and Lyndon Johnson did not say, which may have been obvious to everyone, was that it was all supposed to be free, free as a walk in the very park to which public broadcasting had been compared.[186]

A new Carnegie Commission cannot, on its own, defeat the Monsterverse and put us back on the right path. Many things

184 Carnegie Commission, *Public Television*, 98–99.

185 A Public Trust: *The Landmark Report of the Carnegie Commission on the Future of Public Broadcasting* (New York: Bantam Books, 1979); *On the Cable: The Television of Abundance: Report of the Sloan Commission on Cable Communications* (New York: McGraw-Hill, 1971); *Quality Time?: The Report of the Twentieth Century Fund Task Force on Public Television* (New York: The Twentieth Century Fund Press, 1993); and Lawrence K. Grossman and Newton N. Minow, *A Digital Gift to the Nation: Fulfilling the Promise of the Digital and Internet Age* (New York: The Century Foundation Press, 2001). Larry Grossman worked as head of both NBC News and PBS; see Lawrence K. Grossman, *The Electronic Republic: Reshaping Democracy in the Information Age* (New York: Penguin, 1995).

186 Melody Kramer and Betsy O'Donovan, "F Is for Future: How to Think About Public Media's Next 50 Years," Knight Foundation, accessed October 13, 2020, https://www.knight-foundation.org/public-media-white-paper-2017-kramer-o-donovan; Blair Levin, "Public Media at 50: What's Next for the Information Commons?" Knight Foundation, accessed October 13, 2020, https://www.knightfoundation.org/public-media-white-paper-2017-levin; Pearson Cross, "In Defense of Public Broadcasting," Commentary, *Independent*, Lafayette, LA, June 26, 2017, http://theind.com/article-25240-In-defense-of-public-broadcasting.html.

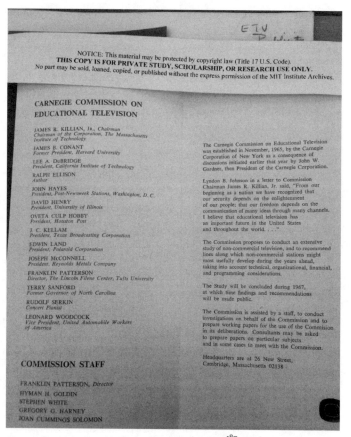

CARNEGIE COMMISSION ON EDUCATIONAL TELEVISION

JAMES R. KILLIAN, Jr., *Chairman*
Chairman of the Corporation, The Massachusetts Institute of Technology

JAMES B. CONANT
Former President, Harvard University

LEE A. DuBRIDGE
President, California Institute of Technology

RALPH ELLISON
Author

JOHN HAYES
President, Post-Newsweek Stations, Washington, D.C.

DAVID HENRY
President, University of Illinois

OVETA CULP HOBBY
President, Houston Post

J. C. KELLAM
President, Texas Broadcasting Corporation

EDWIN LAND
President, Polaroid Corporation

JOSEPH McCONNELL
President, Reynolds Metals Company

FRANKLIN PATTERSON
Director, The Lincoln Filene Center, Tufts University

TERRY SANFORD
Former Governor of North Carolina

RUDOLF SERKIN
Concert Pianist

LEONARD WOODCOCK
Vice President, United Automobile Workers of America

The Carnegie Commission on Educational Television was established in November, 1965, by the Carnegie Corporation of New York as a consequence of discussions initiated earlier that year by John W. Gardner, then President of the Carnegie Corporation.

Lyndon B. Johnson in a letter to Commission Chairman James R. Killian, Jr. said, "From our beginning as a nation we have recognized that our security depends on the enlightenment of our people; that our freedom depends on the communication of many ideas through many channels. I believe that educational television has an important future in the United States and throughout the world. . . ."

The Commission proposes to conduct an extensive study of non-commercial television, and to recommend lines along which non-commercial stations might most usefully develop during the years ahead, taking into account technical, organizational, financial, and programming considerations.

The Study will be concluded during 1967, at which time findings and recommendations will be made public.

The Commission is assisted by a staff, to conduct investigations on behalf of the Commission and to prepare working papers for the use of the Commission in its deliberations. Consultants may be asked to prepare papers on particular subjects and in some cases to meet with the Commission.

Headquarters are at 26 New Street, Cambridge, Massachusetts 02138

COMMISSION STAFF

FRANKLIN PATTERSON, *Director*
HYMAN H. GOLDIN
STEPHEN WHITE
GREGORY G. HARNEY
JOAN CUMMINGS SOLOMON

Carnegie Commission (1967) brochure—MIT Library Archives[187]

will need to happen in many different arenas for there to be real, positive change. However, a new Carnegie Commission–like initiative could go a long way toward identifying more of what needs to be done in different areas and putting the most egregious offenders on notice.

---

187 "James R. Killian Papers," MIT Archives Space, MIT Libraries, accessed October 13, 2020, https://archivesspace.mit.edu/repositories/2/resources/916; https://current.org/tag/carnegie-i/.

▓ ▓ ▓

Vachel Lindsay wanted museums to embrace moving pic-tures—and art critics and art historians to write those movies. They should get their "ideas and refreshment in such places as the Ryerson Art Library of the Chicago Art Institute. They should begin with such books as Richard Muther's *History of Modern Painting*, John C. Van Dyke's *Art for Art's Sake*, Marquand and Frothingham's *History of Sculpture*, A. D. F. Hamlin's *History of Architecture*. They should take the business of guidance in this new world as a sacred trust, knowing they have the power to influence an enormous democracy." Lindsay believed moving images were meant to be wielded for good. "It has come then, this new weapon of men, and the face of the whole earth changes," he wrote, in 1915—when films were becoming so popular that "the whole world seems to turn on a reel." He wanted science, too, to turn into movies—anyone and anything involved in the business of spreading knowledge.

> Transubstantiation must begin. Our young magicians must derive strange new pulse-beats from the veins of the earth, from the sap of the trees, from the lightning of the sky, as well as the alchemical acids, metals, and flames. Then they will kindle the beginning mysteries for our cause. They will build up a priesthood that is free, yet authorized to freedom. It will be established and disestablished according to the intrinsic authority of the light revealed.[188]

---

188 Lindsay, *Art of the Moving Picture*, 135, 175, 187.

Part III
Forward

7. Our Rights

To the thinkers and writers and actors active in the first Enlightenment, the Monsterverse presented as kings and clerics and nobles: people who defined the expansive powers they claimed as mandated by God, royal blood, or class strata, not as rights natural to us as everyday people—not inalienable, not, as the *philosophes* came to say, imprescriptible. Visions of a new world defined by liberty, equality, and justice that all enjoyed were freshly forming in this era. And it was the Enlightenment's publishing project, a single and vast encyclopedia, that facilitated the new insights that were required, the key "epistemological shift that transformed the topography of everything known to man."[189]

Today it is also publishing—online and writ large—that is transforming our understanding of ourselves and our ways of approaching knowledge and society. The struggle over the control of information is once again becoming—has it ever not been?—the most important battle of our time. Our universe in all its fullness looks different now, of course. We are centuries into an appreciation (and the critique) of social contracts and constitutions and declarations and charters that define—and define as law—things like freedom. But the ease with which we can post or tweet something that might reach millions of readers and users quickly and seemingly freely should not suggest that the world, even the Western world, is much freer,

189 Robert Darnton, *The Business of Enlightenment: A Publishing History of the Encyclopédie, 1775–1800* (Cambridge, MA: Harvard University Press, 1979), 7.

more equal, or more just than it was in 1535, 1789, 1917—or ever.

The disseminators of knowledge who came before us glow like icons next to the temple flame. These were our real forebears, and we need to connect to their work for inspiration. We need their inspiration because we have work to do as publishers, translators, and disseminators ourselves. Our Monsterverse today is only partially visible—in part because this freedom we do have (to post, to tweet, to search and to find, to record, to receive, and to send) does seem so far-reaching, so free of the kinds of controls that existed over publishing earlier, as we've discussed in chapters 1, 2, and 3. It is only very recently that other epic figures in the struggle—Edward Snowden, for example; Chelsea Manning; Julian Assange—have let us see, as Tyndale wanted the king to see, the parlous nature of this system of ours in something like its totality, and the fragility of that thing we consider to be ostensibly now a natural right, that thing called freedom.[190]

We have managed—through networks and media and communication—to create not just a worldwide web linking many people and movements in a good way but also a system for almost absolute surveillance: surveillance by corporate interests, government interests, and sometimes both in tandem. When Snowden first started to poke around and see the comprehensive nature of that surveillance, *in America*, no less, he was astonished at its reach, at the complicity of so many corporate-*cum*-govern-

---

190 And whatever you think of Assange, it's worth noting that his indictment is the cognate of Aaron Swartz's—pushed by a government Monsterverse working on behalf of that same government Monsterverse, as opposed to a blinded nonprofit and a knowledge institution temporarily gone mad. Assange's criminal indictment was for one count, conspiracy to commit computer intrusion—talk about a Lewis Carroll world! (Lord! Lord! How ironic!)—at 18 U.S. Code § 371, 1030(a)(1), 1030(a)(2), 1030(c)(2)(b)(ii). See *United States v. Assange*, United States District Court, Eastern District of Virginia [under seal], March 6, 2018, viewable at https://www.justice.gov/opa/press-release/file/1153486/download.

ment actors, and at the absence of any functioning safeguards in place—notwithstanding the multiple branches of our government, our Constitution, our case law, and our common sense. He was looking at the actual dashboard:

> [The U.S. government's mass surveillance system, mainly XKEYSCORE] was, simply put, the closest thing to science fiction I've ever seen in science fact: an interface that allows you to type in pretty much anyone's address, telephone number, or IP address, and then basically go through the recent history of their online activity. In some cases you could even play back recordings of their online sessions, so that the screen you'd be looking at was their screen, whatever was on their desktop. You could read their emails, their browser history, their search history, their social media postings, everything. You could set up notifications that would pop up when some person or some device you were interested in became active on the Internet for the day. . . .
>
> The two decades since 9/11 have been a litany of American destruction by way of self-destruction, with the promulgation of secret policies, secret laws, secret courts, and secret wars, whose traumatizing impact—whose very existence—the US government has repeatedly classified, denied, disclaimed, and distorted. . . . The attempts by elected officials to delegitimize journalism have been aided and abetted by a full-on assault on the principle of truth. . . . What is real is being purposefully conflated with what is fake, through technologies that are capable of scaling that conflation into unprecedented confusion, such that

we may have reached the final but grotesque fulfillment of the original American promise that all citizens would be equal before the law: the equality of oppression through total automated law enforcement.[191]

Snowden is a canary in a coal mine toxic with gas by the time he began to sing. But we cannot allow the sense of grotesque dystopia he describes to become something that paralyzes us forever, like a kind of polio. We have to work once again, work now with the best of the passions of those we can identify in our heroes and with the most sophisticated and effective forms of collective action now that we know. For us to achieve the promise of our moment now, of our new Enlightenment, we have to take a number of measures, and in my book, at least, we have to set out in particular on this five-point plan:

1. Define our Enlightenment-era rights;
2. Build our new knowledge Commons;
3. Construct our new network of facts and evidence—our Republic of Images;
4. Empower the archives at the heart of all this knowledge; and
5. Define our new moment—and process—for knowledge institutions to act together.

Perhaps it is no accident that many of the humanist achievements that propelled the Enlightenment forward occurred contemporaneously with many of the scientific ones in the 1700s. Perhaps it is even less of an accident that two of them,

---

191 Edward Snowden, *Permanent Record* (New York: Metropolitan Books, 2019), 7, 78, 196, 279.

together, brought rational thinking a step forward within years of each other, in the 1710s and 1720s.

The cornerstone of Enlightenment scientific thinking was laid by Isaac Newton, who published his *Mathematical Principles of Natural Philosophy*—in Latin, *Philosophiæ Naturalis Principia Mathematica*—in 1687, then revised it in 1713 and again in 1726. And around the same time, as it happened, the first copyright act—the Copyright Act of 1710, also known as the Statute of Anne—was published, and both in the United Kingdom. This first copyright act defined something that should give us, even in these darkest of times, some serious cause for optimism—and the metaphor to use for it comes, in fact, from Newton.

In publishing contracts, as in music contracts, film contracts, or contracts for other types of human creative endeavor, the rights that you as a creator grant or license to a private interest are traditionally designed to be limited in time. Representative language might be something along the lines of:

> The Author hereby grants to the Publisher, its successors and assigns, during the full term of copyright and renewals and extensions thereof: [a] Exclusive license to print, publish and sell the Work in book form in the English language. . . .

These rights are granted or assigned for a set period; ultimately, they are meant to expire. They may also, at some point, revert, as contract language stipulates, back to you as to the author/designer/creator of the work, if the licensee fails to exploit them.

> In the event that the Publisher shall fail to keep the work in print and for sale for a period of twelve [12] months

and if thereafter, after written notification from the Author, the Publisher shall fail again to place the Work in print and for sale within a period of [12] months from the date of receipt of such notification, all rights granted to the Publisher hereunder shall thereupon revert to the Author. . . .

More on this follows.

And what of user data and user behavior and user content in modern Internet relationships, as the corporations governing those relationships have succeeded in defining them to date? They are called "terms of use" for a reason. The answer is—utter bamboozlement. Shysterism.

Danger.

Spotify, for example, requires that

You grant Spotify a non-exclusive, transferable, sub-licensable, royalty-free, ***perpetual***, ***irrevocable***, fully paid, worldwide license to use, reproduce, make available to the public (e.g. perform or display), publish, translate, modify, create derivative works from, and distribute any of your User Content in connection with the Service through any medium, whether alone or in combination with other Content or materials, in any manner and by any means, method or technology, whether now known or hereafter created.[192]

Pandora says that:

---

192 "Spotify Terms and Conditions of Use," Spotify, last modified February 7, 2019, https://www.spotify.com/us/legal/end-user-agreement/, emphasis added.

When you use the Services, we keep track of your listening activity, including the number and titles of songs to which you have listened, the songs, albums, or artists that you like (thumb up) or dislike (thumb down), the stations you create or listen to, the songs you skip, and how frequently and for how long you listen to the stations in your station list. We may also keep track of your interactions with the Services, which may include the features you use, the advertising in which you see or show interest, and the content you view. We do this for a variety of reasons, such as to gain an understanding of the types of music, content, or features you and/or other similar listeners tend to like or dislike, for compensating artists and other rightsholders for use of their content, to provide you with relevant and interesting advertising, and to improve the Services generally, which includes enhancing our music selection algorithms in an effort to provide you and other listeners with the music most suited to your tastes. As this data is essential to the function of the Services, ***you may not opt out of our collection and use*** of such data or information. By accessing or otherwise using any portion of the Services, you hereby consent to the foregoing collection and use of your listening activity and behavior for the purposes set forth above and also as outlined in our privacy policy.[193]

Various companies will suggest that their hold on user data and information is fleeting and under user control, but far more often the opposite is true: the work of these companies, and

---

193 "Services Terms of Use," Pandora, last modified February 1, 2019, https://www.pandora.com/legal, emphasis added.

their commercial partners—Facebook, for example[194]—is geared toward making your data *their* data, and facilitating what some have called "the end of forgetting."[195] These rights go to the heart of the new social order and how it is a continuation of the old social order, and why a new social contract is worth calling for.

Could it be that the Declaration of the Rights of Man, which was born of the Enlightenment, might find a cognate in a new declaration, a Declaration of the *Use* Rights of Man, a declaration born of and in this new Enlightenment?

The 1789 Declaration—there is something so beautiful about it:

> The representatives of the French people, organized as a National Assembly, believing that the ignorance, neglect, or contempt of the rights of man are the sole cause of public calamities and of the corruption of governments, have determined to set forth in a solemn declaration the natural, unalienable, and sacred rights of man, in order that this declaration, being constantly before all the members of the Social body, shall remind them continually of their rights and duties; in order that the acts of the legislative power, as well as those of the executive power, may be compared at any moment with the objects and purposes of all political institutions and may thus be more respected, and, lastly, in

194 See "Data Policy," Facebook, last modified April 19, 2018, https://www.facebook.com/full_data_use_policy.

195 Jonah Bossewitch and Aram Sinnreich, "The End of Forgetting: Strategic Agency Beyond the Panopticon," *New Media & Society* 15, no. 2 (2012): 224–42, https://doi.org/10.1177/1461444812451565; The Open Mind, special, "The Web Means the End of Forgetting, Part I," hosted by Richard Heffner, featuring Jeffrey Rosen, aired December 1, 2010, on PBS, https://www.pbs.org/video/the-open-mind-the-web-means-the-end-of-forgetting-part-i/.

order that the grievances of the citizens, based hereafter upon simple and incontestable principles, shall tend to the maintenance of the constitution and redound to the happiness of all. . . . The National Assembly recognizes and proclaims, in the presence and under the auspices of the Supreme Being, the following rights of man and of the citizen:

Men are born and remain free and equal in rights. Social distinctions may be founded only upon the general good.[196]

—which is an echo of Jean-Jacques Rousseau's opening to his 1762 masterpiece, *The Social Contract*:

Man is born free; and everywhere he is in chains.[197]

Information, it has been famously said, "wants to be free."[198] Perhaps it is more correct to say that information is born free, too, and yet everywhere it, too, is in chains. Considered in this light, William Tyndale and Aaron Swartz were not heretics, obviously, or thieves. They were simply active in the process of accelerating events—accelerating the arrival of freedoms the importance of

---

196 "Declaration of the Rights of Man—1789," Avalon Project, Lillian Goldman Law Library, Yale University, accessed October 13, 2020, https://avalon.law.yale.edu/18th_century/rightsof. asp; "Declaration of the Rights of Man and of the Citizen," Wikimedia Foundation, last modified July 26, 2020, 03:46, https://en.wikipedia.org/wiki/Declaration_of_the_Rights_of_ Man_and_of_the_Citizen.

197 "One thinks himself the master of others, and still remains a greater slave than they. How did this change come about? I do not know. What can make it legitimate? That question I think I can answer." See "*The Social Contract*," Wikimedia Foundation, last modified July 8, 2020, 04:03, https://en.wikipedia.org/wiki/The_Social_Contract; Jean-Jacques Rousseau, *The Social Contract: Or, Principles of Political Right, 1762*, trans. G. D. H. Cole, Marxists Internet Archive, accessed October 13, 2020, https://www.marxists.org/reference/subject/economics/rousseau/social-contract/.

198 The remark is often attributed to publisher Stewart Brand; see "Information wants to be free," Wikimedia Foundation, last modified June 16, 2020, https://en.wikipedia.org/wiki/ Information_wants_to_be_free.

which will be as plain to see for us in the future as the value of the Thirteenth or Nineteenth Amendments appears to us today.

There is, then, a physics of intellectual property. We refer to video, very much a focus of this book, as a time-based medium for a reason. Information is frequently represented in physical terms, as ideas and expressions progressing through time. That's also why we cite and annotate video with time code, music with notes and instructions that move in time order, and text with pages that are read in time order, first to last.[199] The prescient author, musician, and copyright activist John Perry Barlow described information as moving, as in motion:

> Information is an activity. Information is a life form. . . . Information has *to move.* . . . The way in which information spreads is also very different from the distribution of physical goods. It moves *more like something from nature* than from a factory. It can concatenate like falling dominoes or grow in the usual fractal lattice, like frost spreading on a window, but it cannot be shipped around like widgets, except to the extent it can be contained in them. . . .
>
> Even when it has been encapsulated in some static form like a book or a hard disk, information is still

---

199 For more on this, see Peter B. Kaufman, *A Manual of Video Style: A Guide to the Use of Moving Images in Scholarly Communication* (Cambridge, MA: MIT Press, forthcoming). For the conservation challenges of time-based media, which is to say preserving the physical containers over time, see Caitlin Dover, "What Is 'Time-Based Media'?: A Q&A with Guggenheim Conservator Joanna Phillips," *Checklist* (blog), Guggenheim Foundation, March 4, 2014, https://www.guggenheim.org/blogs/checklist/what-is-time-based-media-a-q-and-a-with-guggenheim-conservator-joanna-phillips; "Time-Based Media Working Group," Met Museum, accessed October 13, 2020, https://www.metmuseum.org/about-the-met/conservation-and-scientific-research/time-based-media-working-group; "Time-based Media & Digital Art," Smithsonian Institute, accessed October 13, 2020, https://www.si.edu/tbma/; and Peter B. Kaufman, *Towards a New Audiovisual Think Tank for Audiovisual Archivists and Cultural Heritage Professionals* (Hilversum: Netherlands Institute for Sound and Vision, 2018), https://www.beeldengeluid.nl/en/knowledge/hub/av-think-tank.

something that happens to you as you mentally decompress it from its storage code. But whether it's running at gigabits per second or words per minute, the actual is a process that must be performed by and upon a mind, *a process that must take place in time.*[200]

Unlike the physical—"static," in Barlow's term—*containers* in which human ideas and information find themselves, the ideas and information in those containers are moving, and moving, I would posit, or riff, from a privately owned or privately licensed state, which is their temporary condition, into their proper and permanent position, where they become part of the knowledge Commons (the public's domain): that, is from the right side of the rights spectrum, where use and other freedoms are limited, toward the left—and ultimately all the way to the left.[201]

The movement of all information, in a social or societal or global context, in other words, is inherently and naturally toward the Commons, the shared public resource that is and always must be perpetually available to all. Ever since the earliest days of patent and copyright law, the law has "imposed a durational limit on patent and copyright protection." Scholars of the law tell us that "the Framers of the U.S. Constitution

---

200 John Perry Barlow, "The Economy of Ideas," *Wired*, March 1994, https://www.wired.com/1994/03/economy-ideas/, emphasis added. Russian filmmaker Andrei Tarkovsky spoke of time—rather than film, rather than images, moving images, words, or sound—as his medium; see Tarkovsky, *Sculpting in Time: Reflections on the Cinema* (New York: Alfred A. Knopf, 1989). For Barlow, "Reality is an edit."

201 Peter B. Hirtle, "Copyright Term and the Public Domain in the United States," Copyright Information Center, Cornell University Library, accessed October 13, 2020, https://copyright.cornell.edu/publicdomain; https://fairuse.stanford.edu/overview/public-domain/welcome/; Corynne McSherry, "The Public Domain Is the Rule, Copyright Is the Exception," *Deeplinks* (blog), Electronic Frontier Foundation, January 23, 2020, https://www.eff.org/deeplinks/2020/01/public-domain-rule-copyright-exception.

recognized the importance of the public domain. By providing that patents and copyrights could only be granted 'for limited Times,' they ensured that all patented inventions and copyrighted works of authorship would enter the public domain at the end of that limited period," just as they had in England.[202] And a full appreciation of this phenomenon is written into the law—from the very first copyright law, across the pond, to the laws that currently govern our media, technology, and freedom of expression. Thus does law describe this almost physical phenomenon of virtually all works of the mind falling—"falling"—into the public domain.

Were this to be a visible fall, as in fruit from a tree in a garden, the visuals might remind us of another Enlightenment moment. Isaac Newton described it:

> After dinner, the weather being warm, we went into the garden & drank tea under the shade of some apple tree; only he & myself.
>
> Amid other discourse, he told me, he was just in the same situation, as when formerly the notion of gravitation came into his mind. Why sh[oul]d that apple always descend perpendicularly to the ground, thought

---

202 Tyler T. Ochoa, "Origins and Meanings of the Public Domain," 28 *U. Dayton L. Rev.* 215 (2002), online at Santa Clara Digital Law Commons, https://digitalcommons.law.scu.edu/fac-pubs/80/; James Boyle, *The Public Domain: Enclosing the Commons of the Mind* (New Haven, CT: Yale University Press, 2005), http://thepublicdomain.org/thepublicdomain1.pdf. Ochoa writes, citing Lawrence Lessig and others: "The difference between government ownership of the public domain in land and common ownership of the public domain in intellectual property is explained by differences in the nature of the 'property' involved. Real property is a limited resource subject to the 'Tragedy of the Commons,' in which common ownership leads to an inefficient allocation of resources. Hence, government control, and a policy of privatization, serves the goal of economic efficiency. Intellectual property, by contrast, is a 'public good' which can be used by any number of persons without depriving anyone else of its use." See Lawrence Lessig, *The Future of Ideas: The Fate of the Commons in a Connected World* (New York: Random House, 2001), http://www.the-future-of-ideas.com/download/lessig_FOI.pdf.

he to himself; occasion'd by the fall of an apple, as he sat in contemplative mood.

Why sh[oul]d it not go sideways, or upwards? But constantly to the Earth's centre? Assuredly the reason is, that the Earth draws it. There must be a drawing power in matter. And the sum of the drawing power in the matter of the Earth must be in the Earth's centre, not in any side of the Earth.

Therefore does this apple fall perpendicularly or towards the centre? If matter thus draws matter; it must be proportion of its quantity. Therefore the apple draws the Earth, as well as the Earth draws the apple.[203]

Like Newton's laws, the original copyright law entered our discourse in the early 1700s. And the law as we have written it since then imposes some time limits on invention, creativity, and the private ownership of expression, before things do "fall," as inevitably as ripening apples, into the public domain. The physics of intellectual property, then, a corollary to the Newtonian *Principia*—treatises that underlay so much of the science behind the Enlightenment—needs its own Newtonian type of reframing. Newtonian *Principia* for intellectual property would suggest that the natural laws of gravity for ideas and inventions require any and all of them to eventually—some sooner than others, but all, eventually—to fall, drift, settle, end up, crash into . . . the public domain. The common good, in other words, is where these things ultimately arrive, by intent, by social design,

---

203 William Stukely, *Memoirs of Sir Isaac Newton's Life* (London: 1752), online at The Newton Project, September 2004, http://www.newtonproject.ox.ac.uk/view/texts/normalized/OTHE00001; Steve Connor, "The Core of Truth Behind Sir Isaac Newton's Apple," *Independent*, London, January 18, 2010, https://www.independent.co.uk/news/science/the-core-of-truth-behind-sir-isaac-newtons-apple-1870915.html.

even with today's systems of licenses and protections. That was the design of the very first copyright law. That is the design, all the obfuscatory language and the misleading information about it notwithstanding, underlying the latest copyright laws and updates in the West and in other parts of the world as well. Intellectual property, as we call it, is not meant to be private, except for a term, and then it's meant to be public forever.

So could it be said that the state of nature for an idea or an invention or any other human creation is, ultimately, in the public domain? That, after all the agita goes forth exploiting and commercializing something, and after all the rights have been recognized and registered and then . . . expire, ashes to ashes and dust to dust, that the thing itself ultimately settles into stasis as a public good? If Newton had written his *Principia* about what some of us call "intellectual property," would the force described in it governing these things be like . . . gravity? Meaning that everything we create, ultimately, falls into the lap of/belongs to . . . society?

The answer is, in a society that is a democracy, where there is not a king or crown vested with ultimate power and authority and ownership, and where we the people are the governors of first and last resort: yes. This is ultimately quite explosive a concept, because it frames every effort to restrict public access to a mind-born thing, idea, invention, or work of the imagination as temporary and—in effect, given our invocation of Newton—unnatural.[204]

---

204 For more on Newton's *Philosophiae Naturalis Principia Mathematica*, see "*Philosophiæ Naturalis Principia Mathematica*," Wikimedia Foundation, last modified June 30, 2020, 17:58, https://en.wikipedia.org/wiki/Philosophi%C3%A6_Naturalis_Principia_Mathematica; George Smith, "Newton's *Philosophiae Naturalis Principia Mathematica*," *The Stanford Encyclopedia of Philosophy* (Winter 2008 Edition), ed. Edward N. Zalta, https://plato.stanford.edu/archives/win2008/entries/newton-principia/; and "Philosophiæ naturalis principia mathematica (Adv.b.39.1)," University of Cambridge Digital Library, accessed October 13, 2020,

If that is all so, then some new Newtonian laws, new New Enlightenment laws, for intellectual property—or what we are calling the physics of intellectual property—might make some sense. The three Newtonian laws of motion might have cognate laws of . . . information! Such that "Every object in a state of uniform motion will remain in that state of motion unless an external force acts on it" could read much the same in information terms, with a kicker or two:

> *Every object in a state of uniform motion will remain in that state of motion, directed toward the public domain, unless an external force [a contract or a license] acts upon it.*

"Force equals mass times acceleration" could read as:

> *Free up that mofo info!*

And "For every action there is an equal and opposite reaction" could be reformulated as:

> *Eventually, all of our work will become part of common humanity, or humanity's Commons.*

A new Social Network Contract. New laws of information—a physics of intellectual property! A new . . . *Use* Rights of Man! Tyndale and Swartz, Diderot and Stallman—two on one side of the original Enlightenment, two on the

https://cudl.lib.cam.ac.uk/view/PR-ADV-B-00039-00001. Newton and his work are cited some 790 times throughout the *Encyclopédie*; see especially D'Alembert's article "Newtonianisme": Jean Le Rond d'Alembert, "Newtonianisme ou Philosophie Newtonienne," ARTFL Encyclopédie, University of Chicago, accessed October 13, 2020, https://artflsrvo3.uchicago.edu/philologic4/encyclopedie1117/navigate/11/679/?byte=1375304.

other—were simply trying to accelerate time itself. One day, someone might actually draft a formula free of arbitrary time dimensions legislated by private interests, such that the proper pull of our public domain might be explained. Perhaps it would be a formula like Newton's law of universal gravitation— $F_{gravity} = G\frac{Mm}{r^2}$ —wherein, irrespective of the form (song, photo, poem, play, book, film, drawing, tapestry), there is some math that predicts when every creative act becomes fully part of our free common heritage.[205] As a friend of mine used to say, "It'll all be the same in a thousand years," but that's too long to wait.

This concept of IP ownership as something we ultimately have in common—of social ownership, at least, not-ultimately-private ownership—for knowledge that we produce and share in the twenty-first century (as we have done now for hundreds of years) leads one to declare, in this complex Internet age, and with others who have said as much, that new rules are required, new rules of use, new terms of service (as they are often described, in the vulgate), new, in effect, manuals, guidebooks, directions, and agreements binding members of society and the companies and other private interests that seek to exploit their creativity, in ways quite different from the ways in which they have been written up to now.[206] The rights of creators, of members of society, to their own work and data in an era where almost anything can be zipped out onto the Internet for distribution and replicated almost instantly—they need restating, for, again, the Internet era and the network connectivities that

---

205 "Newton's law of universal gravitation," Wikimedia Foundation, last modified July 28, 2020, 14:18, https://en.wikipedia.org/wiki/Newton%27s_law_of_universal_gravitation.

206 See Peter Baldwin, *The Copyright Wars: Three Centuries of Trans-Atlantic Battle* (Princeton, NJ: Princeton University Press, 2014), online at the Internet Archive, January 24, 2018, https://archive.org/details/thecopyrightwars0000bald/page/n2.

it has ushered about constitute a change as transformative as that occasioned by the printing press, and that was the last real media change before the Constitution and its Bill of Rights was drafted and approved and published. Now, some 230 years later, again (there are no coincidences), these founding documents face a media and communications—and, with these a data-collection—environment, especially in the developed world, that would have been unimaginable by the Founding Fathers. And let us remember, they had some imagination![207]

If we should be seeking in some sense an update of the rights enshrined in these, our own terms of service as a society, what sections should we look at? This is not a call to amend the master contract, which is our Constitution—just to interrogate, closely and then even more closely, our true place as parties to it. It is more to remind ourselves that however majestic the document is upon which we have built our society here at home, it is also a document, a terms-of-service agreement, that served to

---

207 In France, the American Revolution was "looked upon as a kind of providential confirmation of ideas long accepted but hitherto demonstrated only in books." In 1783, the Marquis de Lafayette "conspicuously placed a copy of the Declaration in his house, leaving beside it a vacant space to be filled, as we are told, by a declaration of rights for France when, if ever, France should have one. Whether, in 1789, Lafayette placed a copy of the Declaration of the Rights of Man and the Citizen in the vacant space beside the Declaration of Independence I do not know." Carl L. Becker, *The Declaration of Independence: A Study in the History of Political Ideas* (New York: Vintage, 1922, rev. 1942, paperback, 1970), 231. The lines from Tyndale to the Founding Fathers' work are also direct. The framers read Tyndale's prose and repeated his language—and the hopes they harbored and qualities they wished for the Americans to come were colored by the messages that his words articulated, his work being no less an achievement than our own Constitution. See Mark A. Noll, *In the Beginning Was the Word: The Bible in American Public Life, 1492–1783* (New York: Oxford University Press, 2015), and Daniel L. Dreisbach, *Reading the Bible with the Founding Fathers* (New York: Oxford University Press, 2016). As for the *Encyclopédie*, it was not yet translated into English professionally for publication during the eighteenth century, but the Founding Fathers—John Adams, Benjamin Franklin, Alexander Hamilton, Thomas Jefferson, and James Madison—owned copies of French-language editions. Hamilton cites the *Encyclopédie* article on "Empire" in *Federalist* No. 22. See *Federalist* No. 22, December 14, 1787, https://guides.loc.gov/federalist-papers/text-21-30 and Paul Merrill Spurlin, *The French Enlightenment in America: Essays on the Times of the Founding Fathers* (Athens, GA: University of Georgia Press, 1984), 108–120.

ensure an early world of savage inequity, one in which slavery and other forms of brutality were condoned and normalized, and in which the most basic rights of society were kept away from women and nonwhites—not only then, at the time of its drafting, but for centuries thereafter. "The Constitution," writes historian David Waldstreicher, "never mentions slavery."

> The word does not appear. And yet slavery is all over the document. Of its eighty-four clauses, six are directly concerned with slaves and their owners. Five others had implications for slavery that were considered and debated by the delegates to the 1787 Constitutional Convention and the citizens of the states during ratification. This is many more words, with greater implications for slavery, than contained in the Articles of Confederation, the previous, notoriously weak national charter drafted in 1776 and passed eventually by the Constitutional Congress. All but one of these clauses protects slavery; only one points toward a possible future power by which the institution might be ended. In growing their government, the framers and their constituents created fundamental laws that sustained human bondage.[208]

Historian Eric Foner reminds us that, "of the fifty-five delegates [to our 1787 Constitutional Convention, where the document was drafted], nearly half, including a number of northerners, possessed slaves. George Washington, who presided, owned over two hundred, three of whom accompanied

---

208 David Waldstreicher, *Slavery's Constitution: From Revolution to Ratification* (New York: Hill & Wang, 2009), 3.

him to Philadelphia. . . ."[209] In other words, our terms-of-service agreements, so-called "end-user" agreements, those that we so often approve (even as we ignore them, since consent is usually implicit and opt-out)—these terms are in effect a kind of cipher, a symbol, a metaphor, a reflection, for and of the larger terms of service which we, too, have all too often ignored.[210] The Use Rights, or perhaps, the *User* Rights, of Man! Historians have remarked upon the fact that written constitutions often function as "weapons of control" rather than as "documents of liberation and rights"—and the use rights to which media and knowledge corporations subject us to may in fact be no different.[211]

How these use rights intersect with the Constitution and especially our Bill of Rights is an area for fruitful inquiry. The corporate behavior we've begun to describe concerns the Fourth Amendment, for example, and though it may not be a search, and it may not be a seizure, whatever goes on is certainly "unreasonable," especially when these companies not only collaborate with each other to exploit this user data but share information and work hand in glove with federal, local, and international governments. Calls have mounted for the reversion of these data rights as though they were basic rights an author grants to a publisher (which they are), and as this is not a govern-

---

209 Eric Foner, *The Second Founding: How the Civil War and Reconstruction Remade the Constitution* (New York: W. W. Norton, 2019), 1–2.

210 As Les McCann wrote, "Possession is the motivation that is hanging up the goddamned nation." Hear "Compared to What?": "Les McCann and Eddie Harris Compared To What," riksurly, July 23,2010, YouTube, video, 8:19, https://youtu.be/kCDMQqDUtv4.

211 Foner, *The Second Founding*, 2. See, in particular, the work of Linda Colley and James Rivington, "Linda Colley: Interview," *British Academy Review* 28 (Summer 2016), https://www.thebritishacademy.ac.uk/linda-colley-interview. Writing and code, even more generally than written constitutions, have always played a role. As anthropologist Claude Lévi-Strauss put it, ancient writing's main function—perhaps its first function—was "to facilitate the enslavement of other human beings." See Jared Diamond, *Guns, Germs, and Steel: The Fates of Human Societies* (New York: W. W. Norton, 1999), 235.

ment protecting us by virtue of a covenant designed to benefit our welfare but instead a set of private corporations in effect infringing upon our rights and overstepping the limits of what should be acceptable behavior in a modern web-connected world.[212] This is overreach in principle and practice—"surveillance capitalism," as it is now being called—connected to the neoliberal order architected for so long under steadily diminishing regulation. The data collection and retention policies of these companies, together with their nonstop collaboration with governments, especially our own, would have given the Founding Fathers pretty powerful dyspepsia. Indeed, perhaps it *is* a search and a seizure. As Harvard Business School professor Shoshana Zuboff tell us, we thought we were searching Google all this time, but actually Google has been searching us.[213] It's time to proceed in lockstep, as it were, with John Locke, who, after all, described his work so very modestly as just a search for "a modified form of the original compact."[214]

---

212 Jaron Lanier, *Who Owns the Future?* (New York: Simon & Schuster, 2014). See also Lanier, *Ten Arguments for Deleting Your Social Media Accounts Right Now* (New York: Henry Holt, 2018).

213 Shoshana Zuboff, *The Age of Surveillance Capitalism: The Fight for a Human Future at the New Frontier of Power* (New York: Public Affairs, 2019); Shoshana Zuboff, interview (part 1) by Amy Goodman, Democracy Now, March 1, 2019, https://www.democracynow.org/2019/3/1/age_of_surveillance_capitalism_we_thought; Shoshana Zuboff, interview (part 2) by Amy Goodman, Democracy Now, March 1, 2019, https://www.democracynow.org/2019/3/1/big_tech_stole_our_data_while; Ry Crist, "Amazon and Google Are Listening to Your Voice Recordings. Here's What We Know About That," CNet, July 13, 2019, https://www.cnet.com/how-to/amazon-and-google-are-listening-to-your-voice-recordings-heres-what-we-know/. This is not necessarily the place to refer to conceptions of property from other societies—Native American societies especially—but it might be said that the more progressive and spiritual approaches have always been onto something good.

214 Quoted in Carl Becker, *The Declaration of Independence*, 231. See also Becker, "Everyman His Own Historian," *American Historical Review* 37, no. 2 (January 1932): 221–36, http://www.historians.org/info/aha_history/clbecker.htm. Becker famously reminded professional historians in the 1930s of their "ancient and honorable company of wise men of the tribe, of bards and story-tellers and minstrels, of soothsayers and priests," where every man, as he put it, has been and always will be "his own historian"—and, might we add, data librarian?

8. *Our Commons*

Digitally today we gambol across the Internet like children let out early from school. We go about liking a post on Instagram, posting a video on YouTube, reading an article on Wikipedia, bumping to some new sounds on Spotify, and (for those of us who act our age) looking up a news story on CNN or googling a fact, the weather, or a sports score. Yet, while it *seems* as though we are roaming through the fields now gaily and freely, we are actually running across other people's lawns, crossing the private railroad company's trainyards and trestles, sprinting across endless box-store parking lots, one after another. And these owners are chasing us, just like in the movies—only they are running after us and capturing our data, filming us, in a way, as we all scramble across our rectangles, rather than trying to call the police or beat us some about the head.

And while it may seem at first glance that all of these platforms are the same—they appear free, or freely accessible, for the most part; they all appear to us on the same rectangle of screen and through the same audio speakers; their logos and iconography are all part of our common brand awareness now; they are all, to continue the metaphor, *outside*—they are not the same. If intellectual property—and copyrighted IP in particular—is something, at the end of days, we will ultimately be able to enjoy together, we should understand the mechanisms that facilitate our ability to share these materials today. Very few sites on the Internet are free as in "freedom": nonprofit;

noncommercial; ad-free; open to all at all times. The sites that *are* free, in this sense, are our digital parks now, our forests, our civic centers, our real public spaces, and they need our nurture. This includes platforms for the distribution of knowledge online—and also mechanisms for the collective and collaborative production of knowledge. And increasingly, the two go hand in glove.

For the Commons, only Wikipedia, of those in the above list, is part of that process of production. It is our air. It does not belong to someone else. Wikipedia promotes a self-conscious approach to rights—to contributor rights, to use rights, to *user* rights—as its first order of business. Not only is the actual process of knowledge creation on Wikipedia one that actually produces more equity and fairness within the act of authoring and editing—never closed to anyone, never static; not only is it an encyclopedia that even ten years ago rivalled and usually surpassed the quality of the *Encyclopedia Britannica* and other longstanding print and online references; today this powerful website, the fifth or sixth or tenth most visited site in the world, shapes knowledge creation as well as reflects the state of what we know.[215]

It is also, and rather significantly for this volume, the most gigantic and successful realization *ever known* of the original Enlightenment project. A commentator on Twitter discovered that you can cause a disturbance—and provide moments of

---

215 Roy Rosenzweig, "Can History Be Open Source? Wikipedia and the Future of the Past," *Journal of American History* 93, no. 1 (June 2006): 117–46, https://rrchnm.org/essay/can-history-be-open-source-wikipedia-and-the-future-of-the-past/; Neil Thompson and Douglas Hanley, "Science Is Shaped by Wikipedia: Evidence from a Randomized Control Trial," MIT Sloan School of Management Research Paper No. 5238-17, February 13, 2018, available at SSRN, http://dx.doi.org/10.2139/ssrn3039505; Richard Cooke, "Wikipedia Is the Last Best Place on the Internet," *Wired*, February 17, 2020, https://www.wired.com/story/wikipedia-online-encyclopedia-best-place-internet/.

serious fear and confusion—by taking almost any Wikipedia article and putting its descriptions of things that exist today into the past tense. Take Wikipedia's article on water, for example. Today it reads:

> **Water** is an inorganic, transparent, tasteless, odorless, and nearly colorless chemical substance, which is the main constituent of Earth's hydrosphere and the fluids of all known living organisms. It is vital for all known forms of life, even though it provides no calories or organic nutrients.

Now read it this way:

> **Water** was an inorganic, transparent, tasteless, odorless, and nearly colorless chemical substance, which was the main constituent of Earth's hydrosphere and the fluids of all known living organisms. It was vital for all known forms of life, even though it provided no calories or organic nutrients.

Or take oxygen.

> **Oxygen** is the chemical element with the symbol O and atomic number 8. It is a member of the chalcogen group in the periodic table, a highly reactive nonmetal, and an oxidizing agent that readily forms oxides with most elements as well as with other compounds. After hydrogen and helium, oxygen is the third-most abundant element in the universe by mass.

But now:

Oxygen was the chemical element with the symbol O and atomic number 8. . . . After hydrogen and helium, oxygen was the third-most abundant element in the universe by mass. . . . Oxygen was continuously replenished in Earth's atmosphere by photosynthesis, which used the energy of sunlight to produce oxygen from water and carbon dioxide.

And more past-tense tension:

The **Supreme Court of the United States (SCOTUS)** was the highest court in the federal judiciary of the United States of America. It had ultimate (and largely discretionary) appellate jurisdiction over all federal and state court cases that involve a point of federal law, and original jurisdiction over a narrow range of cases, specifically "all Cases affecting Ambassadors, other public Ministers and Consuls, and those in which a State shall be Party." The Court held the power of judicial review, the ability to invalidate a statute for violating a provision of the Constitution. It was also able to strike down presidential directives for violating either the Constitution or statutory law.

Democracy (Greek: δημοκρατία, *dēmokratiā*, from *dēmos* "people" and *kratos* "rule") was a form of government in which the people had the authority to choose their governing legislation. Who people are and how authority was shared among them were core issues for democratic theory, development and constitution. Some cornerstones of these issues were freedom of assembly and speech, inclusiveness and equality, membership, consent, voting, right to life and minority rights. . . . Generally, there were two types of democracy: direct and representative. In a direct democracy, the people directly deliberated and decided on legislature. In a representative democracy, the people elected representatives to deliberate and decide on legislature, such as in parliamentary or presidential democracy.

Or:

The **United States of America** (USA), commonly known as the United States (U.S. or US) or America, was a country mostly located in central North America, between Canada and Mexico. It consisted of 50 states, a federal district, five major self-governing territories, and various possessions. At 3.8 million square miles (9.8 million km²), it was the world's third or fourth-largest country by total area. With a 2019 estimated population of over 328 million, the U.S. was the third most-populous country in the world. The Americans were a racially and ethnically diverse population that was shaped through centuries of immigration. The capital was Washington, D.C., and the most populous city was New York City.

The dystopic nature of this exercise is effective. It also works because many of us have come to recognize the lingua franca, structure, cadence, and content of a Wikipedia article, and rely on the site to provide us with entry points into learning more. Moreover, they are the *key* entry points online, as each of the above surfaces first in a Google search for the noun.[216]

Wikipedia's terms of service enshrine the values that we should seek from any publishing platform—if our creations are meant to be our own, if contributing to knowledge is a part of what we want to accomplish, if the means of production are meant to be our own as well. It summarizes its terms as follows:

Part of our mission is to:
- **Empower and Engage** people around the world to collect and develop educational content and either publish it under a free license or dedicate it to the public domain.
- **Disseminate** this content effectively and globally, free of charge.

---

216 "Water," Wikimedia Foundation, last modified July 24, 2020, 17:00, https://en.wikipedia.org/wiki/Water; "Oxygen," Wikimedia Foundation, last modified July 25, 2020, 19:30, https://en.wikipedia.org/wiki/Oxygen; "Supreme Court of the United States," Wikimedia Foundation, last modified July 27, 2020, 20:41, https://en.wikipedia.org/wiki/Supreme_Court_of_the_United_States; "Democracy," Wikimedia Foundation, last modified July 24, 2020, 02:51, https://en.wikipedia.org/wiki/Democracy; "United States," Wikimedia Foundation, last modified July 28, 2020, 12:39, https://en.wikipedia.org/wiki/United_States. For more, see Peter B. Kaufman, "Dystopedia," *Commonplace* (blog), Knowledge Futures Group, April 17, 2020, https://commonplace.knowledgefutures.org/pub/ngtzl14z/release/1. The original Twitter suggestion is here: @lbcyber, "Fun fact: You can make any Wikipedia article dystopian by changing it to the past tense." Twitter, April 7, 2019, 6:16 p.m., https://twitter.com/lbcyber/status/1115015586243862528?s=20. For a Swiftian version of this kind of dystopic writing (this one around climate change), replete with a past-tense "lexicon of archaic terms" like these examples, see Naomi Oreskes and Erik M. Conway, *The Collapse of Western Civilization: A View from the Future* (New York: Columbia University Press, 2014). "Baconianism," for example, is/was "a philosophy, generally attributed to the English jurist Sir Francis Bacon (1561–1616), that held that through experience, observation, and experiment, one could gather reliable knowledge about the natural world and this knowledge would empower its holder. The fallacy of Baconianism was clearly demonstrated by the powerlessness of scientists, in the late twentieth and twenty-first centuries, to effect meaningful action on climate change despite their acute knowledge of it" (152).

You are free to:
- **Read and Print** our articles and other media free of charge.
- **Share and Reuse** our articles and other media under free and open licenses.
- **Contribute To and Edit** our various sites or Projects.

Under the following conditions:
- **Responsibility**—You take responsibility for your edits (since we only *host* your content).
- **Civility**—You support a civil environment and do not harass other users.
- **Lawful Behavior**—You do not violate copyright or other laws.
- **No Harm**—You do not harm our technology infrastructure.
- **Terms of Use and Policies**—You adhere to the below Terms of Use and to the applicable community policies when you visit our sites or participate in our communities.

With the understanding that:
- **You License Freely Your Contributions**—you generally must license your contributions and edits to our sites or Projects under a free and open license (unless your contribution is in the public domain).
- **No Professional Advice**—the content of articles and other projects is for informa-

tional purposes only and does not constitute
professional advice.[217]

And when it will be able to host and play video, much as
Amazon and Facebook and Alphabet/Google/YouTube do—
which is coming, by the way—Wikipedia will become the
most important media platform of all time.[218]

In 2017, the Metropolitan Museum of Art in New York City
released more than three hundred thousand images of items in
its collections with a license that allows anyone, anywhere to
use and modify them freely and for free—a license that facilitated their incorporation into Wikipedia. The thinking—it
was not as sudden a shift as all that; Wikipedians had been
working with the museum, as with other cultural institutions,
from 2009, and social tagging at museums and so-called cultural informatics kicked off even before that—was that the
Met could become more relevant to people's lives by having
its knowledge circulate around the world, and on platforms
even beyond its own control, than if it were to continue to
husband its resources on its own website alone. Still, the concept of releasing art and culture information—images and text,
but also metadata—into a world that could manipulate that
information and make things out of it is not that easy a concept

217 "Terms of Use," Wikimedia Foundation, last modified June 7, 2019, 19:07, https://foun-
dation.wikimedia.org/wiki/Terms_of_Use/en. See also Phoebe Ayers, Charles Matthews, and
Ben Yates, *How Wikipedia Works: And How You Can Be a Part of It* (San Francisco: No Starch
Press, 2008), online at the Internet Archive, https://ia800501.us.archive.org/20/items/How-
WikipediaWorks/HowWikipediaWorks.pdf.

218 And it's coming soon! "Wikimedia Product/Perspectives/Experience/Rich Content,"
Wikimedia Foundation, June 21, 2019, 22:33, https://www.mediawiki.org/wiki/Wikimedia_
Audiences/Perspectives/Experience/Rich_Content; and Peter B. Kaufman, *Video for Wikipedia
and the Open Web: A Guide to Best Practices for Cultural and Educational Institutions* (New
York: Open Video Alliance/Ford Foundation, October 2010), https://upload.wikimedia.org/
wikipedia/commons/a/a2/Videowikipedia_vi.pdf.

for every museum curator (or for any lover of facts, truth, and knowledge, for that matter) to embrace.

The Met's objective was also to introduce authoritative, canonical, definitive images of its holdings to the online world—and counter the persistent duplication of low-grade and otherwise faulty images of its artwork around the world, the so-called "Yellow Milkmaid Syndrome." The term comes from a 2011 white paper that the European Commission–supported cultural agency Europeana published to drum up support for its own plan—realized the following year, five years before the Met's public initiative—to release material relating to European museums and cultural-heritage organizations freely and openly on the web. Harry Verwayen, today executive director of Europeana and then one of the paper's co-authors, summarized the challenge at the time, "the release of open metadata from the perspective of the business model of the cultural institutions."

> Why does it make sense for them to open up their data? The study showed that this depends to a large extent on the role that metadata plays in the business model of the institution. By and large, all institutions agreed that the principle advantages of opening their metadata is that this will increase their relevance in the digital space, it will engage new users with their holdings, and perhaps most importantly, that it is in alignment with their mission to make our shared cultural heritage more accessible to society.
>
> But by themselves these arguments were not in all cases sufficiently convincing to make the bold move to open the data. There is also a fear that the authenticity of the works would be jeopardised if made available

for anyone to re-use without attribution, and a loss of potential income if all control would be given away. All understandable arguments from institutions who are increasingly under financial pressure. Nevertheless one could feel that the balance was tilting towards opening access.

An illustrating anecdote was provided by the Rijksmuseum. *The Milkmaid*, one of Johannes Vermeer's most famous pieces, depicts a scene of a woman quietly pouring milk into a bowl. During a survey the Rijksmuseum discovered that there were over 10,000 copies of the image on the Internet—mostly poor, yellowish reproductions. As a result of all of these low-quality copies on the web, according to the Rijksmuseum, "people simply didn't believe the postcards in our museum shop were showing the original painting. This was the trigger for us to put high-resolution images of the original work with open metadata on the web ourselves. Opening up our data is our best defence against the 'Yellow Milkmaid.'"

Open metadata for 20 million items in European collections from more than 2,200 institutions were released to the world that year.[219]

---

219 Harry Verwayen, Martijn Arnoldus, and Peter B. Kaufman, "The Problem of the Yellow Milkmaid: A Business Model Perspective on Open Metadata," *Europeana White Paper* No. 2 (The Hague: Europeana, 2011), https://pro.europeana.eu/files/Europeana_Professional/Publications/Whitepaper_2-The_Yellow_Milkmaid.pdf; Sam Leon, "The Revenge of the Yellow Milkmaid: Cultural Heritage Institutions Open Up Dataset of 20m+ Items," November 17, 2012, Open Knowledge Foundation, https://blog.okfn.org/2012/09/17/the-revenge-of-the-yellow-milkmaid-cultural-heritage-institutions-open-up-dataset-of-20m-items/. The Yellow Milkmaid Syndrome even has its own Tumblr now: Sarah Stierch, "Yellow Milkmaid Syndrome," accessed October 13, 2020, https://yellowmilkmaidsyndrome.tumblr.com/.

The Met took this initiative further. The Museum brought on a Wikipedian-in-residence to advocate within the Wikipedia community for more Met imagery and material to appear in Wikipedia. Through organized edit-a-thons that Wikipedia sponsored at the museum, as well as through individual initiatives among Wikipedia editors, Met Museum materials began to be published in key articles—on George Washington, Vincent van Gogh, Babylon, Benjamin Franklin, Henry VIII—across the vast encyclopedia. Images viewed by a hundred or two hundred web users a month on the Met's own website suddenly were being seen by hundreds of thousands of web users of Wikipedia and elsewhere. Visitors to the museum in 2018 numbered 7 million; and to the Met website, 30 million; but to the Wikipedia pages featuring Met images and data, 190 million.[220] The Met also began to explore opportunities to collaborate with other institutions interested in pushing technology, and artificial intelligence in particular, to spread art and culture knowledge—and to collaborate with the crowd. A new series of initiatives—involving MIT and others—launched in 2019 to accelerate experimentation between knowledge institutions and society.[221]

---

220 Author interview with Loic Tallon, then chief digital officer of the Metropolitan Museum of Art, February 5, 2019.

221 Loic Tallon, "xTalk Oct. 16, 2018: If Open is the Answer, What Was the Question?" MIT xTalks Office of Digital Learning, video, YouTube, 40:36, October 24, 2018, https://youtu.be/FU2o8YgusaE; Ivory Zhu, "The Met is More Than a Building! 5 Things You Missed if You Missed Loic Tallon's xTalk," Open Learning newsletter, MIT Open Learning, October 22, 2018, https://openlearning.mit.edu/news-events/blog/met-more-building-5-things-you-missed-if-you-missed-loic-tallons-xtalk; Chuck Leddy, "New Collaboration Sparks Global Connections to Art Through Artificial Intelligence," *MIT News*, February 5, 2019, http://news.mit.edu/2019/mit-collaboration-sparks-global-connections-art-artificial-intelligence-0205; "The Met x Microsoft x MIT," Metropolitan Museum of Art, accessed October 13, 2020, https://metmuseum.org/about-the-met/policies-and-documents/open-access/met-microsoft-mit; "The Met x MIT - a digital renaissance | Microsoft In Culture" Microsoft, video, YouTube, 1:49, February 5, 2019, https://youtu.be/c9KVfIjjBEc; Sara Castellanos, "Metropolitan Museum of Art Employs AI as Tool of Engagement," *Wall Street Journal*, February 6, 2019, https://www.wsj.com/articles/metropolitan-museum-of-art-employs-ai-as-tool-of-engagement-11549447200; Nancy Kenney,

The Commons is growing almost exponentially fast.[222] More than 1.4 billion works are online now, licensed with a Creative Commons license. Wikipedia hosts more than 40 million pieces of freely licensed content.[223] Search tools are being built to discover freely licensed content exclusively.[224] For knowledge institutions to embrace the Commons will be to recognize—in some direct way, but also in some symbolic, shamanistic, almost spiritual way—the power of the real public sphere, the power of society, and the power of the people (for whom, after all, we design our knowledge institutions). The system/the network/the apparatus allowing us to make this turn, and to secure it, is only twenty years old. The bright shiny objects of the Internet—Instagram (founded in 2010), Facebook (2004), Twitter (2006), YouTube (2005), Netflix (1997), WeChat (2011), and all the others—have fixed our attention, as happens, but it's the combination of Wikipedia and Creative Commons, together with the relentless drumbeat of the Free Software Foundation, the Electronic Frontier Foundation, and other advocacy groups, that really have our best future in mind. And that future includes the past, as it is fair to say that the

---

"Met unveils its AI experiment with Microsoft and MIT," *Art Newspaper*, February 5, 2019, https://www.theartnewspaper.com/news/met-unveils-its-ai-experiment-with-microsoft-and-mit; Eileen Kinsella, "The Met Museum Envisions a Future Where Artificial Intelligence Helps You Find #Art Posts for Your Instagram," *Artnet News*, February 5, 2019, https://news.artnet.com/art-world/the-met-ai-1456774; and Loic Tallon, "Sparking Global Connections to Art through Artificial Intelligence," *Medium*, February 5, 2019, https://medium.com/@loictallon/sparking-global-connections-to-art-through-artificial-intelligence-c8866522457d.

222 "State of the Commons," Creative Commons, accessed October 13, 2020, https://stateof.creativecommons.org/.

223 Ryan Merkley, "A Transformative Year: State of the Commons 2017," Creative Commons blog, May 8, 2018, https://creativecommons.org/2018/05/08/state-of-the-commons-2017/.

224 Home page, Creative Commons Search, accessed October 13, 2020, https://ccsearch.creativecommons.org/. This new tool exists to search across the billion-plus CC-licensed items in the Commons; of course, many more items that billions of humans have created over hundreds of centuries are in the public domain.

majority of all creative works created by mankind are (much stronger language than "should be") already part of the Commons today.

This kind of movement by knowledge institutions—hundreds in Europe, the Met, and now more institutions in the United States—is being propelled now not only by Commons activists, Wikipedia editors, and key organizations like the Wiki Education Foundation, all of whom are seeking, in the spirit of this book, greater access to knowledge, but also by cultural and educational institutions themselves, institutions whose leaders and funders are seeking greater connectivity to a public that in turn might be seeking access to knowledge that they possess, control, or can contribute. The advantages for marketing culture and education via the inheritor to the Enlightenment *Encyclopédie*—which happens, again, to be one of the most popular web platforms in the world—are clear enough, but so too is the burgeoning impulse to install authoritative, curated assets for the world to see through the mushroom clouds and shrapnel of lies big and small, fakery, deceptions, misrepresentations, half-truths, and (at best) incomplete information all exploding now online. In many ways, knowledge institutions together—museums, libraries, archives, galleries, universities—represent a kind of Fifth Estate, beyond the four estates of the executive, the legislature, the judiciary, and the press. Each of these institutions can contribute to our self-knowledge as humans, and in essential ways; together they deserve a name.

Projects are under way now to much more systematically bring your favorite knowledge institution, anywhere in the world that it may be, out to Wikipedia and also to bring Wikipedia into the knowledge institution—training faculty and students to write with it, training teachers to both teach and strengthen it, and training the world to read it (and indeed any information) with a careful and critical eye. The statistics provided today by Wikipedia's newest calculator, for the GLAM sector—galleries, libraries, archives, and museums—would have made Diderot proud. The British Museum images in Wikipedia are spread across pages that to date have 5.7 billion views. The Imperial War Museum: 7.2 billion. The Library of Congress: 36 billion. NASA: 30.1 billion. Media from Public Library of Science journals—1.9 billion.[225] And the effort, true to its roots, also runs across subject matter as varied as that of the original *Encyclopédie*, but more modern now. One such effort, on improving Wikipedia's content in and related to women's studies, reached 346 million readers in about a year.[226] Imagine if all the cultural and educational institutions in eighteenth-century France had had staff members who were writing for the Enlightenment encyclopedia—and buying subscriptions!—rather than just a tiny coterie of upper-class white men. And imagine if their understanding of liberty (and they, too, had some imagination!) was such that their contributions, like today's to Wikipedia, would have been governed by Wikipedia's four freedoms:

---

225 "BaGLAMa 2," Toolforge, accessed July 30, 2020, https://tools.wmflabs.org/glamtools/baglama2/.

226 See Jami Mathewson, "Women's studies and Wikipedia: a year in review," WikiEdu, May 9, 2018, https://wikiedu.org/blog/2018/05/09/womens-studies-and-wikipedia-a-year-in-review/ and Ryan McGrady, "Improve Women's Suffrage Articles on Wikipedia for a New National Archives Exhibit," WikiEdu, November 19, 2018, https://wikiedu.org/blog/2018/11/19/improve-womens-suffrage-on-wikipedia/; Will Kent, "The Success of Our First Wikipedia Fellows Cohort," WikiEdu, May 11, 2018, https://wikiedu.org/blog/2018/05/11/the-success-of-our-first-wikipedia-fellows-cohort/; Helen Siaw, "Wikipedia as a Tool for Public Engagement with Science," WikiEdu, November 14, 2018, https://wikiedu.org/blog/2018/11/14/wikipedia-as-a-tool-for-public-engagement-with-science/; and Cassidy Villeneuve, "Wikipedia: An Important Frontier for Scientific Knowledge," WikiEdu, September 12, 2018, https://wikiedu.org/blog/2018/09/12/wikipedia-an-important-frontier-for-scientific-knowledge/.

To ensure the graceful functioning of this ecosystem, works of authorship should be **free**, and by *freedom* we mean:

- the **freedom to use** the work and enjoy the benefits of using it[;]
- the **freedom to study** the work and to apply knowledge acquired from it[;]
- the **freedom to make and redistribute copies**, in whole or in part, of the information or expression[; and]
- the **freedom to make changes and improvements**, and to distribute derivative works[.][227]

And imagine if all things published and posted then and since had had Wikipedia's requirement not of simply being true, but of being *verifiable*.[228] Imagine how much more speedily this whole process of global enlightenment would be moving! When the museum is built for our time and our work—the Extraordinary Museum of Knowledge, or the Ziggurat, in MIT vice president Sanjay Sarma's words, of Facts—what culture of ours would we want featured and displayed?[229] What

---

227 "Definition," Freedom Defined, Wikimedia Foundation, last modified February 17, 2015, 18:57, http://freedomdefined.org/Definition. These definitions root back to software activist and former MIT resident Richard Stallman, as Wikipedia acknowledges: "History of Wikipedia," Wikimedia Foundation, last modified July 7, 2020, 06:32, https://en.wikipedia.org/wiki/History_of_Wikipedia. Stallman's proposal for a free encyclopedia is online here: Richard Stallman, "The Free Universal Encyclopedia and Learning Resource," Gnu.org, https://www.gnu.org/encyclopedia/anencyc.txt, and is reproduced as the Appendix to this book.

228 "Wikipedia: Verifiability," Wikimedia Foundation, last modified July 30, 2020, 13:57, https://en.wikipedia.org/wiki/Wikipedia:Verifiability.

229 See Peter B. Kaufman, *MOOCs and Open Education Resources: A Handbook for Educators* (Lakeville, CT: Intelligent Television, 2016), online at http://intelligenttelevision.com/files/59-moocs_and_open_educational_resources_handbook_kaufman_100616.pdf.

would be the items and artifacts we'd be most proud of? What would we want our museum visitors to be able to do with them? Amazon shipping envelopes? Netflix DVDs? Or Wikipedia, which by then will have become the Bible, Koran, and Netflix of information? For the Commons is not only a destination and ultimately the living museum of all creativity, it is also a dynamic showcase for one of the newest forms of human innovation: Commons-based peer production, and the Commons-based peer production of knowledge in particular.[230]

---

230 Eric von Hippel, *Free Innovation: How Citizens Create and Share Innovations* (Cambridge, MA: MIT Press, 2017), available at SSRN: https://ssrn.com/abstract=2866571, and von Hippel, *Democratizing Innovation* (Cambridge, MA: MIT Press, 2005), available at SSRN: https://ssrn.com/abstract=712763; Dietmar Harhoff and Karim R. Lakhani, eds., *Revolutionizing Innovation: Users, Communities, and Open Innovation* (Cambridge, MA: MIT Press, 2016); Rishab Aiyer Ghosh, ed., *CODE: Collaborative Ownership and the Digital Economy* (Cambridge, MA: MIT Press, 2005); James Surowiecki, *The Wisdom of Crowds* (New York: Anchor, 2005); Yochai Benkler, *The Wealth of Networks: How Social Production Transforms Markets and Freedom* (New Haven, CT: Yale University Press, 2006), free and online at http://www.benkler.org/Benkler_Wealth_Of_Networks.pdf.

9. *Our Network*

Should our ecosystem of knowledge depend on commercial platforms if it is meant to benefit and support the public good? Answer: no.[231] How, then, can we build a healthier system that is noncommercial in nature: a network of the most powerful and most energetic nonprofits, the ones with the oldest pedigrees, a mashup of models like the National Science Foundation, the National Endowment for the Humanities, the National Institute of Health, the Institute of Museum and Library Services, Wikipedia, the Internet Archive, public media, universities, museums, libraries, archives, parks, public spaces, advocacy groups, and more?

Journalism, as a profession, has begun to confront this truth now, in a field where advertising is being siphoned away from newspapers and magazines by the largest commercial Internet behemoths. As Emily Bell of Columbia University's Journalism School put it at the start of 2019, "The assumption in the US that news will eventually find a market model that does work has been one of the most consistent and damaging misconceptions advanced over the past twenty years."[232]

---

231 Or, as Greg Jackson has written, "Is it a problem that our mental representation of the world is the product of a for-profit entertainment industry? Yes." Greg Jackson, "Vicious Cycles," *Harper's Magazine*, January 2020, https://harpers.org/archive/2020/01/vicious-cycles-theses-on-a-philosophy-of-news/.

232 Emily Bell, "The Cairncross Review Admits What America Won't About Journalism," *Columbia Journalism Review*, February 15, 2019, https://www.cjr.org/tow_center/the-cairn-cross-review.php; Frances Cairncross, "The Cairncross Review: A Sustainable Future for Journalism," white paper, February 12, 2019, https://assets.publishing.service.gov.uk/

The system we have is not working. Google, Apple, Microsoft, Adobe, Facebook, and Twitter: they all can fritter away our time and our dynamism, our better selves. Instagram, Snapchat, DeepTalk, DuuDuu (the name of my new start-up that measures just how much of our time and energy the corporate entities that harvest and sell our data points suck up for themselves)—all weaken our imagination.[233]

Our citizens around the world are ready for a network that unites our screens and speakers and various devices (including the cardboard and paper ones) into this New Enlightenment, built for and of and by the people. In the same way that the rules for how we protect the environment and manage our health care and our credit systems need to be rewritten, we now need to attend to rules for the underwriting of knowledge, of education, of culture. Education is our core strength. It's the bones and the muscles, the neural networks and the organs of our society. Knowledge is everything.

The conversation may be about more than about making knowledge accessible. It may be about more than the elemental activist commitment, beneficent as it is, to making digital knowledge resources free because they are easy and inexpensive to duplicate and distribute. It may be that meaning and purpose is to be found in a deeper and larger conversation, now under way at last, about the need to reappraise and indeed replace the neoliberal action and funding agenda that

---

government/uploads/system/uploads/attachment_data/file/779882/021919_DCMS_Cairncross_Review_.pdf. In 2020, the McClatchy Group, the United States's second-largest newspaper group, filed for bankruptcy protection. See Lukas J. Alpert, "Newspaper Publisher McClatchy Files for Chapter 11 Bankruptcy," *Wall Street Journal*, February 13, 2020, https://www.wsj.com/articles/newspaper-publisher-mcclatchy-files-for-chapter-11-bankruptcy-11581598316.

233   Peter B. Kaufman, "The Other (Information) Emergency," *Medium*, October 11, 2019, https://medium.com/@pbkauf/the-other-information-emergency-77e6291b0247.

has dominated much of the discourse around education and philanthropy, and dominated the ways we speak of supporting noncommercial activity through philanthropic giving. Larry Kramer, president of the Hewlett Foundation, has written that "Today's prevailing intellectual paradigm—which has come to be labeled 'neoliberalism'—is no longer up to the task. However well this free-market orthodoxy suited the late 20th century, when it achieved broad acceptance, it has proved unable to provide satisfactory answers to problems like wealth inequality, wage stagnation, economic dislocation due to globalization, and loss of jobs and economic security due to technology and automation. Worse, it has become one of the principal sites of hyperpartisan conflict."[234]

Kramer expounds further on this neoliberal agenda and its attendant perversities:

> Its core premises: that society consists of atomized individuals competing rationally to advance their own interests; that this behavior, in aggregate, produces good social outcomes and the greatest economic growth; that free markets are therefore the best way to allocate societal resources and government should intervene only to remedy market failures. Disagreements about what constitutes such failures and when and how to correct them

---

234 Larry Kramer, "Beyond Neoliberalism: Rethinking Political Economy," William and Flora Hewlett Foundation, April 26, 2018, https://hewlett.org/library/beyond-neoliberalism-re-thinking-political-economy/. For the "network of philosophers, economists, journalists, and private foundations across the Atlantic world" that helped to develop this paradigm, and the funding dynamo behind their "abstract ideas" and the lasting and "tangible political changes" that resulted, see Angus Burgin, *The Great Persuasion: Reinventing Free Markets since the Depression* (Cambridge, MA: Harvard University Press, 2012), esp. 5, 99, 173, 181, 198, 224–225, and Nancy MacLean, *Democracy in Chains: The Deep History of the Radical Right's Stealth Plan for America* (New York: Viking, 2017).

persisted, but the general premises were widely embraced by policymakers and politicians (reflected, for example, in the so-called Washington Consensus). Today, this consensus is breaking down. Neoliberal policies have contributed to generating profound wealth inequality and have little to offer to address the perceived negative consequences of globalization and emerging technologies like artificial intelligence and robotics.

The "force for openness and opportunity" that many have seen in the Internet remains, but we now have to confront the fact that we are all implicated in creating what can be seen as a—the—"neoliberal, commercial, privatized web," an online world where "the outsourcing of information practices from the public sector facilitates privatization of what we previously thought of as the public domain."[235] Advertising, as Ethan Zuckerman has said, is "the original sin of the web." The "fallen state of our Internet," he maintains, is a "direct, if unintentional, consequence of choosing advertising"—commercial advertising—"as the default model to support online content and services."[236] In the name of making the world—as Face-

---

235 "As the search arena is consolidated under the control of a handful of corporations, it is more crucial to pay close attention to the types of processes that are shaping the information prioritized in search engines. In practice, the higher a web page is ranked, the more it is trusted. Unlike the vetting of journalists and librarians, who are entrusted to fact check and curate information for the public according to professional codes of ethics, the legitimacy of websites' ranking and credibility is simply taken for granted." Safiya Umoja Noble, *Algorithms of Oppression: How Search Engines Reinforce Racism* (New York: New York University Press, 2018), 13, 36–37, 155.

236 On more of the mistakes we've made with the Internet, see Ethan Zuckerman, "The Internet's Original Sin," *The Atlantic*, August 14, 2014, https://www.theatlantic.com/technology/archive/2014/08/advertising-is-the-internets-original-sin/376041/. See also Maciej Cegłowski, "Notes from an Emergency," speech delivered to re:publica Conference, Berlin, May 10, 2017, online at *Idle Words*, http://idlewords.com/talks/notes_from_an_emergency.htm and Stephen Segaller, *Nerds 2.0.1: A Brief History of the Internet* (New York: TV Books, 1998).

book's original stock filing said—"more open and connected," we have also created . . . a Frankenstein.[237] As a consequence, any information—from MIT, from a museum, a newspaper, public broadcaster; or from any wackadoodle wingnut—that "purports to be credible" is "actually a reflection of advertising interests . . . delivered to users through a set of steps (algorithms) implemented by programming code and then naturalized as 'objective'."[238] And it is delivered to users in a highly unregulated, largely commercial media environment—stripped, also thanks to the success of the neoliberal agenda, of any meaningful government/regulatory oversight. Google and its parent company, Alphabet, let us remember, have spent more on Washington lobbyists than any other corporation in America.[239]

We now depend almost exclusively on commercial third-party vendors (Google/YouTube; Amazon's CloudFront;

---

237 Facebook's 2012 SEC filing is here: "Registration Statement on Form S-1: Facebook, Inc.," United States Securities and Exchange Commission, filed February 1, 2012, https://www.sec.gov/Archives/edgar/data/1326801/000119312512034517/d287954ds1.htm. See Sheera Frenkel, Nicholas Confessore, Cecilia Kang, Matthew Rosenberg, Jack Nicas, "Delay, Deny and Deflect: How Facebook's Leaders Fought Through Crisis," *New York Times*, November 14, 2018, https://www.nytimes.com/2018/11/14/technology/facebook-data-russia-election-racism.html. For more on Frankenstein, see MIT Press's "ASU and MIT Launch a Collaborative, Multimedia Version of Frankenstein," MIT Press, June 14, 2018, https://mitpress.mit.edu/blog/asu-and-mit-launch-collaborative-multimedia-version-frankenstein.

238 Noble, *Algorithms of Oppression*, 36–37.

239 Nicholas Confessore, "The Unlikely Activists Who Took On Silicon Valley—and Won," *New York Times Magazine*, August 19, 2018, https://www.nytimes.com/2018/08/14/magazine/facebook-google-privacy-data.html. Especially in the light of footnote 74, above, it is interesting to see how media critic Jay Rosen speaks of "staggering malpractice" of today's major and mainstream media—a remarkable (and remarkably honest) charge, redolent of social responsibility, Hippocratic oaths, "codes of ethics," and the like. Jay Rosen (@jayrosen_nyu), "This is a level of malpractice by @ABC News that is simply staggering. Just pumping into the national debate lie after lie, fantasia after fantasia, completely unchecked. No summary or excerpt can do it justice. You have to read." Twitter, October 31, 2018, 9:49 p.m., https://twitter.com/jayrosen_nyu/status/1057811793941331968.

Vimeo) for rich media distribution.[240] Is that in our interest? For ten days in 2018, MIT OpenCourseWare videos—in many ways the most important video resource body in education—were rendered largely invisible to the world. YouTube had changed its terms of service without prior notice, and, before some emergency haggling and hondling, MIT OCW videos went completely dark.

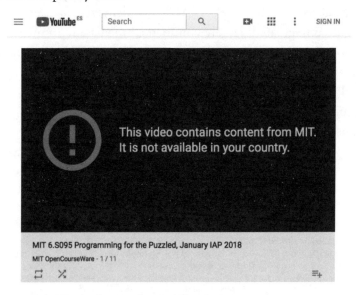

MIT OCW video disappears from YouTube—I—June 2018

One public comment on a blog post after YouTube took down MIT OCW for ten days that June was: "You can find entire lectures on Archive.org. . . . With that said I suggest MIT starts P2P streaming, and relieving us of YouTube's tentacles. This should serve as a stark prompt to MIT to not depend entirely on YouTube serving OCW videos. . . . Shouldn't MIT

---

240 See especially Amazon's definition of its products and users: "Amazon CloudFront," Amazon Web Services, accessed October 13, 2020, https://aws.amazon.com/cloudfront/.

MIT OCW video disappears from YouTube—II—June 2018

be leading the charge in developing P2P streaming? (Asking out loud)."[241] In this light, is it worth noting here and for our argument as a whole how "Democracy Now!" and "The Open Mind," among other noncommercial and educational video collections, work with the Internet Archive—a powerful node

---

241 See the following MIT posts and tweets from June 2018: "MIT OpenCourseWare Videos on YouTube Have Been Restored," Open Matters (blog), MIT OpenCourseWare, June 21, 2018,   https://mitopencourseware.wordpress.com/2018/06/21/mit-opencourseware-videos-on-youtube-have-been-restored/; "Statement on OCW Videos Blocked on YouTube," Open Matters (blog), MIT OpenCourseWare, June 18, 2018, https://mitopencourseware.wordpress.com/2018/06/18/statement-on-ocw-videos-blocked-on-youtube/; MIT OpenCourseWare (@MITOCW), "While we all wait for our videos to be up and running, let's take a look at new physics course on quantum theory! http://ow.ly/QxZK5ohKcR2 (Image by Steven G. Johnson on Wikipedia. Used with permission.)" Twitter, June 18, 2018, 2:55 p.m., https://twitter.com/MITOCW/status/1008785197649842176; MIT OpenCourseWare (@MITOCW), "Monday morning update: We are still trying to resolve the problem with our videos. Here's an article on the situation: https://goo.gl/pgTZ7d. Thank you for your patience. If you head to our site, you can still download the videos on iTunes or @internetarchive," Twitter, June 18, 2018, 10:24 a.m., https://twitter.com/MITOCW/status/1008717037160534016; MITOpenCourseWare (@MITOCW), "You may have noticed that we are having some trouble with our videos! Please stand by. The elves are working around the clock to fix the issue. There is still a ton of content you can use @MITOCW that doesn't have video: http://ocw.mit.edu. Hang in there folks!" Twitter, June 16, 2018, 7:10 a.m., https://twitter.com/MITOCW/status/1007943441035268096. MIT has not commented publicly about the YouTube blackout, but others similarly affected have said the reason was YouTube presenting their organizations with a monetization agreement to sign. See Ernesto Van Der Sar, "YouTube's Blocks MIT Courses, Blender Videos, and More (Updated)," TorrentFreak, June 18, 2018, https://torrentfreak.com/youtubes-piracy-filter-blocks-mit-courses-blender-videos-and-more-180618/.

of our network. The Internet Archive helps by facilitating systematic batch uploads of video.[242]

Hewlett's Larry Kramer writes:

> The academy is vastly larger [than in the late 1940s] and more specialized and heterogeneous, while public trust in what it produces has declined. The number of journals and outlets for publishing is exponentially greater. Our media are fragmented and politicized, and standards for assessing factual accuracy—much less intellectual quality—have eroded. Ideas and arguments increasingly are distributed through the medium of the Internet, which turns choices about what we see over to uncurated social media guided by algorithms designed to maximize ad revenue. *The noise one needs to break through to be heard today is practically deafening.*[243]

What then should be the relationship between the production and distribution of knowledge and the commercial architecture of today's web, and of both to the larger architecture of the public good? Stanford University historian and open-access advocate John Willinsky, studying the relationships of scholarship to rights, licenses, and publishing over millennia, has written that "historical efforts to increase and improve access—through copying and translation, paper and

---

242 See "Democracy Now!" Internet Archive, accessed October 13, 2020, https://archive.org/details/democracy_now_vid; "The Open Mind," Internet Archive, accessed October 13, 2020, https://archive.org/details/open_mind; and "ias3 Internet archive S3-like API," Internet Archive, accessed October 13, 2020, https://archive.org/help/abouts3.txt.

243 Kramer, "Beyond Neoliberalism," emphasis added. Carbon-date it to April 1947; see Greg Kaza, "The Mont Pelerin Society's 50th Anniversary," Foundation for Economic Education, June 1, 1997, https://fee.org/articles/the-mont-pelerin-societys-50th-anniversary/.

printing, libraries and academies—were among the more constant and inventive activities of learned institutions."[244] We should always be identifying the relationship of our work to the Commons and, more specifically, always be interrogating the rights and licenses governing access to academic knowledge. One scholar asks us to do just that, freeing up more university knowledge, and then to

> imagine [the energy of the network underlying the Internet] . . . turned loose not only on the cultural artifacts of the twentieth century, but on the universe of scholarly literature. Think of the people who would work on Buster Keaton, or the literary classics of the 1930s, or the films of the Second World War, or footage on the daily lives of African Americans during segregation, or the music of the Great Depression, or theremin recordings, or the best of vaudeville. But think also of those who are fascinated by Civil War history, of the analysis of the works of Dickens, or the latest paper on global warming, or Tay-Sachs disease. . . .

"Where are the boundaries," he then demands, "of the academy now?"[245] Open as a constant is good; and increasing

244 John Willinsky, *The Intellectual Properties of Learning: A Prehistory from Saint Jerome to John Locke* (Chicago: University of Chicago Press, 2017), 8.

245 James Boyle, "Mertonianism Unbound: Imagining Free, Decentralized Access to Most Cultural and Scientific Material," in *Understanding Knowledge as a Commons: From Theory to Practice*, Charlotte Hess and Elinor Ostrom, eds. (Cambridge, MA: MIT Press, 2011), 127–28, emphasis added. See also: Boyle, *The Public Domain: Enclosing the Commons of the Mind* (New Haven, CT: Yale University Press, 2010), online at http://www.thepublicdomain.org/enclosing-the-commons-of-the-mind/. For how sure are we, in the world of Open 2.0, or in any world, that knowledge should be construed first and foremost as . . . property? (I am grateful to Jeff Ubois of the MacArthur Foundation for posing this question so well and so directly.) See, for example, Nina Paley (a self-described "copyright abolitionist"), "Copyright is Brain

openness as a natural law of knowledge institutions may be grounds for optimism. And as time goes on, artificial intelligence and its many concomitant manifestations will give rise to additional moral, ethical, and human rights issues—probably far surpassing the ones around Google and Facebook and Apple that we obsess about today.

The challenge we face is how to build the best future for knowledge, but the real context for this challenge is the crisis we face—an epistemic crisis, a knowledge crisis, a truth crisis—brought to the fore by an untended and largely commercial media ecosystem, itself the result of the neoliberal project to deregulate media and technology while subjecting expertise and the university project in particular to skepticism and doubt. And, as we are all implicated—as information studies scholar Safiya Umoja Noble writes,

> commercial control over the Internet, often considered a "commons," has moved further away from the public through a series of national and international regulations and intellectual and commercial borders that exist in the management of the network. Beyond the Internet and the control of the network, public information—whether delivered over the web or not—continues to be outsourced to the public sphere, eroding the public information commons that has been a basic tenet of U.S. democracy.[246]

—we should all dig out of it together. Active measures are needed

---

Damage," talk delivered at TEDx Maastricht, video, YouTube, 18:23, October 21, 2015, https://www.youtube.com/watch?v=XO9FKQAxWZc.

246 "The privatization and commercial nature of information has become so normalized that it not only becomes obscured from view but, as a result, is increasingly difficult to critique within the public domain." Noble, *Algorithms of Oppression*, 50–51.

to surface the knowledge that we produce as knowledge institutions with centuries of trust and well-earned brand loyalty behind us. Do knowledge institutions have a responsibility to engage with free and liberal licenses, and free and open standards, for their content, their software, their work product? You bet we do. Increasingly, the funders of our work will mandate open/free access provisions as a condition for accepting their support.[247] And what access should we be guaranteeing to the disabled and disadvantaged?[248] And more broadly, for the materials that we all curate—even loosely defined—do we consider facilitating present access to past culture as some kind of professional obligation?[249]

In these new Sargasso Seas of online lies and fakery, the effort of one lone Ahab, or indeed a *Pequod*, will not be sufficient; rather, educational and cultural institutions captained by visionary educators need to work together to strategize and reinforce each other. Ahab alone ended poorly.[250] In the long history of the access-to-knowledge

247 See the essential work of the Smithsonian's Effie Kapsalis, "The Impact of Open Access on Galleries, Libraries, Museums, and Archives," white paper, Smithsonian Emerging Leaders Development Program, April 27, 2016, https://siarchives.si.edu/sites/default/files/pdfs/2016_03_10_OpenCollections_Public.pdf; the published requirements of the European Commission, "Guidelines to the Rules on Open Access to Scientific Publications and Open Access to Research Data in Horizon 2020," white paper, March 21, 2017, http://ec.europa.eu/research/participants/data/ref/h2020/grants_manual/hi/oa_pilot/h2020-hi-oa-pilot-guide_en.pdf; and the Open Research Funders Group in the United States: Home page, Open Research Funders Group, http://www.orfg.org/.

248 See, for one statement, European Broadcasting Union, "Broadcasters and Disability Organisation Draw Up Common Recommendation on Future EU Rules for Audiovisual Access Services," press release, February 16, 2017, https://www.ebu.ch/news/2017/02/broadcasters-and-disability-organisation-draw-up-common-recommendation-on-future-eu-rules-for-audiovisual-access-services.

249 See the work of Communia/The European Thematic Network on the Digital Public Domain: Giancarlo F. Frosio, "Final Report," Communia, March 31, 2011, http://communia-project.eu/final-report/.

250 "The harpoon was darted; the stricken whale flew forward; with igniting velocity the line ran through the groove;—ran foul. Ahab stood to clear it; he did clear it; but the flying turn caught him round the neck, and voicelessly as Turkish mutes bowstring their victim, he was shot out of the boat, ere the crew knew he was gone. Next instant, the heavy eye-splice in the rope's final end flew out of the stark-empty tub, knocked down an oarsman, and smiting the sea, disappeared in its depths." Not good. Herman Melville, *Moby-Dick. Or, the Whale* (New York: Modern Library, 1950) 565.

movement, there has always been a moral imperative to share what we know, especially in the age of the Internet (which makes it so easy to do so). But now, in this moment, the imperative is overarching, encompassing everything. Violence and lawlessness are rising, and basic civil norms and codes of social conduct are disintegrating across the country and everywhere. The Monsterverse—while not completely visible—is more active and powerful now than ever.

Philosophers speak of the ways in which we are able to directly affect, for the better, the power structure of the public sphere and deliberative politics worldwide through the production and redistribution of media—of how the public square and public space are continually defined and redefined; where access to knowledge is over and over again denied, debated, and fought over; and where the responsibilities for tying the public record to truth and reason sometimes lie in the hands of moral and Solomonic stewards and sometimes in the hands of fools.[251] Collective action is required to publish our truths—all that can be found in books, journals, courseware, sound video, imagery—freely and openly and immediately, everywhere.[252] As we indicated in Chapter 1, this need for collective action is becoming more and more evident to all who consider themselves stakeholders, however modestly, in the great Enlightenment project of liberty, equality, fraternity—and peace. As MIT professor and the founder of the web, Tim Berners-Lee, has put it, "The web has become a public square, a library, a doc-

---

251 Jürgen Habermas, *The Structural Transformation of the Public Sphere: An Inquiry into a Category of Bourgeois Society*, trans. Thomas Burger with Frederick Lawrence (Cambridge, MA: MIT University Press, 1991), and Habermas, "Political Communication in Media Society: Does Democracy Still Enjoy an Epistemic Dimension? The Impact of Normative Theory on Empirical Research," *Communication Theory* 16, no. 4 (November 2006): 411–26, online (behind a paywall) at https://doi.org/10.1111/j.1468-2885.2006.00280.x.

252 Peter B. Kaufman, "In the Post-Truth Era, Colleges Must Share Their Knowledge," *Chronicle of Higher Education*, April 2, 2017, http://www.chronicle.com/article/In-the-Post-Truth-Era/239628.

tor's office, a shop, a school, a design studio, an office, a cinema, a bank, and so much more."

> Of course with every new feature, every new website, the divide between those who are online and those who are not increases, making it all the more imperative to make the web available for everyone. And while the web has created opportunity, given marginalised groups a voice, and made our daily lives easier, it has also created opportunity for scammers, given a voice to those who spread hatred, and made all kinds of crime easier to commit.

The National Academies of Science, Engineering, and Medicine have discussed forming "a consortium of professional scientific organizations to fund the creation of a media and internet operation that monitors networks, channels, and web platforms known to spread false and misleading scientific information so as to be able to respond quickly with a countervailing campaign of rebuttal based on accurate information through Facebook, Twitter, and other forms of social media."[253] In 2020, they have begun collaborating with—who else?—Wikipedia on edit-a-thons about climate change. Berners-Lee himself is calling for a new "Contract for the Web," and has enumerated the commitments required for governments, corporations, and individuals to build the web we want.

---

253 See Shanto Iyengar and Douglas S. Massey, "Scientific Communication in a Post-Truth Society," *Proceedings of the National Academy of Sciences* 116, no. 16 (November 26, 2018): 7656–61, https://doi.org/10.1073/pnas.1805868115.

Governments will:

Ensure everyone can connect to the internet so that anyone, no matter who they are or where they live, can participate actively online.

Keep all of the internet available, all of the time so that no one is denied their right to full internet access.

Respect people's fundamental right to privacy so everyone can use the internet freely, safely and without fear.

Companies will:

Make the internet affordable and accessible to everyone so that no one is excluded from using and shaping the web.

Respect consumers' privacy and personal data so people are in control of their lives online.

Develop technologies that support the best in humanity and challenge the worst so the web really is a public good that puts people first.

Citizens will:

Be creators and collaborators on the web so the web has rich and relevant content for everyone.

Build strong communities that respect civil discourse and human dignity so that everyone feels safe and welcome online.

Fight for the web so the web remains open and a global public resource for people everywhere, now and in the future.[254]

Such sweeping new visions for action, and collective action at that, should be racing across the horizon of all knowledge institutions like wildfire: across the horizons of museums, libraries, public broadcasters, archives—really any organization with a mission or mandate to educate. The original Enlightenment owed its success to its own variety of network, as the digital humanities scholars have shown.[255] Our New Enlightenment will unspool across our new network of knowledge.

---

254 "Contract for the Web," World Wide Web Foundation, accessed October 13, 2020, https://fortheweb.webfoundation.org/. See also Brewster Kahle, "Locking the Web Open: A Call for a Decentralized Web," Brewster Kahle's Blog, August 11, 2015, http://brewster.kahle.org/2015/08/11/locking-the-web-open-a-call-for-a-distributed-web-2/.

255 "Mapping the Republic of Letters," Stanford University, accessed October 13, 2020, http://republicofletters.stanford.edu/; Maria Teodora Comsa, Melanie Conroy, Dan Edelstein, Chloe Summers Edmondson, and Claude Willan, "The French Enlightenment Network," *Journal of Modern History* 88, no. 3 (September 2016): 495–534, online (behind a paywall) at https://doi.org/10.1086/687927; and Dan Edelstein and Chloe Edmondson, *Networks of Enlightenment: Digital Approaches to the Republic of Letters* (New York: Oxford University Press, 2019), https://global.oup.com/academic/product/networks-of-enlightenment-9781786941961.

10. *Our Archive*

Who controls our access to the libraries of content developed and produced and archived over the last hundred-plus years? Who controls, or has tried to control, our search across these screens and servers for the moving pictures and sounds we are looking for? The forces of the Monsterverse are arrayed on every battlefield. We have to recognize these forces for what they are.

And we have to gird for war.

As we digitize all of our cultural heritage materials for access, we link our institutions and ourselves together online, and are in fact building one big supercomputer—futurologist Kevin Kelly has called it a "planetary electric membrane"—comparable to the individual human brain. It is an organism of collective human intelligence in the business now of processing the hundreds of thousands of full-length feature films we have made, the millions of television shows, the tens of millions of recorded songs, tens of billions of books, and billions of web pages—and looking at the world every day through camera lenses and microphones, including 3 billion phones and counting—all recording our own sounds and visions. It is a supercomputer so large that if we think of it as one connected thing, it processes some 3 million emails every second and generates so many exabytes of data each year that it consumes 5 percent of the world's electrical energy. And what it wants is . . . more knowledge. Increasing sentience, or intelligence.

Who is writing the software that makes this contraption useful and productive? We are. When we post and tag photos, for example, we are teaching the machine to give names to images, and the thickening links between caption and picture form a "neural net" that can continue learning! The 100 billion times per day humans click on one page or another is a way of teaching the web what we think is important. Each time we forge a link between words, we teach it an idea. We may think we are merely wasting time when we surf mindlessly or blog an item, but each time we click a link we strengthen a node somewhere in the supercomputer's mind. "Google is learning. . . . We teach it while we think it is teaching us. . . . Every search for information is itself a piece of information Google can learn from."[256]

An understanding of our rights and our power needs to course through the knowledge sector. The Rebel Alliance— should we found it—must have this understanding, and a deep awareness of the pedigree of our integrity, the duration of our centuries-old struggle, at its core. While Wikipedia doesn't formally recognize the *Encyclopédie* anywhere as its exquisite forerunner, the Internet Archive roots its name and founding principles—even core graphics—in the Library of Alexandria, from the Ptolemaic period, some 2,300 years ago, in Egypt, 7,400 miles away from where the Internet Archive is based in current-day San Francisco. The Internet Archive was funded initially, and still, in the main, by its founder, Brewster Kahle, from the sale of a type of search engine he created called, not incidentally, Alexa.

---

256 Kevin Kelly, *What Technology Wants* (New York: Viking, 2010); Daniel Soar, "It Knows," *London Review of Books* 33, no. 19 (October 6, 2011), https://www.lrb.co.uk/v33/n19/daniel-soar/it-knows.

Today the Archive, an independent nonprofit, runs on an operating budget of approximately $10 million per year. Its goal is to provide "universal access to all knowledge." Its primary operation is to archive the worldwide web—not a bad ambition, given that everyone seems to be ignoring the essential mandate of collecting, keeping, and learning from the past. Today the archive holds 330 billion web pages, 20 million books and texts, 4.5 million audio recordings (including 180,000 live concerts), 4 million videos (including 1.6 million television news programs), 3 million images, and 200,000 software programs.[257] Any user anywhere can create a free account and archive her own media—it's as close to a public resource as we can get.

Is this important? It is no accident that the etymology of the word "archive" comes from the Greek ἄρχω—"to begin, rule, govern"—and thus no accident that "archive" shares the same root as the words "monarch" and "hierarchy."[258] Archives started in the "archon"—the seat of government—and the centrality of the power of the archive is likely to be the story of the twenty-first century.[259] If this book is in part about the power of the moving image and the web, then it is at least worth noting that this—the archive as pure power—is the critical message of one of the highest-dollar-grossing moving images of all time. Set in the future (but how far?), the Na'avi people in *Avatar* plug into and connect

---

257 "About the Internet Archive," Internet Archive, accessed October 13, 2020, https://archive.org/about/; Stephanie Ann Frampton, "Alexandria in the Googleplex: The Pre-History of the Universal Library," *Eidolon*, December 22, 2017, https://eidolon.pub/alexandria-in-the-googleplex-or-the-pre-history-of-the-universal-library-cf6a2a5c3198.

258 See "Archon," Wikimedia Foundation, last modified July 17, 2020, 02:50, https://en.wikipedia.org/wiki/Archon.

259 The battles over that history have already begun. See Peter B. Kaufman and Jeff Ubois, "The Devolution Will Be Televised," *The Nation*, October 18, 2017, https://www.thenation.com/article/the-devolution-will-be-televised/.

with the sounds of the past—they make *zahaylu*—as the primordial way for them to heal, regenerate their powers, and enlighten themselves. It seems to work. We too have to imagine a collective of knowledge institutions forging alliances to make available all of their holdings to similar seekers and the weak and the injured at our own Tree of Knowledge.

The Internet Archive mirrors the Library of Alexandria's ambitions. "Starting as early as 300 BCE," we have been told, "the Ptolemaic kings who ruled Alexandria had the inspired idea of luring leading scholars, scientists, and poets to their city by offering them life appointments at the Museum"—located right in the center of the city—featuring a library where "most of the intellectual inheritance of Greek, Latin, Babylonian, Egyptian, and Jewish cultures had been assembled at enormous cost and carefully archived for research." Ptolemy III (246–221 BCE), according to one historian, "is said to have sent messages to all the rulers of the known world, asking for books to copy." As a result, Euclid developed his geometry in Alexandria; Archimedes discovered pi and laid the foundation for calculus; Eratosthenes posited that the earth was round and calculated its circumference to within 1 percent; Galen revolutionized medicine. Alexandrian astronomers postulated a heliocentric universe; geometers deduced that the length of a year was 365 1/4 days and proposed adding a "leap day" every fourth year; geographers speculated that it would be possible to reach India by sailing west from Spain; engineers developed hydraulics and pneumatics; anatomists first understood clearly that the brain and the nervous system were a unit, studied the function of the heart and the digestive system, and conducted experiments in nutrition. The level of achievement was staggering. And:

The Alexandrian library was not associated with a particular doctrine or philosophical school; its scope was the entire range of intellectual inquiry. It represented a global cosmopolitanism, a determination to assemble the accumulated knowledge of the whole world and to perfect and add to this knowledge.[260]

The concatenating links of past and present abound. The *Encyclopédie* launched in 1750 with a prospectus that included a map of human knowledge. It was built upon the knowledge maps of Francis Bacon—to whom Diderot and D'Alembert quite frequently alluded.[261] Bacon sought to organize knowledge—memory, reason, imagination, that sort of thing—and here we go again. Google's mission is one they put out there simply for us:

Organize the world's information and make it universally accessible and useful.

260 Stephen Greenblatt, *The Swerve: How the World Became Modern* (New York: W. W. Norton, 2011), 86–88, 280. See also Jonathan Bloom and Sheila Blair, *Islam: A Thousand Years of Faith and Power* (New York: TV Books, 2000). Suitably enough, there is a mirror site of the Internet Archive's complete holdings at the Bibliotheca Alexandrina, the modern Library of Alexandria in Egypt today. See Raimond Spekking, "Mirror of the Internet Archive in the Bibliotheca Alexandrina," photograph, Wikimedia file created July 18, 2008, appearing in "Internet Archive," Wikimedia Foundation, last modified July 28, 2020, 22:50, https://en.wikipedia.org/wiki/Internet_Archive#/media/File:Internet_Archive_-_Bibliotheca_Alexandrina.jpg; and "Bibliotheca Alexandrina," Wikimedia Foundation, last modified July 21, 2020, 22:16, https://en.wikipedia.org/wiki/Bibliotheca_Alexandrina. As historian Roger Bagnall writes, "The disparity between, on the one hand, the grandeur and importance of this library, both in its reality in antiquity and in its image both ancient and modern, and, on the other, our nearly total ignorance about it, has been unbearable." Roger S. Bagnall, "Alexandria: Library of Dreams," *Proceedings of the American Philosophical Society* 146, no. 4 (Dec. 2002), 348–362.

261 One hundred and seventy-four times. See especially the article on "Baconisme, ou le Philosophie de Bacon," contributed by Abbé Jean Pestre: ARTFL Encyclopédie, University of Chicago, accessed October 13, 2020, https://artflsrv03.uchicago.edu/philologic4/encyclopedie1117/navigate/2/92/?byte=140013.

And it's terrifying.[262] Should one private, profit-seeking company, one state, one religion, or one church have a role like this ceded to it by the people? (The answer, again, is still no.) The company's work on its taxonomy of knowledge objects, its "knowledge graph," is in many senses founded upon the knowledge base of structured data that Metaweb developed and ran publicly as Freebase from 2007 to 2010. Google bought that out from Danny Hillis and his colleagues, who today, at MIT and elsewhere, are trying to develop a not-for-profit alternative that may take billions of dollars to underwrite.[263] At the time of that purchase, that free knowledge base was said to be able to sort and classify 70 billion facts. Today, the challenge is orders of magnitude greater.[264] We have to understand how to make knowledge as easily searchable and discoverable as other products are in our society, from music and sports videos to pornography and shoes.

What we have that the Carnegie Commission did not have is the new network, some woke alliance members, and extraordinary computing power. (What they had that we do not is a sense of deep, catalyzing fear—but we will be getting that again.) Where artificial intelligence may take us is for other work in the future, but for now, what if we were to steal a page

---

262 "Our Approach to Search," Google Search, accessed October 13, 2020, https://www.google.com/search/howsearchworks/mission/.

263 Danny Hillis, SJ Klein, Travis Rich, and Joel Gustafson, "The Underlay," MIT, accessed October 13, 2020, https://underlay.mit.edu/; Home page, Knowledge Futures Group, accessed October 13, 2020, https://mitpress.mit.edu/kfg; Joel Gustafson, "The Underlay: The Inevitable Future of Knowledge," talk delivered at Lab Day, MIT, Cambridge, MA, August 2018. Protocol Labs, video, YouTube, 2:28, October 22, 2018, https://www.youtube.com/watch?v=C2jz9pfwh7Q; Ray Schroeder, "Search in the Post-Truth Era," *Inside Higher Ed*, November 14, 2018, https://www.insidehighered.com/digital-learning/blogs/online-trending-now/search-post-truth-era.

264 "Knowledge Graph," Wikimedia Foundation, last modified July 27, 2020, 18:14, https://en.wikipedia.org/wiki/Knowledge_Graph; Joel Gustafson, "What is a Distributed Knowledge Graph?" KFG Notes, October 15, 2020, https://notes.knowledgefutures.org/pub/belji1gd/release/2.

from the Monsterverse? What if, as Rebel Alliance members, we were to acknowledge our own lack of progress to date, as a field? While we noodle over the potential *rights* challenges involved in making our assets searchable, our lunch is being eaten. Our breakfast. Our dinner. The commercial sector is actively exploiting the growth potential for such advanced products and services. Pandora, Netflix, iTunes, and IMDb (the Internet Movie Database), among others, enable customers to experience moving images, sounds, texts, and images, and they provide thriving recommendation engines. Google has more than two hundred signals in its Page-Rank algorithm. Amazon's engine resembles in many ways its competitor Netflix's, which has been studied and even opened to the public to improve upon. But in many ways the Holy Grail for us in the knowledge and public education business would be to develop the equivalent of the music genome at the heart of a company like Pandora. Pandora's automated Music Genome Project, for example, the patent application for which is available online, assembles and searches through four hundred separate characteristics of each song and music file to determine relationships between that file and the rest of the sound corpus. These attributes are called "genes" for songs. And each of the songs in Pandora's database—more than four hundred thousand songs from more than twenty thousand artists—has been assessed manually, requiring a minimum of twenty to thirty minutes of assessment per four minutes of music. Even the characteristics of books—that old medium—are being analyzed this way now.[265]

265 Soar, "It Knows"; Brian Dean, "Google's 200 Ranking Factors: The Complete List (2020)," BackLinko, January 22, 2020, https://backlinko.com/google-ranking-factors; "How Search Algorithms Work," Google Search, accessed October 13, 2020, https://www.google.

All of which leads one to ask, where is the knowledge genome? And where are we as educators and knowledge experts in developing it? To know a knowledge genome! To search for "black hole," "tax reform," "greenhouse gas"—and receive facts! Perhaps via . . . Wikidata![266] Facts! Truth! Knowledge! And to see the archive owned by . . . the people!

If this is the Republic of Images now, a video age, and an age also propelled by a need to expand the Commons, we will have to ensure that the moving image not be knotted up by six hundred years of the same mistakes in the contracts and agreements regulating the use and ultimately ownership of

com/search/howsearchworks/algorithms/; Adrian Covert, "Netflix to Open API and Databases to the Public," *Gizmodo*, September 30, 2008, http://gizmodo.com/5057203/netflix-to-open-api-and-databases-to-the-public; Richard Adhikari, "Netflix Circles the Wagons Around Its API," *Tech News World*, June 20, 2012, http://www.technewsworld.com/story/75424.html; Lara O'Reilly, "Netflix Lifted the Lid on How the Algorithm That Recommends You Titles to Watch Actually Works," *Business Insider*, February 26, 2016, http://www.businessinsider.com/how-the-netflix-recommendation-algorithm-works-2016-2; Yves Raimond and Justin Basilico, "Recommending for the World," Netflix Technology Blog, February 17, 2016, http://techblog.netflix.com/2016/02/recommending-for-world.html; Ben Popper, How Netflix Completely Revamped Recommendations for Its New Global Audience," *The Verge*, February 17, 2016, http://www.theverge.com/2016/2/17/11030200/netflix-new-recommendation-system-global-regional; Nathan McAlone, "Why Netflix Thinks Its Personalized Recommendation Engine Is Worth $1 Billion Per Year," *Business Insider*, June 14, 2016, http://www.businessinsider.com/netflix-recommendation-engine-worth-1-billion-per-year-2016-6; "About The Music Genome Project," Pandora, accessed October 13, 2020, http://www.pandora.com/corporate/mgp.shtml; "Music Genome Project," Wikimedia Foundation, last modified June 24, 2020, 22:37, https://en.wikipedia.org/wiki/Music_Genome_Project; William T. Glaser, Timothy B. Westergren, Jeffrey P. Stearns, and Jonathan M. Kraft, Patent no. 7,003,515 B1, issued February 21, 2006, US Patent Office, viewable via Google Patents search: "Consumer item matching method and system," http://www.google.com/patents/US7003515?dq=7,003,515; Home page, the Video Genome Project, accessed October 13, 2020, http://thevideogenomeproject.com/. Note, in this context, calls for an "Archive Genomic Decoder" and an "Openometer Use-A-Tron" in Peter B. Kaufman, *Assessing the Audiovisual Archive Market: Models and Approaches for Audiovisual Content Exploitation* (Hilversum: PrestoCentre, 2013), https://publications.beeldengeluid.nl/pub/1818/.

266 https://www.wikidata.org/wiki/Wikidata:Main_Page; and Thomas Pellissier Tanon et al., "From Freebase to Wikidata: The Great Migration," *WWW 2016*, April 11–15, 2016, online at: https://static.googleusercontent.com/media/research.google.com/en//pubs/archive/44818.pdf; and Denny Vrandecic and Markus Krotzsch, "Wikidata: A Free Collaborative Knowledge Base," online at: https://static.googleusercontent.com/media/research.google.com/en//pubs/archive/42240.pdf.

the value in these media (as book and journal contracts have been). Book contracts we discussed earlier in this volume. But zoom in on a particular piece of moving-image media—we can focus, for example, on the monumental American public broadcasting documentary about the civil rights movement, *Eyes on the Prize*—and the very real complexity of video's copyright and contracts anatomy becomes apparent pretty quickly. To a civilian viewer, the documentary might be entertaining, informative, and educational. To the people involved in producing it, the film also represents myriad relationships of talent, materials, imagination, and technical experience, behind which lies a matrix of rights and responsibilities often governed by dozens of contracts and agreements involving talent, agents, lawyers, guilds, and unions, representing thousands, sometimes millions, of dollars of underwriting or investment. Rightsholders and other financial stakeholders can include producers, directors, cinematographers, cameramen, film and video editors, writers of scripts, writers of songs, writers of music, actors, singers, musicians, dancers, choreographers, narrators, and animators, as well as whole cohorts of content from music and book publishing and the film business who may have sold or otherwise licensed rights to the production—to say nothing of the dozens, sometimes hundreds, of artists, designers, engineers, consultants, and staff who are often rewarded when they help the production to complete its journey from idea to finished work. F. Scott Fitzgerald wrote of the "savage tensity" that often would be present when Hollywood studio bosses would first screen the movies they were producing: these screenings, he wrote, were "the net result of months of buying, planning, writing and rewriting, casting, constructing, lighting, rehearsing and shooting—the fruit alike of brilliant hunches or of counsels of despair, of lethargy, conspiracy and sweat."[267]

The anatomy of rich media is now getting the attention it deserves. One will find, to bear out Fitzgerald, that a typical two-hour feature film can have as many as five thousand different shots, all told, edited together—and a typical feature-length documentary, which will present much more licensed content, as many as two thousand.[268] Perhaps that complexity can best be visualized itself in a moving-image illustration that explores the anatomy of a media production—and visualizes the sources and online uses for those sources together. The number and types of existing/potential creative- and economic-property stakeholders involved in the professional production of media are numerous; licensing experts in public media have calculated that there can be as many as almost eighty different rightsholders for a single minute of a finished public-television documentary.[269]

---

267 F. Scott Fitzgerald, *The Last Tycoon* (New York: Scribners, 1941), 53. Neal Gabler, in his biography of Walt Disney and Disney studios, describes "the nervousness" that accretes from "years of imagining, scrutinizing, retelling, fiddling, mobilizing, and pushing"; Gabler, *Walt Disney: The Triumph of the American Imagination* (New York: Alfred A. Knopf, 2006), 272.

268 See Cinemetrics and the work of Yuri Tsivian, at http://cinemetrics.lv/about.php; http://cinemetrics.lv/database.php. See also the case study of Ric Burns's *Andy Warhol*: http://cinemetrics.lv/movie.php?movie_ID=5977. Ray Bradbury gave an interview about his masterpiece *Fahrenheit 451* in which he pointed that out. "The whole problem of TV and movies today is summed up by the film *Moulin Rouge*. It came out a few years ago and won a lot of awards. It has 4,560 half-second clips in it. The camera never stops and holds still. So it clicks off your thinking; you can't think when you have things bombarding you like that. The average TV commercial of sixty seconds has one hundred and twenty half-second clips in it [. . .]. We bombard people with sensation. That substitutes for thinking." The interviewer says, "But you foresaw all of that in the fifties. I mean, the people in *Fahrenheit 451* are addicted to their wall screens . . ." "That's right," Bradbury says. "A Conversation with Ray Bradbury," in Ray Bradbury, *Fahrenheit 451: The 50th Anniversary Edition* (New York: Del Rey Books, 1991), 184–185. His publisher released a limited edition of two hundred copies of the novel bound in asbestos, to keep them safe and fireproof from the book burners—the "men with matches," in the words of the novel—of the Monsterverse; http://www.openculture.com/2018/07/asbestos-bound-fireproof-edition-ray-bradburys-fahrenheit-451-1953.html.

269 Author interviews with Joe Basile, director of rights and clearances, Thirteen/WNET, December 8, 2009, and *Eyes on the Prize* clearance attorney Sandra Forman, July 26, 2016.

These rightsholders include talented individuals, companies, music bands, and other groups whose work is audible and visible on the screen, and who often have business contracts with producers and distributors describing the compensation and credits they receive and the rights they have licensed to their work for specific media uses (television, radio, DVD, and online, for example) and, even in this networked world, certain delineated territories (such as North America or Japan) in which they have granted those rights. And, in the United States anyway, unions and guilds that engage in collective bargaining with networks and producers often represent them to determine the appropriate pay scales and more general equity participation on behalf of their members. Video stakeholders subject to engagement agreements include actors, singers, dancers, and producers, via the American Federation of Television and Radio Artists (AFTRA); scriptwriters, via the Writers Guild of America (WGA); directors, via the Directors Guild of America (DGA); and songwriters and lyricists, composers and arrangers, musicians and music publishers, via the American Federation of Music (AFM). Possibly subject to various additional collective bargaining agreements are producers, cinematographers and cameramen, film and video editors, animators, voice narrators, choreographers, artists, designers, engineers, consultants, and other staff. The collective bargaining agreements these unions and guilds have negotiated on behalf of their clients, and the roles they have played and still play in protecting the rights of those clients (and their own interests), profoundly affect the ways in which media has been and is being put online.

Vendors and suppliers of images, sounds, photographs, and artwork form another circle of stakeholders. These licensors often have receivables tied to the number of end users the licensee is likely to reach or the number of uses (television,

The anatomy of a video clip. Produced by Intelligent Television, Inc., 2016. Watch at: https://youtu.be/1SENjXXA4To.

home video/DVD, educational video/DVD, mobile platforms, etc.) through which the licensee's work will be made available. These footage suppliers and archives include Getty Images and AP Images, for example. Most are commercial businesses. Some represent unique collections of classic media that can be used—under current law and standard practice—only through a license obtained from their company. A licensing director at a US public media station once sought to help a producer use a clip of the film *Rebel Without a Cause* in his television show, and Metro-Goldwyn-Mayer billed his company over $100,000 for the educational/public television broadcast rights to seventy seconds. Such licenses, too, often lie at the core of public-media productions. And all of these stakeholders, licensors, and beneficiaries involved in producing audiovisual media have interests that are affected when their productions enter the digital universe online—where, once posted, they can be replicated ad infinitum almost for free, anywhere. The original economic model on which most every one of these contracts was predicated goes right out the window. New publishing and production regimes that make explicit reference to the Commons may help investors and underwriters appreciate the new future they face—and the power of Wikipedia in particular as a portal to the world of ideas.

One day, the powerful algorithms at work toward commercial objectives may be turned on education and the exploration of culture. Netflix, it is said, an archive as much as YouTube, has "the ability to 'personalize' its interactions" with its tens of millions of customers.[270]

Will educational and culture need to stay so far behind?

The challenge of making things free for the vast archive *and* the Commons is multilayered. There have been, over the past thirty years or so, multiple levels of progress—first, to put content online; next, to put it online for free; next, to put it online for free with a CC license or with another generous license; and lastly, to put it online for free with the most liberal type of license that facilitates that content's full integration into the Commons. Passing into each of these circles has involved, as it should, some self-congratulation on the part of each licensor making progress.

When MIT OpenCourseWare first started, Creative Commons and Wikipedia and our general knowledge about how to enable sharing were not as advanced as they are today; indeed, as I've written elsewhere, that knowledge then was as primitive as a coelacanth.[271] This became apparent some years ago when educators and producers endeavored to fit popular MIT OpenCourseWare lecture videos about Isaac Newton's laws of

---

270 Joe Nocera, "Can Netflix Survive in the New World It Has Created?" *New York Times Magazine*, June 15, 2016, http://www.nytimes.com/2016/06/19/magazine/can-netflix-survive-in-the-new-world-it-created.html.

271 Peter B. Kaufman, *MOOCs and Open Education Resources: A Handbook for Educators* (Lakeville, CT: Intelligent Television, 2016), 7, online at http://intelligenttelevision.com/files/59-moocs_and_open_educational_resources_handbook_kaufman_100616.pdf.

physics into the appropriate articles in Wikipedia. Wikipedia editors told us we had to renegotiate the standard MIT OCW terms of service and all the relevant agreements with the MIT physics lecturer before Wikipedia would allow MIT's video into the encyclopedia. Intelligent Television post-produced video of the lectures to fit them into Wikipedia articles, and the terms were reworked with the professor's approval and blessing—but the rights and permissions statement published in the encyclopedia looks (as it should) more like an exception was made to include these videos and OCW in Wikipedia, rather than, as should obviously be the case, the rule.[272]

That OCW should exist as an artifact with some imperfection in "openness" or "free-as-in-freedom" today is no travesty. Far from it. The entire universe of digital scholarly and educational resources—from JSTOR and HathiTrust to the Khan Academy and beyond—provides invaluable knowledge and information to millions worldwide, and much of that is free to the public. Yet one cannot but wonder, at a time when so much is wrong with the world, whether a little tweak—a goose, a nudge—in the licensing requirements for the production of this knowledge could not be put into effect, so that the educational materials produced expressly as such could become fully blessed at their birth—with a licensing sacrament—by becoming fully free. Richard Stallman has noted how software called "open-source" is more often than not free, but the educational projects described as "open courseware" and

---

272 And the video had to be transferred into the F/LOSS video codec Ogg Theora. See "File:Thirdlaw.ogv," Wikimedia Foundation, retrieved December 23, 2010, https://en.wikipedia.org/wiki/File:Thirdlaw.ogg; "Newton's laws of motion," Wikimedia Foundation, last modified June 21, 2020, 14:28, https://en.wikipedia.org/wiki/Newton's_laws_of_motion. For the underlying OCW rights info, see "FAQ: Intellectual Property," MIT Open CourseWare, accessed October 13, 2020, http://ocw.mit.edu/help/faq-intellectual-property/.

"open access" are, more often than not, not.[273] It might do great good to make open courseware—and any educational material licensed for it—completely free at all times, once all the underlying creations have been secured and their creators properly compensated. Without these or some similar kind of these myriad agreements, artists and creators of content at all levels—directors, musicians, composers, actors, archivists, researchers, and publishers, to name just a few—would have no basis on which to be paid, and the work that they do, which informs, entertains, and indeed enlightens us, might all but cease. We don't need to eradicate these kinds of contracts, just reimagine them, such that they explicitly make reference, each and every one, to the Commons where their work is destined at last to lie. Let us reimagine these agreements such that they protect both the public good and the abilities of creators, and so that they reduce the corporate overreach of our age by companies that make a grab for rights beyond their natural purview—because no one is stopping them from doing so.

Iterating toward openness in this regard would involve applying best practices to the past as well as the present and future.[274] Systematically exploring how to extend the license

273 Richard Stallman, "Libre Software, Libre Education," talk delivered at Columbia University, New York, NY, October 17, 2014. Video online at https://audio-video.gnu.org/video/2014-10-17-libre-software-libre-education.ogv.

274 "Wikimedia has received an e-mail confirming that the copyright holder has approved publication under the terms mentioned on this page. This correspondence has been reviewed by an OTRS member and stored in our permission archive. The correspondence is available to trusted volunteers as ticket #2011051010013473." The presence of these lecture clips on Wikipedia became even more important after MIT withdrew Lewin's lectures from OCW online because of a sex scandal with online learners in which Lewin was reportedly involved; see Leon Lin, "MIT Cuts Ties with Walter Lewin After Online Harassment Probe," *The Tech*, December 9, 2014, http://tech.mit.edu/V134/N60/walterlewin.html and Leon Lin, "MIT Says It Removed Lewin Videos for Fear of Continued Harassment," *The Tech*, January 14, 2015, http://tech.mit.edu/V134/N62/lewin.html. The impermanence of these video lectures—of MOOCs—for whatever reason should give us all pause, and it may be another argument for more liberal licenses that facilitate unrestricted duplication. See "A Handy Guide on How to Download

from early and contemporary productions to encompass these fuller freedoms could be an extraordinary task to assign to a production team—and one that would benefit world knowledge forever. Reclearing past productions like this would be relatively straightforward. The *Eyes on the Prize* documentary series had to be recleared for continued broadcast and DVD distribution in recent years—the Ford Foundation sponsored the process—with funds that amounted to a small fraction of the original production budget but which were substantial nonetheless.[275] The larger point here involves regret that the process had to be undertaken at all—and also that a second effort at clearing was more expensive to conduct years later than it would have been at the time, had the knowledge and the sense of a longer future, of our New Enlightenment, been present at the moment of production. It would have been possible, and simpler, to anticipate, and to formally recognize right at the time of the work's creation, its ultimate entrance into the public domain. Things need to be produced with the confi-

Old Coursera Courses Before They Disappear," Open Culture, June 17, 2016, http://www. openculture.com/2016/06/a-handy-guide-on-how-to-download-old-coursera-courses-before-they-disappear.html. On video impermanence more generally and the adverse effects it always brings about, see Jeff Ubois, "Finding Murphy Brown: How Accessible are Historic Television Broadcasts?" *Journal of Digital Information* 7, no. 2 (2006), still online at https://journals.tdl. org/jodi/index.php/jodi/article/view/172. There are various ways to better archive all our work and future-proof it with the Commons in mind; see Brian Stelter, "C-Span Puts Full Archives on the Web," *New York Times*, March 15, 2010, http://www.nytimes.com/2010/03/16/arts/television/16cspan.html.

275 Part of the story of *Eyes on the Prize* is the value of the music in telling the story. "Music was a part of the [Civil Rights] movement in a way that you cannot separate," Rena Kosersky, music clearance supervisor for *Eyes on the Prize*, has said. Documentary filmmaker and programmer Thom Powers has written about Bernice Johnson Reagon, a member of the Student Nonviolent Coordinating Committee's Freedom Singers, recalling in one episode how "during the thick of the struggle there was more singing than talking." Clearing licenses for 130 songs for broadcast and DVD distribution took some doing. See Thom Powers, "'Eyes on the Prize' Off the Shelf," *Boston Globe*, January 16, 2005, http://archive.boston.com/news/globe/ideas/articles/2005/01/16/eyes_on_the_prize_off_the_shelf/ and Thom Powers, "Case Study on #SaveDocs: Eyes on the Prize," DocNYC, http://www.docnyc.net/news/case-study-on-save-docs-eyes-on-the-prize/.

dence that they will enter—they must enter—the public record of civilization. Imagine a library book being pulled from the shelves for clearance reasons: that the rights to peruse the words within had expired! But that is exactly what happens to our film and television programs—and our music and sound—because of the adolescent approach we take to rights in our new Republic of Images.

Looking forward with all the knowledge we can indeed gain from hindsight, we might ask if it is more expensive to produce works from the get-go that are freely licensed and licensable. One doesn't need extra cameras or lights or software. Only a select few line items—legal costs, rights acquisition, insurance policies, accounting, staff—in a production budget are affected by the pursuit of open licenses, and these, if the right licenses are embraced at the start—and appropriate and thorough briefings given to the production teams and administrators about research, clearance procedures, citations, and record keeping—only marginally or hardly at all.[276]

The early history—the foundation—of cinema and radio, when screen culture was just beginning to take root a century ago, is indicative. In early cinema, media consumers in theaters multitasked endlessly, interacting with the screen, lecturers, musicians, and other audience members throughout the playing time of a picture.[277] Early filmmakers treated their media as unfinished and customizable. Historians of film tell

---

276 See Kenn Rabin's advice for the International Documentary Association, "Raiding the Lost Archives, Wisely and Legally: A Short Guide to Clearing Copyrighted Footage," March 3, 2013, http://www.documentary.org/magazine/raiding-lost-archives-wisely-and-legally-short-guide-clearing-copyrighted-footage; and Sheila Curran Bernard's resources online at: https://www.sheilacurranbernard.com/archival-storytelling.html.

277 Roy Rosenzweig, *Eight Hours for What We Will: Workers and Leisure in an Industrial City, 1870–1920* (Cambridge: Cambridge University Press, 1983), 191–221.

us, for example, that pioneering filmmaker D. W. Griffith's "incessant adding and subtracting of footage implies that he saw these films as *essentially open texts*, capable of showing one face to Boston and another to New York. . . . By the late silent period, exhibitors could choose alternate endings for a number of major films. Some audiences, viewing Garbo as Anna Karenina in Clarence Brown's 'Love' (1927), saw Anna throw herself under a train. Other theaters showed Anna happily reunited with Count Vronsky."[278] That the bulk of modern Internet usage today involves time-shifting watchers of Netflix and collecting and curating video on file-sharing networks should tell us something.[279]

To imagine this fairer future for media, the long historical perspective is crucial. While the challenges that Internet technology presents can seem huge to us, in fact there has always been a sense of challenge present with technological innovation. Lawyer Fred von Lohmann has noted that the Internet is one of the biggest disruptive innovations in copyright—but it is certainly not the first or only one. "People forget that broadcast radio, cable television, the VCR, the player piano—every one

---

278 Richard Koszarski, *An Evening's Entertainment: The Age of the Silent Feature Picture, 1915–1928* (Berkeley: University of California Press, 1990), 137, emphasis added. See also Eileen Bowser, *The Transformation of American Cinema 1907–1915* (Berkeley: University of California Press, 1990) and Melvyn Stokes and Richard Maltby eds., *American Movie Audiences: From the Turn of the Century to the Early Sound Era* (London: British Film Institute, 1999). That *Anna Karenina*, by Leo Tolstoy, arises in this book is a reminder that Tolstoy may have been the first of many great educators to commit to open content; he renounced copyright in most of his work before his death. See Rosamund Bartlett, *Tolstoy: A Russian Life* (New York: Houghton Mifflin, 2011) 331. But we get ahead of ourselves . . . .

279 "Global Internet Phenomena," blog, Sandvine, accessed October 13, 2020, https://www.sandvine.com/trends/global-internet-phenomena/; "Cisco Annual Internet Report (2018–2023) White Paper," Cisco.com, last updated March 9, 2020, http://www.cisco.com/c/dam/en/us/solutions/collateral/service-provider/visual-networking-index-vni/complete-white-paper-c11-481360.pdf; Robert Steele, "If You Think Piracy Is Decreasing, You Haven't Looked at the Data. . . ," *Digital Music News*, July 16, 2015, http://www.digitalmusicnews.com/2015/07/16/if-you-think-piracy-is-decreasing-you-havent-looked-at-the-data-2/.

of those technologies created a panic among copyright owners, incumbents of the era, upon their introduction."[280] Many of the institutions that grew up at that time—institutions that seem to have always been present—arose as a function of earlier copyright panics, and prove that we are constantly adapting.

Many people and institutions today are incentivized already to put their material online and to make that material more openly available for use and reuse. They might not have their rights houses fully in order, and they might not label what they are doing with a formal "open educational resources" or "OER" brand, but they are seeking to make—and making—their material more available. Rightsholders are all concerned, as a rule, with the same thing—clear definitions, clear rules of the road, ways for people who invest to be compensated, and avoiding surprises. Setting out the obstacles to making educational material more accessible—building a full toolkit for putting content online and then into the Commons—should be a priority for advocates and funders in the years ahead.[281] Such a toolkit should include all kinds of sextants, compasses, and telescopes—especially a set of richly annotated production contracts and agreements, for example, where the language representing barriers to making material more openly available could be identified and highlighted as such, and boilerplate language about institutional commitments to openness that

---

280 "Interview with Fred von Lohmann, Electronic Frontier Foundation, recorded at OnCopyright2010," online at https://www.beyondthebookcast.com/wp-images/vonLohman-Transcript.pdf.

281 This work can build on earlier guides including *Otherwise Open: Managing Incompatible Content within Open Educational Resources* (Version 1.0, September 1, 2009) (San Francisco: Creative Commons, 2009), viewable at the Internet Archive: https://archive.org/details/OtherwiseOpenManagingIncompatibleContentWithOpenEducationalResources; and Peter Hirtle, Emily Hudson, and Andrew T. Kenyon, *Copyright and Cultural Institutions: Guidelines for Digitization for U.S. Libraries, Archives, and Museums* (Ithaca, NY: Cornell University Library, 2009), online at http://ecommons.cornell.edu/handle/1813/14142.

can be developed and copied is included. Cornell law professor James Grimmelman launched one such a model effort to annotate the Google Book Search agreement, for example.[282] This is the key—a library of foundational documents, annotated for promoting free/libre access to online education.

The development and production of all of our work takes place in a crucible of experimentation. In many ways today we are traveling up and down the Rhine river valley in the earliest years of print. Princeton historian and media scholar Anthony Grafton recounts how printers would experiment with printing all kinds of things during these years—sometimes becoming so competitive as to assault each other (while printing Bibles, no less, which emerged as a cutthroat business!).[283] We are still in the early years of movable type here—notwithstanding the achievements we've chronicled above. And the key to more achievements in this area is, predictably perhaps, more experimentation.

---

282 Grimmelman's work is at https://james.grimmelmann.net/publications.

283 "The history of media & social change—Anthony Grafton in INT's ENLIGHTEN- MENT MINUTES," Intelligent Channel, September 8, 2013, YouTube video, 6:38, https:// youtu.be/VosaOdqbVf4.

11. *Our Moment*

We have to convene more regular conversations, publish more systematic financial and legal analyses, produce more frequent programming, curate more substantial exhibitions, and teach more detailed courses—all about the ways in which we might restore control over the information economy we have been so busily victimized by until today.

At MIT we have convened a working group on open (Open 2020, as we've called it), to advance the discussion points herein and the future of knowledge and open learning—inviting visionary stakeholders from throughout the university and experts and creative advocates from outside the institute, inviting in funders and underwriters and other strategic partners. The people we are inviting and assembling—from Wikipedia and the Wikimedia Foundation; from the Internet Archive, Creative Commons, the Public Broadcasting Service, and National Public Radio; legal experts on rights, including free speech and copyright; historians of education and media; librarians, publishers, museum curators, technologists—are like a Constituent Assembly or a Continental Congress, but even more like a freely assembled Rebel Alliance, a nonprofit Sanhedrin of activists and teachers who together (with you) are leading us out of this mess as stakeholders in the future of the non-neoliberal web.[284] Another new MIT-originated initiative is the Knowledge Futures Group, established in 2019 to address precisely these issues of public control over publishing and search.[285]

So much of what is fascinating on the web is produced by us, but somehow it is owned or being run—published, sold, licensed, rented out, agented—by others. We in this sector operate some of the best business schools in the world, so why do we not have our own McKinsey Group, one that could study the fish soup of a financial ecosystem that is scholarly publishing and university librarianship and information science and turn it back into its original aquarium? We have some of the best and most accomplished graduates out there, so why do we not have our own advertising agency, equipped to sell access and time on our digital platforms to a short client list of the companies whose interests could conceivably align with ours? Or our own lobbying group—based in Washington and state capitols, to campaign for better decisions about the issues that affect us and our world so deeply? Or our own legal and business advocacy group, which could—more effectively than the Association of American Universities or American Association of University Professors, the American Alliance of Museums, the Society of American Archivists or Association of Moving Image Archivists, America's Public Television Stations, the advocacy workers we all hire, the agents and representatives

---

284 "Open 2020 Working Group Home," MIT Wikis, last modified February 14, 2020, https://wikis.mit.edu/confluence/display/open2020/Open+2020+Working+Group+Home. Talk of a new public interest technology network also has begun. Natasha Singer, "Top Universities Join to Push 'Public Interest Technology,'" *New York Times*, March 11, 2019, https://www.nytimes.com/2019/03/11/technology/universities-public-interest-technology.html.

285 Home page, Knowledge Futures Group, accessed October 13, 2020, https://www.knowledgefutures.org/.

we enlist, the labor unions and other collectives that have, basically, missed the forest for the trees—argue for our rights,[286] and maybe one day pull off actions the equal of a Pullman Strike to bring more awareness to the systemic problems we face as a sector and thus as a nation?[287]

Who should be able to say, even a bit, that they own our knowledge? To have some kind of metaphorical purchase on it is fine. To have rights to control some of it, even exclusive rights, for a time—okay. But to own it? Outright? And ostensibly in perpetuity?

No.

Efforts are under way, especially now in the United Kingdom and the Netherlands, to establish a so-called public sphere— or "public space"—for public-service and educational content. Visionaries at cultural and educational institutions and in journalism and related fields are now joining cutting-edge leaders in audiovisual production, so we may actually be getting somewhere. Indeed, the pandemic has brought forth collaborative projects of the sort that true public service broadcasting was founded for— projects involving television and radio, museums, universities, hospitals now, concert halls, and schools: the entire knowledge industry, and much of the culture sector. Here is the BBC:

---

286 More at Peter B. Kaufman, "Marketing Culture in the Digital Age: A Report on New Business Collaborations Between Libraries, Museums, Archives and Commercial Companies" (New York: Mellon Foundation, 2005), http://msc.mellon.org/msc-files/MarketingCultureinDigitalAge-%20Ithaka.pdf. See also Peter B. Kaufman, "On Building a New Market for Culture: Virtue and Necessity in a Screen-Based Economy" (London: JISC, 2009), https://sca.jiscinvolve.org/wp/files/2009/07/sca_intelligenttv_sponsorship_report_vi-final.pdf.

287 Nick Salvatore, *Eugene V. Debs: Citizen and Socialist, The Working Class in American History* (Urbana: University of Illinois Press, 1982). See also Peter Baldwin, "Why Are Universities Open Access Laggards?" *Bulletin of the German Historical Institute* 63 (Fall 2018): 67–80, https://www.arcadiafund.org.uk/wp-content/uploads/2018/11/why-are-universities-open-access-laggers.pdf.

Our core role is to bring trusted news and information to audiences in the UK and around the world in a fast-moving situation, and counter confusion and misinformation.

We will help people in the UK deal with the impact of the crisis on their own lives, by providing advice, education and support.

We will keep people entertained, providing laughter, escapism, companionship, shared experiences and a sense of connection to the outside world.

At a time when British culture is having to close its doors, the BBC [. . .] can give British culture an audience that can't be there in person. We propose to run an essential arts and culture service—Culture in Quarantine—that will keep the Arts alive in people's homes [. . .]

This arts and culture service will include guides to shuttered exhibitions or permanent collections in museums and galleries; performances from world-class musicians and comedians; new plays created especially for broadcast featuring exceptional talent; the experience of book festivals with privileged access to authors and great ideas switched online; and quarantine diaries from creative visionaries. We will also be offering jewels from the archive, ensuring that brand new theatre and dance performances will join with modern classics to create a repertory theatre of broadcast.[288]

---

288 "BBC Sets Out Plan to Inform, Educate, and Entertain during Unprecedented Times," BBC, March 3, 2020, https://www.bbc.co.uk/mediacentre/latestnews/2020/bbc-keeping-na-tion-informed-educated-entertained; Jonty Claypole, "Culture in Quarantine: Bringing Arts and Culture into the Home," BBC, March 18, 2020, https://www.bbc.co.uk/blogs/aboutthebbc/entries/9b107488-0154-4435-a9a1-81bd16224086; "BBC to Deliver Biggest Push on Education in Its History," BBC, April 3, 2020, https://www.bbc.co.uk/mediacentre/lat-estnews/2020/coronavirus-education; "BBC Announces Package of Measures to Maintain

The great Czech writer and playwright and later president of Czechoslovakia, Václav Havel, next to Nelson Mandela perhaps our only modern philosopher-king, spoke of the possibility that certain elements of our human experience "do not— without our really being aware of it—point somewhere further, beyond their apparent limits" and whether "right here, in our everyday lives" "certain challenges are not already encoded, quietly waiting for the moment when they will be read and grasped." The real question, he maintained, "is whether the 'brighter future' is really always so distant":

> What if, on the contrary, it has been here for a long time already, and only our blindness and weakness has prevented us from seeing it around us and within us, and kept us from developing it?[289]

But—we need more. The forces that line up to shut down these kinds of experiments—often led by rightsholders seeking to monetize content before everything is available online—are strong: years ago, they put the kibosh on an early, majestic experiment at the BBC in 2005, and they have been busy before and since. Consortial efforts are required because the world's strongest vested interests—whether Elsevier, Wiley, Disney, Sony, Warner, or any of a hundred others—are commercializing our knowledge, locking it away from us, exerting a powerful

---

Creative Health of the Independent Production Sector during the COVID-19 Pandemic," BBC, April 6, 2020, https://www.bbc.co.uk/mediacentre/latestnews/2020/coronavirus-independent-production-sector.

289 Václav Havel, "The Power of the Powerless" in Havel, *Living in Truth: Twenty-Two Essays Published on the Occasion of the Award of the Erasmus Prize to Václav Havel*, ed. Jan Vladislav (London: Faber and Faber, 1987), 122. For background, see https://sourcebooks.fordham.edu/ancient/plato-republic-philosopherking.asp.

counterforce upon its natural, Newtonian trajectory into the Commons. That force lasts longer than the lifetime of single human advocates, and when these nefarious and financially powerful corporations expand and merge and acquire one another, they benefit by receiving not only the assets and revenue of the companies they buy but the accrued man-days of their institutional existences, their connections, their collective suppression strategies—the momentum behind which is considerable. When church and state working together (the church being the publisher, or JSTOR, of its day), neutralize or eliminate our greatest advocates and heroes, the only way we can combat their power is by aggressive and collective action. We have to launch a consortial effort to take back the public broadcasting efforts we seem to have abandoned, writ large, as a global society—a consortial effort to establish, produce, coprogram a new web network, perhaps called "public sphere broadcasting"?[290] One devoted to the public weal—rather than to the bottom line.

We might (this means: we should) therefore want to start (this means we should start right away) a new national, even international, commission of experts from science, media,

---

290 "A Future for Public Service Television: Content and Platforms in a Digital World. A Report on the Future of Public Service Television in the UK in the 21st Century," (London: Goldsmiths, University of London, 2016), https://futureoftv.org.uk/wp-content/uploads/2016/06/FOTV-Report-Online-SP.pdf. This inquiry was chaired by film and television producer Lord (David) Puttnam (*The Killing Fields, Chariots of Fire, Midnight Express*). Puttnam's speech at the launch of the BBC Creative Archive in London in 2005 is available online at: http://www.bbc.co.uk/creativearchive/news/news_april05.shtml. See also: Becky Hogge, "Meet Mr. Rights," *The Guardian*, September 20, 2004, online at: https://www.theguardian.com/technology/2004/sep/20/mondaymediasection.bbc. My speech at the 2005 launch of the Creative Archive is also online here: http://www.bbc.co.uk/creativearchive/news/news_april05.shtml. See also: Becky Hogge, "How the BBC Can Create a Better Digital Public Sphere," July 19, 2016, online at: https://www.opendemocracy.net/ourbeeb/becky-hogge/how-bbc-can-create-better-digital-public-sphere; and James Bennett, "Create Public Service Algorithms," part of "100 Ideas for the BBC: Imagining a Bolder Future for Public Service Broadcasting" (2015), online at: https://www.opendemocracy.net/100ideasforthebbc/blog/2015/09/14/create-public-service-algorithms/.

technology, and the arts to explore the proper role for the university and sister knowledge institutions in our modern and broken information ecosystem. This would be an echo of the Carnegie Commission on educational broadcasting that MIT's former president James Rhyne Killian called for and chaired in the 1960s. Though it was bold, and produced a report full of passion, effectively paving the way for our current system of public broadcasting, the Carnegie Commission operated in a world that could not have imagined our current epistemic crisis. On the other hand, its members could not have imagined the possibilities that the networked world presents to us today. Visionaries almost a decade ago called for the great global meta-university—a great global meta-archive of knowledge—as well. MIT's former president Charles Vest spoke of "a transcendent, accessible, empowering, dynamic, communally constructed framework of open materials and platforms on which much of higher education worldwide can be constructed or enhanced. . . . The meta-university will enable, not replace, residential campuses, especially in wealthier regions. It will bring cost efficiencies to institutions through the shared development of educational materials. It will be adaptive, not prescriptive. It will serve teachers and learners in both structured and informal contexts. It will speed the propagation of high-quality education and scholarship. It will build bridges across cultures and political boundaries. It will be particularly important to the developing world."[291]

We have to start consciously collaborating with one another

---

[291] Charles M. Vest, "Open Content and the Emerging Global Meta-University," *EDU-CAUSE Review* 41, no. 3 (May/June 2006): 18–30, http://er.educause.edu/articles/2006/1/open-content-and-the-emerging-global-metauniversity. See also Charles M. Vest, *Pursuing the Endless Frontier: Essays on MIT and the Role of Research Universities* (Cambridge, MA: MIT Press, 2005).

and producing—but immediately—for this new knowledge network. Signs of what is possible are evident everywhere. The Internet Archive, always a host and sponsor of such coproductions, is working with Wikipedia now, digitizing books so that links to sources in Wikipedia link all the way through to the books themselves—and render up images and text on the cited pages. This takes the *Encyclopédie*'s vision and ambition to a whole new level. The reference link to a biography by Taylor Branch at the bottom of a Wikipedia article on Martin Luther King, Jr. (the Wikipedia article [https://en.wikipedia.org/wiki/Martin_Luther_King_Jr.] is the first link to surface on a Google search), now hotlinks to the readable online book at https://archive.org/details/atcanaansedgeameoobran. There is magic happening here, under our eyes. The National Academies of Sciences, Engineering, and Medicine in Washington—"private, nonprofit institutions," as they describe themselves, "that provide independent, objective analysis and advice to the nation to solve complex problems and inform public policy decisions related to science, technology, and medicine," now host two-day Wikipedia edit-a-thons on nothing less important than climate change. "For more than four decades, the National Academies have helped to establish climate change as a national issue through their consensus study reports," the academies tells us. "Their work has resolved long-standing questions about the science, defined the urgency for understanding the short- and long-term impacts of climate change, and charted ways in which we can prepare for and respond to climate change." To address the pandemic and global disinformation crisis, the World Health Organization has begun to cooperate, at long last, with Wikipedia. But now—after all these decades—now is the time to get into the production business: and in fact, the *production-of-networked-knowledge business.*[292]

By producing for the network we will make it happen and grow. Today all these knowledge institutions we have are involved in education—physical, online, public, K-8, university level, high school, advanced, you name it. But are we also in the health care business? The banking business? Education policy? Foreign policy? Climate change?

You bet we are.

We are everywhere the Monsterverse is.

Is race discrimination our topic? Gender discrimination? Abortion? Gun laws? Climate Change? Tax reform?[293]

You bet they are. And until such time as there is a real opportunity for regulations over these network news sources and platforms that purvey blatant falsehoods, it's not our job to be defending against misinformation, backed up in a crush like peewee soccer players against our own goal. It's our job instead to be playing *offense*, and thus to be publishing—as universities, museums, libraries, archives—as much true information, verifiable narrative, research, and data as possible, and in methods that facilitate their freest distribution and redistribution.

The real question is, how great will the forces against progress be? And how violent the reaction to a concerted effort by leaders

292 Klint Finley, "The Internet Archive Is Making Wikipedia More Reliable," *Wired*, March 3, 2019, https://www.wired.com/story/internet-archive-wikipedia-more-reliable/; Whitney Kimball, "The Internet Archive Fights Wiki Citation Wars With Books," *Gizmodo*, November 4, 2019, https://gizmodo.com/the-internet-archive-fights-wiki-citation-wars-with-boo-1839609540; "The National Academies of Sciences, Engineering, and Medicine with support from Wikimedia DC," Eventbrite, accessed October 13, 2020, https://www.eventbrite.com/o/the-national-academies-of-sciences-engineering-and-medicine-with-support-from-wikimedia-dc-28766063707. See also Donald G. McNeil Jr., "Wikipedia and W.H.O. Join to Combat Covid-19 Misinformation," *New York Times*, October 22, 2020, https://www.nytimes.com/2020/10/22/health/wikipedia-who-coronavirus-health.html.

293 Kristen Bialik, "State of the Union 2019: How Americans See Major National Issues," Fact Tank (blog), Pew Research Center, February 4, 2019, https://www.pewresearch.org/fact-tank/2019/02/04/state-of-the-union-2019-how-americans-see-major-national-issues/.

in our movement—and only the brave need apply—to reclaim our rights, reinsure and reinforce the Commons, establish a true and self-aware knowledge network, run our archive, and seize our moment? The battle over the control of knowledge is the defining struggle of our time. My guess is that it will be sizable.

When the Massachusetts Institute of Technology, where I work now, was first established, our country was riven by violent conflict over power and freedom. The very day, in fact—April 10, 1861—that the Massachusetts Commonwealth granted the founding members of the Association of Industrial Art and Science the institute's formal charter, Brigadier General Pierre Gustave Toutant Beauregard, commander of the Provisional Army in Charleston, was busy, on behalf of the new Confederacy—seven of our thirty-four states had already seceded, and four more would follow—demanding the surrender of a US Union garrison stationed off the South Carolina coast. The Union commander, Robert Anderson, who had been an instructor of Beauregard's at West Point, refused to lay down Union arms, and on April 12—two days into MIT's existence—Beauregard's unit started shelling Fort Sumter. It was a student shelling a teacher; but it was also the start of the Civil War.[294]

It would be four years before the war would end, and four years before MIT would recruit its first students and hold its first classes. But, born in that crucible, that violent Civil War spring, MIT kept a

---

294 "MIT History," MIT Libraries, accessed October 13, 2020, https://libraries.mit.edu/mithistory/mit-facts/. Beauregard would become general of the Army of the Potomac; by July he would be leading Confederate troops in the first Battle of Bull Run. See Edward L. Ayers, *In the Presence of Mine Enemies: War in the Heart of America, 1859–1863*, Valley of the Shadow Project (New York: W. W. Norton, 2003); and "P. G. T. Beauregard, Wikimedia Foundation, last modified July 29, 2020, 14:36, https://en.wikipedia.org/wiki/P._G._T._Beauregard. It turns out some of the Confederate soldiers in that cannonade had also been students of MIT founder William Barton Rogers. See "MIT Charter, 1861," MIT Museum, accessed October 13, 2020, http://museum.mit.edu/150/74.

remarkably steady hand at the helm of knowledge sharing and public engagement, steering its own institution and leading minds around the globe toward solving the world's largest problems. The original consortium that set up the institute—William Barton Rogers and his Back Bay Brahmins (James M. Beebe, E. S. Tobey, S. H. Gookin, E. B. Bigelow, M. D. Ross, various Daltons, Dupees, and Cabots)—believed, uniquely then and perhaps even now among institutions of higher learning, that "professional competence" would best be "fostered by coupling teaching and research," that is, by "focusing attention on real-world problems."[295] But they also intended for the educational programs they designed, as they wrote to each other at the time, "to fall within the reach of a large number whom the scantiness of time, means, and opportunity, would exclude from the great seats of classical and scientific education in the Commonwealth."[296] In so doing, the establishment also honored and echoed the sentiments of John Lowell and his Boston Society for the Diffusion of Useful Knowledge.

One hundred and sixty years later, the institute remains committed in its very mission statement to "generating, disseminating, and preserving knowledge" and to "working with others to bring this knowledge to bear on the world's great challenges."[297] MIT has become a "world-class educational institution"; and it avers that "teaching and research—with relevance to the practical world and transforming society for the better as guiding principles—continue to be its primary

---

295 "Origins and Leadership," MIT Facts, accessed October 13, 2020, http://web.mit.edu/facts/origins.html.

296 Objects and Plan for an Institute of Technology (1861), online at: https://libraries.mit.edu/mithistory/digital/.

297 "Massachusetts Institute of Technology: Mission" MIT, March 2001, http://web.mit.edu/mission.html.

purpose."[298] Yet with equal tenacity many of the overarching problems facing the institute and the country in the 1860s—as Civil War historian Eric Foner lists them: "the enduring legacy of slavery, the nature of presidential leadership, the relationship between morality and politics, and the definition of American nationality and citizenship"[299]—remain eerily familiar, as relevant, as unsolved, as urgent now as they were then.

Addressing collective action in the face of the direst challenges of the age will not allow us to sit still or be silent. Speaking of the Constitution, historian David Waldstreicher reminds us that "with respect to slavery, the federalists had fashioned a silence, not a consensus—or at most a consensus to be silent."[300] We've seen what happened afterwards. Such silence in the face of power is never good, nor is inaction in the face of aggression. We have witnessed, in the years after Trump's election fired up the incubators and greenhouses for all this violence and hate, an upsurge in vitriol like nobody's business. In the words of the astute critic James Poniewozik, that was what the election of Donald Trump was designed to do. "Trump got elected," Poniewozik writes. "But TV became president." And "the only job [Trump] was truly elected to do" was "monitoring, stoking, and embodying the cultural anger machine."[301]

That anger and the concomitant violence we see has been

---

298 "Origins and Leadership," https://web.mit.edu/facts/origins.html.

299 Eric Foner, *The Fiery Trial: Abraham Lincoln and American Slavery* (New York: W. W. Norton, 2010), xv.

300 David Waldstreicher, *Slavery's Constitution: From Revolution to Ratification* (New York: Hill & Wang, 2009), 153–54. Editorializing, Waldstreicher writes that "the Constitution requires of us what the philosopher Antonio Gramsci called the pessimism of the intellect and the optimism of the will" (56).

301 Poniewozik reminds us that Hannah Arendt saw this same tendency in the intellectuals of Europe during the 1930s: "brilliant and witty praise of violence, power, and cruelty." James Poniewozik, *Audience of One: Donald Trump, Television, and the Fracturing of America* (New York: Liveright, 2019), 240, 260.

in power. It may be that people who have experience wielding power unjustly jump to guilt, and that guilt makes them violent. One of the greatest historians of the South, C. Vann Woodward, speaks of the Civil War South as having "writhed in the torments of its own conscience until it plunged into catastrophe to escape."[302] And it was tormented—according to Woodward—by the power that its people wielded over others.

Now, what may ensue in the years ahead may be a polite little scuffle. As the young Confederate Army mustered its strength to fire that spring, its leaders sent this note from the Charleston harbor to the Union garrison stationed offshore:

April 12, 1861 – 3.20 a.m.
FORT SUMTER, S.C.,

SIR: By authority of Brigadier-General Beauregard, commanding the Provisional Forces of the Confederate States, we have the honor to notify you that he will open the fire of his batteries on Fort Sumter in one hour from this time.

We have the honor to be, very respectfully, your obedient servants,

JAMES CHESTNUT, JR.   STEPHEN D. LEE
Aide-de-Camp   Aide-de-Camp[303]

---

302 C. Vann Woodward, *The Burden of Southern History* (Baton Rouge: Louisiana State University Press, 1960), 21.

303 "Gen. P. G. T. Beauregard to Maj. Robert Anderson," American Battlefields Trust, accessed October 13, 2020, https://www.battlefields.org/learn/primary-sources/gen-p-g-t-beauregard-maj-robert-anderson.

But, on the other hand, it could be violent. It could be violent like the fatal fights over the television towers in Romania, Lithuania, and Russia, where dozens died in the struggle for screen control.[304] It equally could be the more American story of Edmund Ruffin, who joined the Palmetto Guards of Charleston, as historian John Hope Franklin has written, "and assumed the duties of a regular recruit." The company selected him to fire the first shot on Sumter, and he was delighted. When Ruffin pulled the lanyard on the sixty-four-pound columbiad at 4:30 in the morning of April 12, 1861, he did what thousands of Southerners were willing to do. They, like Ruffin, had nothing more to say. They were ready to fight, even if on the wrong side, and this is what they would do.[305]

304 John Budris, "'Is This What the 15 People at the TV Tower Died For?'" *New York Times*, August 2, 1992, https://www.nytimes.com/1992/08/02/magazine/is-this-what-the-15-people-at-the-tv-tower-died-for.html; "The Romanian Revolution, Broadcast Live," Google Arts & Culture, accessed October 13, 2020, https://artsandculture.google.com/exhibit/the-romanian-revolution-broadcast-live-tvr-the-romanian-public-broadcaster/wRsiAKoC?hl=en; *Los Angeles Times*, "Stray Shot Killed American Lawyer During Fight at Television Complex," *Orlando Sentinel*, October 6, 1993, https://www.orlandosentinel.com/news/os-xpm-1993-10-06-9310060656-story.html.

305 John Hope Franklin, *The Militant South, 1800–1861* (Cambridge, MA: Harvard University Press, 1956).

Coda

Newton M. Minow, the chairman of our Federal Communications Commission when commercial and public broadcasting were in their toddler years in America and full of hope, told me a story when I was visiting with him in Chicago years ago.

He was walking with President Kennedy in the White House Rose Garden, just a few days before the president was shot and killed in Texas. And during that walk in the White House Rose Garden in 1963, Kennedy was recalling a story of a similar walk that another statesman, French Marshal Hugo Lyautey, had taken many years before in a rose garden as well.

Marshal Lyautey was a kind of French Lawrence of Arabia, from my mother's hometown of Nancy in Alsace-Lorraine, and for a while he was the face and symbol of the hauteur of Western imperialism in Northern Africa. A ruthless colonialist, Lyautey was also strangely and ambiguously a sensitive and sometimes beloved man for his time and place—he lies entombed in Northern Africa, with an Arabic kiss scripted on his casket there.

Kennedy told his first media and communications czar that the *marechal* was walking around his property, taking his morning constitutional (as French generals are wont to do) and he stopped in the middle of his garden to inspect—imperiously, no doubt—a bare spot between some bushes. Lyautey said to the groundskeeper who had been following him closely, "This spot is bare, so I would like you to plant a tree right there:

a beautiful mimosa, one that will grow a thousand pink and white fragrant flowers. Bring a sapling and put it in the ground this time tomorrow morning!"

The gardener hemmed and hawed and said something to the effect of, "*Oui, mais . . . . Ah. Uh. Marechal!* You know that such a tree, if we plant it here tomorrow, will not bloom for fifty, seventy-five, or even a hundred years."

Marshal Lyautey, as you might imagine, fixed the gardener with a cold stare, taking in this news, and then said, with a growl, "If that truly *is* the case, *mon cher*, then you had better set about planting that tree this very afternoon."[306]

---

306 For more on Newton Minow, television, and society, see "Broadcasting in the Public Interest: The Newton Minow Collection," https://americanarchive.org/special_collections/newtonminow.

Appendix

From: Richard Stallman <rms@gnu.org>
Subject: Re: Evaluation of Gcompris
To: vtamara@gnu.org
Date: Mon, 18 Dec 2000 15:21:47 -0700 (MST)
Reply-to: rms@gnu.org

The Free Universal Encyclopedia and Learning Resource
Richard Stallman

The World Wide Web has the potential to develop into a universal encyclopedia covering all areas of knowledge, and a complete library of instructional courses. This outcome could happen without any special effort, if no one interferes. But corporations are mobilizing now to direct the future down a different track—one in which they control and restrict access to learning materials, so as to extract money from people who want to learn.

To ensure that the web develops toward the best and most natural outcome, where it becomes a free encyclopedia, we must make a conscious effort to prevent deliberate sequestration of the encyclopedic and educational information on the net. We cannot stop business from restricting the information it makes available; what we can do is provide an alternative. We need to launch a movement to develop a universal free encyclopedia, much as the Free Software movement gave us the free software operating system GNU/Linux. The free encyclopedia will provide an alternative to the restricted ones that media corporations will write.

The rest of this article aims to lay out what the free encyclopedia needs to do, what sort of freedoms it needs to give the public, and how we can get started on developing it.

• An encyclopedia located everywhere.

In the past, encyclopedias have been written under the direction of a single organization, which made all decisions about the content, and have been published in a centralized fashion. It would not make sense to develop and publish the free encyclopedia in those ways—they fit poorly with the nature of the World Wide Web and with the resources available for writing the encyclopedia.

The free encyclopedia will not be published in any one place. It will consist of all web pages that cover suitable topics, and have been made suitably available. These pages will be developed in a decentralized manner by thousands of contributors, each independently writing articles and posting them on various web servers. No one organization will be in charge, because such centralization would be incompatible with decentralized progress.

• Who will write the encyclopedia?

In principle, anyone is welcome to write articles for the encyclopedia. But as we reach out for people to help, the most promising places to look are among teachers and students. Teachers generally like to teach, and writing an article a year for the encyclopedia would be an enjoyable change from their classroom duties. For students, a major school paper could become an encyclopedia article, if done especially well.

• Small steps will do the job.

When a project is exciting, it is easy to imagine a big contribution that you would like to make, bite off more than you can chew, and ultimately give up with nothing to show for it.

So it is important to welcome and encourage smaller contributions. Writing a textbook for a whole semester's material is a big job, and only a small fraction of teachers will contribute that much. But writing about a topic small enough for one meeting of a class is a contribution that many can afford to make. Enough of these small contributions can cover the whole range of knowledge.

• Take the long view.

The encyclopedia is a big job, and it won't be finished in a year. If it takes twenty years to complete the free encyclopedia, that will be but an instant in the history of literature and civilization.

In projects like this, progress is slow for the first few years; then it accelerates as the work that has been done attracts more and more people to join in. Eventually there is an avalanche of progress. So we should not feel discouraged when the first few years do not bring us close to completion. It makes sense to choose the first steps to illustrate what can be done, and to spread interest in the long-term goal, so as to inspire others to join in.

This means that the pioneers' job, in the early years, is above all to be steadfast. We must be on guard against downgrading to a less useful, less idealistic goal, just because of the magnitude of the task. Instead of measuring our early steps against the size of the whole job, we should think of them as examples, and have confidence that they will inspire a growing number of contributors to join and finish the job.

• Evangelize.

Since we hope that teachers and students at many colleges around the world will join in writing contributions to the free encyclopedia, let's not leave this to chance. There are already scattered examples of what can be done. Let's present these examples systematically to the academic community, show the vision of the free universal encyclopedia, and invite others to join in writing it.

• What should the free encyclopedia contain?

The free encyclopedia should aim eventually to include one or more articles for any topic you would expect to find in another encyclopedia. In addition, since there is no practical limit to the amount of encyclopedic material that can be on the web, this encyclopedia should eventually also cover the more advanced and specialized topics you might expect to find in specialized encyclopedias, such as an "Encyclopedia of Physics," "Encyclopedia of Medicine," "Encyclopedia of Gardening," or "Encyclopedia of Cooking." It could go even further; for example, bird watchers might eventually contribute an article on each species of bird, along with pictures and recordings of its calls.

However, only some kinds of information belong in an encyclopedia. For example, scholarly papers, detailed statistical data bases, news reports, fiction and art, extensive bibliographies, and catalogs of merchandise, useful as they are, are outside the scope of an encyclopedia. (Some of the articles might usefully contain links to such works.)

Courses in the learning resource are a generalization to hypertext of the textbooks used for teaching a subject to yourself or to a class. The learning resource should eventually include courses for all academic subjects, from mathematics to art history, and practical subjects such as gardening as well, to the extent this makes sense. (Some practical subjects, such as massage or instrumental ensemble playing, may not be possible to study from a "book" without a human teacher—these are arguably less useful to include.) It should cover these subjects at all the levels that are useful, which might in some cases range from first grade to graduate school.

A useful encyclopedia article will address a specific topic at a particular level, and each author will contribute mainly by focusing on an area that he or she knows very well. But we should keep in the back of our minds, while doing this, the vision of a free encyclopedia that is universal in scope—so that we can firmly reject any attempt to put artificial limits on either the scope or the free status of the encyclopedia.

• **Criteria pages must meet.**

To ensure this encyclopedia is indeed a free and universal encyclopedia, we must set criteria of freeness for encyclopedia articles and courses to meet.

Conventional non-free encyclopedias published by companies such as Microsoft will surely be made available on the web, sooner or later—but you will probably have to pay to read an article, and you surely won't be allowed to redistribute them. If we are content with knowledge as a commodity, accessible only through a computerized bureaucracy, we can simply let companies provide it.

But if we want to keep human knowledge open and freely available to humanity, we have to do the work to make it available that way. We have to write a free encyclopedia—so we must first determine the proper interpretation of "free" for an encyclopedia on the Internet. We must decide what criteria of freedom a free encyclopedia and a free learning resource should meet.

• Permit universal access.

The free encyclopedia should be open to public access by everyone who can gain access to the web. Those who seek to gain control over educational materials, so they can profit by restricting access to them, will push us to "compromise" by agreeing to restrict access in exchange for their participation. We must stand firm, and reject any deal that is inconsistent with the ultimate goal. We are in no hurry, and there is no sense in getting to the wrong place a few years sooner.

• Permit mirror sites.

When information is available on the web only at one site, its availability is vulnerable. A local problem—a computer crash, an earthquake or flood, a budget cut, a change in policy of the school administration—could cut off access for everyone forever. To guard against loss of the encyclopedia's material, we should make sure that every piece of the encyclopedia is available from many sites on the Internet, and that new copies can be put up if some disappear.

There is no need to set up an organization or a bureaucracy to do this, because Internet users like to set up "mirror sites" which hold duplicate copies of interesting web pages. What we must do in advance is ensure that this is legally permitted.

Therefore, each encyclopedia article and each course should explicitly grant irrevocable permission for anyone to make verbatim copies available on mirror sites. This permission should be one of the basic stated principles of the free encyclopedia.

Someday there may be systematic efforts to ensure that each article and course is replicated in many copies—perhaps at least once on each of the six inhabited continents. This would be a natural extension of the mission of archiving that libraries undertake today. But it would be premature to make formal plans for this now. It is sufficient for now to resolve to make sure people have permission to do this mirroring when they get around to it.

• Permit translation into other languages.

People will have a use for encyclopedia material on each topic in every human language. But the primary language of the Internet—as of the world of commerce and science today—is English. Most likely, encyclopedia contributions in English will run ahead of other languages, and the encyclopedia will approach completeness in English first.

Trying to fight this tendency would be self-defeating. The easier way to make the encyclopedia available in all languages is by encouraging one person to translate what another has written. In this way, each article can be translated into many languages.

But if this requires explicit permission, it will be too difficult. Therefore, we must adopt a basic rule that anyone is permitted to publish an accurate translation of any article or course, with proper attribution. Each article and each course should carry a statement giving permission for translations.

To ensure accuracy of translation, the author of the original should reserve the right to insist on corrections in a translation. A translator should perhaps have to give the original author a reasonable amount of time to do this, perhaps three months, before publishing the translation in the first place. After that, the translator should continue to make corrections at the author's request, whenever the author asks for them.

In time, as the number of people involved in encyclopedia activity increases, contributors may form Translation Accuracy Societies for various languages, which undertake to ensure the accuracy of translations into those languages. An author could then desig-nate a Translation Accuracy Society to check and correct a certain translation of a certain work. It may be wise to keep the Translation Accuracy Societies separate from the actual translators, so that each translation will be checked by someone other than the translator.

• Permit quotation with attribution.

Each encyclopedia article or course should permit anyone to quote arbitrary portions in another encyclopedia article or course, provided proper attribution is given. This will make it possible to build on the work others have done, without the need to completely replace it.

Different authors may—if they care—set different rules for what constitutes proper attribution to them; that is okay. As long as the rules set for a particular work are not unreasonable or impractical, they will cause no problem.

• Permit modified versions of courses.

Courses must evolve, and the original authors won't keep working on them forever. And teachers will want to adapt course materials to their own curriculum plans and teaching methods. Since courses will typically be large (like a textbook today), it would be unacceptably wasteful to tell teachers, "Write your own from scratch, if you want to change this."

Therefore, modifying an existing course must be permitted; each course should carry a statement giving permission to pub-lish a modified version.

It makes sense to require modified versions to carry proper attribution giving credit to the authors of the previous version, and be labelled clearly as modified, so that there is no confu-sion about whose views they present.

The GNU Free Documentation License would be a good license to use for courses.

• **Permit modified versions of pictures and videos, for courses.**

Pictures and videos, both drawn and photographic, will play an important role in many courses. Modifying these pictures and videos will be pedagogically useful. For example, you could crop a picture to focus attention on a certain feature, or circle or label particular features. Using false color can help make certain aspects easier to see. Image enhancement is also possible.

Beyond that, an altered version of a picture could illustrate a different but related idea. You could start with a diagram useful for one theorem in geometry, and add to it, to produce a diagram that is relevant to another theorem.

Permission to modify pictures and videos is particularly important because the alternative, to make your own picture or video from scratch, is often very hard. It is not terribly hard to write your own text, to convey certain facts from your own angle, but doing the same thing with a picture is not feasible.

Of course, modified versions of pictures and videos should be labeled as modified, to prevent misattribution of their contents, and should give credit properly to the original.

• **Only free software in the encyclopedia.**

Articles, and especially courses, will often include software—for example, to display a simulation of a chemical reaction, or teach you how often to stir a sauce so it won't burn. To ensure that the encyclopedia is indeed free, all software included in articles and courses should meet the criteria of free software (http://www.gnu.org/philosophy/free-sw.html) and open source software (http://www.opensource.org).

• No central control.

People often suggest that "quality control" is essential for an encyclopedia, and ask what sort of "governing board" will decide which articles to accept as part of the free encyclopedia. The answer is, "no one." We cannot afford to let anyone have such control.

If the free encyclopedia is a success, it will become so ubiquitous and important that we dare not allow any organization to decide what counts as part of it. This organization would have too much power; people would seek to politicize or corrupt it, and could easily succeed.

The only solution to that problem is not to have any such organization, and reject the idea of centralized quality control. Instead, we should let everyone decide. If a web page is about a suitable topic, and meets the criteria for an article, then we can consider it an article. If a page meets the criteria for a course, then we can consider it a course.

But what [if] some pages are erroneous, or even deceptive? We cannot assume this won't happen. But the corrective is for other articles to point out the error. Instead of having "quality control" by one privileged organization, we will have review by various groups, which will earn respect by their own policies and actions. In a world where no one is infallible, this is the best we can do.

• Encourage peer review and endorsements.

There will be no single organization in charge of what to include in the encyclopedia or the learning resource, no one that can be lobbied to exclude "creation science" or holocaust denial (or, by the same token, lobbied to exclude evolution or the history of Nazi death camps). Where there is controversy, multiple views will be represented. So it will be useful for readers to be able to see who endorses or has reviewed a given article's version of the subject.

In fields such as science, engineering, and history, there are formal standards of peer review. We should encourage authors of articles and courses to seek peer review, both through existing formal scholarly mechanisms, and through the informal mechanism of asking respected names in the field for permission to cite their endorsement in the article or course.

A peer-review endorsement applies to one version of a work, not to modified versions. Therefore, when a course has peer-review endorsements, it should require anyone who publishes a modified version of the course to remove the endorsements. (The author of the modified version would be free to seek new endorsements for that version.)

• No catalogue, yet.

When the encyclopedia is well populated, catalogues will be very important. But we should not try to address the issue of cataloguing now, because it is premature. What we need this year and for the coming years is to write articles. Once we have them, once we have a large number of volunteers producing a large number of articles, that will be the time to catalogue them. At that time, enough people will be interested in the encyclopedia to provide the manpower to do the work.

Since no one organization will be in charge of the encyclopedia, there cannot be one authoritative catalogue. Instead, anyone will be free to make a catalogue, just as anyone is free to provide peer review. Cataloguers will gain respect according to their decisions.

Encyclopedia pages will surely be listed in ordinary web search sites, and perhaps those are the only catalogues that will be needed. But true catalogues should permit redistribution, translation, and modification—that is, the criteria for courses should apply to catalogues as well.

What can usefully be done from the beginning is to report new encyclopedia articles to a particular site, which can record their names as raw material for real catalogues, whenever people start to write them. To start off, we will use http://www. gnu.org/encyclopedia for this.

• Making links to other pages.

The last and most important rule for pages in the encyclopedia is the exclusionary rule:

> If a page on the web covers subject matter that ought to be in the encyclopedia or the course library, but its license is too restricted to qualify, we must not make links to it from encyclopedia articles or from courses.

This rule will make sure we respect our own rules, in the same way that the exclusionary rule for evidence is supposed to make police respect their own rules: by not allowing us to treat work which fails to meet the criteria as if it did meet them.

The idea of the World Wide Web is that links tie various separate pages into a larger whole. So when encyclopedia articles or courses link to a certain page, those links effectively make the page part of the encyclopedia. To claim otherwise would be self-deception. If we are to take seriously the criteria set forth above, or any criteria whatsoever, we have to base our actions on them, by not incorporating a page into our network of pages if it doesn't fit the criteria.

When a topic ought to be covered in the encyclopedia or

with a course, but it isn't, we must make sure we don't forget that we have a gap. The exclusionary rule will remind us. Each time we think of making a link to the unacceptable page, and we stop because of the exclusionary rule, that will remind us that someone ought to write another page about the same topic—one that is free enough to be part of the encyclopedia. Eventually, one of us will do the job.

On the other hand, many web pages cover material that wouldn't normally be included in an encyclopedia—for example, scholarly papers, detailed statistical data bases, news reports, fiction and art, extensive bibliographies, and catalogs of merchandise. Such pages, regardless of whether they are free enough to be in the encyclopedia, are outside its scope. They do not represent gaps in the encyclopedia. So there is no need to apply the encyclopedia criteria in making links to such pages.

To produce a complete encyclopedia which satisfies the principles of freedom stated here will take a long time, but we will get it done eventually—as long as we remember the goal. The greatest danger is that we will lose sight of the goal and settle for less. The exclusionary rule will make sure we keep going all the way.

• **Uphold the freedom to contribute.**

As education moves on-line and is increasingly commercialized, teachers are in danger of losing even the right to make their work freely available to the public. Some universities have tried to claim ownership over on-line materials produced by teachers, to turn it into commercial "courseware" with restricted use. Meanwhile, other universities have outsourced their on-line services to corporations, some of which claim to own all materials posted on the university web sites.

It will be up to professors to resist this tendency. But there is more than one way to do so. The most obvious basis for objection is to say, "I own this work, and I, not the university, have the right to sell it to a company if I wish." But that places the faculty on the same selfish moral level as the university, so that neither side has a moral advantage in the argument.

If, on the other hand, professors say, "I want to be able to make my work fully available to the public without restriction," they occupy the commanding moral position, which a university can oppose only by setting itself against the public, against learning, and against scholarship.

Resisting the selling of the university will not be easy. Professors had better make use of any advantage they can find—especially moral advantages.

Two other points that will help are that (1) a few prestigious universities will probably gobble up most of the commercial business, so other universities would be deluding themselves to think they can really get a great deal of funds from selling themselves, and (2) business is likely to drive even the elite universities out of the most lucrative parts of the field.

• **Spread the word.**

When you post a potential encyclopedia article or a course, you can reference this plan if you wish, to help spread the word and inspire others to help.

Acknowledgments

This author is grateful to the staffs at MIT Libraries; Columbia University Libraries; Harvard Library; the Scoville Memorial Library in Salisbury, Connecticut; HathiTrust; and the Internet Archive. Special thanks to, at MIT, Anant Agarwal, Catherine Ahearn, Chris Bourg, Amy Brand, Steve Carson, Cecilia D'Oliviera, Larry Gallagher, Clayton Hainsworth, SJ Klein, Shigeru Miyagawa, Curt Newton, Krisha Rajagopal, Sanjay Sarma, Sarah Schwettmann, Tom "T-Money" Smith, the book's inspiration Richard M. Stallman, Ece Turnator, Eric von Hippel, and all the members of our Open 2020 Working Group; at the Hewlett Foundation, Raquel Abdala, TJ Bliss, Cathy Casserly, Angela DeBarger, Larry Kramer, Kent McGuire, Mike Smith, and Vic Vuchic; at Sound & Vision, Johan Oomen, Rachel Somers Miles, Marius Snyders, and Erwin Verbruggen; at Europeana, Harry Verwayen; at JISC, Stuart Dempster and Catherine Grout; at the *Lakeville Journal*, Cynthia Hochswender and Janet Manko; at the Hotchkiss School, Steve McKibben; and, for their encouragement and additional support, Henry Adams, James H. Billington, Jonah Bossewitch, my close associate Ellen Bratina, Ian M. Cuthbertson, Alexandra Elbakyan, Eric Foner, Paul Gerhardt, Al Gottesman, Eddie Griffith, Vladimir Grigoriev, Eddie Harris, Michael Jensen, Colette Kaufman, Eric Kaufman, Alice Kessler-Harris, Naum Kleiman, John Koch, Paul Lawrence, Richard Lourie, Roger Macdonald, Mike Mashon, Les McCann, Yehudi

Menuhin, Frank Moretti, Ben Moskowitz, Jim Neal, Roy Rosenzweig, Ben Shapiro, Joan Shigekawa, Elisabeth Sifton, Peter Suber, Loic Tallon, Bettina Teich, Doug Teich, Roger Teich, Jeff Ubois, John Unsworth, and Gleb Uspensky.

Jan Mitchell, Ira D. and Miriam Wallach, George Soros, and Lorne Michaels supported me as I started to bring these thoughts together. I tried out not a few on Lawrence K. Grossman, Edward Kasinec, and Newton N. Minow along the way. I am grateful to Charlie and Fern Nesson and Pam Samuelson for hearing me out on some of these ideas, and to Charlie and Fern especially for the whiskey in the pool.

I wrote this book for all of these people, and for everyone else. I put some extra oomph into it for Eric Adrien Mitchell, who would have liked it; Carter Cooper, who would have challenged it; Alex Singer, who fought for many of the goals it promotes; and Henry Kaufman: I miss you every day. I wrote it for our strongest fighters: Sophia Kaufman and Charlie Kaufman, and for their mother, Ellen Bratina, all of whom I love. I have always loved you, from the first.

At Seven Stories, my friend, reader, and editor Dan Simon made a home for this book, and he made it better. His colleagues Lauren Hooker, Ruth Weiner, Stewart Cauley, Jon Gilbert, Claire Kelley, Molly Lindley Pisani, Shayan Saalabi, and Eva Sotomayor handled this work with attention and grace. Everyone should have such a publisher.